"ACT *for Adolescents* is a must-read for professionals working their primary caregivers. Turrell and Bell emphasize the accepta therapy (ACT) view of person-in-environment, linking the .... mutual influence of adolescents in their social and physical environments. This perspective in a helping relationship fosters empowerment, and this book guides a flexible, holistic approach that clinicians working with adolescents will benefit from. Readers will gain novel and practical ACT approaches to working with adolescents."

—**Timothy Gordon MSW, RSW**, social worker; ACT instructor at McMaster University in Hamilton, ON, Canada; and peer-reviewed ACT trainer

"Sheri Turrell and Mary Bell have developed a step-by-step approach to using acceptance and commitment therapy (ACT) with teenagers, in individual and group treatment, brimming with new exercises and metaphors, and creatively adapted traditional ACT interventions. Amongst the strengths of this book are its integration of self-compassion training and the powerful ACT matrix model."

—**Benjamin Schoendorff**, international ACT trainer; director of the Contextual Psychology Institute in Montreal, QC, Canada; and coauthor of *The Essential Guide to the ACT Matrix*

"ACT *for Adolescents* is a well-written resource that steps therapists through the hexaflex model, session by session. The authors have a deep understanding of young people and how to approach therapeutic work with them. This book is a way to see the acceptance and commitment therapy (ACT) model through the eyes of two experienced adolescent therapists. A practical approach for setting up group and individual therapy with young people."

—**Louise Hayes, PhD**, senior fellow at Orygen, The National Centre of Excellence in Youth Mental Health; and The University of Melbourne; and coauthor of *The Thriving Adolescent* and *Get Out of Your Mind and Into Your Life for Teens*

"Hats off to Turrell and Bell for giving us a high-quality manual to support clinicians' use of acceptance and commitment therapy (ACT) with adolescents! They've tested and refined their interventions over years, and now provide specific instructions on how to use them in both individual and group treatments. The ACTion group protocol follows a ten-session model, and it's filled with teen-friendly metaphors and supported by online mindfulness exercises. Bravo! Truly what we needed."

> —**Patricia J. Robinson, PhD**, director of training and program evaluation at Mountainview Consulting Group; international ACT trainer; author of numerous articles, chapters, and books; and coauthor of *Inside This Moment* and *Real Behavior Change in Primary Care*

"Turrell and Bell have made a valuable and timely contribution to the field. The authors provide a model that is comprehensive enough in theory and practice to allow a confident foray into using acceptance and commitment therapy (ACT) with adolescent clients. At the same time, the program is flexible and not overly prescriptive, which allows the clinician to walk alongside the adolescent wherever they need to go that day in the service of the therapy goals. Clients will feel that the work is being tailored to them in the moment, which it is, and not some imposed system the adolescent is expected to fit into."

> —**Christopher McCurry, PhD**, clinical child psychologist in private practice, and author of *Parenting Your Anxious Child with Mindfulness and Acceptance* and *Working with Parents of Anxious Children*

"Turrell and Bell are adolescent pros! In *ACT for Adolescents*, they provide a readable, organized, and practical protocol for treating adolescents using acceptance and commitment therapy (ACT). They clearly describe sophisticated interventions, and include dozens of powerful and engaging experiential exercises that will surely engage and resonate with young people. This book can be used as a treatment manual, allowing the reader to implement ACT immediately and effectively with teens, with step-by-step instructions to guide the therapist through each session. The entire protocol can be implemented in a group setting, and specific modifications are suggested for group work. The authors are clearly gifted therapists, and their experience, wisdom, and respect for adolescents comes through on every page. Any therapist who works with adolescents will find powerful tools that can be used immediately to improve their outcomes with adolescents in this very accessible book."

> —**Britt H. Rathbone, MSSW, LCSW-C**, expert adolescent therapist, trainer, author, and coauthor of *What Works with Teens*, *Dialectical Behavior Therapy for At-Risk Adolescents*, and *Parenting a Teen Who Has Intense Emotions*

ACT *for* Adolescents

Treating Teens and
Adolescents in Individual
and Group Therapy

SHERI L. TURRELL, PhD
MARY BELL, MSW, RSW

CONTEXT PRESS
An Imprint of New Harbinger Publications, Inc.

Distributed in Canada by Raincoast Books

Copyright © 2016 by Sheri L. Turrell and Mary Bell
        Context Press
        An imprint of New Harbinger Publications, Inc.
        5674 Shattuck Avenue
        Oakland, CA 94609
        www.newharbinger.com

DOTS, "The Acetate," "Demons on the Boat," "Observe, Breathe, Expand," "Struggle Switch," and the exercises in "Defusion Exercises: How to Unstick" are modified from ACT MADE SIMPLE by Russ Harris, copyright © 2009 Russ Harris. "Quicksand Metaphor" adapted from GET OUT OF YOUR MIND AND INTO YOUR LIFE by Steven C. Hayes and Spencer Smith, copyright © 2005 Steven C. Hayes and Spencer Smith. "LLAMA" and "The Wrinkled Sock" are modified from THE WORRY TRAP by Chad LeJeune, copyright © 2007 Chad LeJeune. "The Rocks" adapted from ACT FOR DEPRESSION by Robert Zettle, copyright © 2007 by Robert Zettle. All used by permission of New Harbinger Publications.

"The Tiger" adapted from METACOGNITIVE THERAPY FOR ANXIETY AND DEPRESSION by Adrian Wells, copyright © 2009 by The Guilford Press. Adapted by permission of The Guilford Press.

Cover design by Amy Shoup; Acquired by Tesilya Hanauer; Edited by Ken Knabb; Indexed by James Minkin

Library of Congress Cataloging-in-Publication Data on file

Printed in the United States of America

18   17   16

10   9   8   7   6   5   4   3   2   1   First printing

Contents

Foreword

I have done hundreds of acceptance and commitment therapy workshops, and always get this question: "What about ACT for kids?" My pattern of responding is sadly predictable. It comes in the form of an apologia—name any topic in psychology and search that topic in our scientific database; now, add the words "and adolescents" to the search and watch the number of results plummet, sometimes to zero. My answer is true, but not useful. It's really about the question behind the question: "How can I apply what I find in ACT to the adolescents I see in my clinic?"

I have spent a career working to develop broadly applicable psychological principles and have advocated adherence to established treatment principles. But there is a problem with this strategy. Outside of replications of highly controlled randomized clinical trials, which are exceedingly rare, we are always extrapolating. And some extrapolations are easier than others. Many exercises, metaphors, and other interventions can be moved with little or no modification from one population to another. The extrapolation to adolescents is more challenging.

Adolescents present with problems that must be understood in the context of a host of variables that differ in kind or at least in magnitude from those we find in adults. At minimum, psychological struggles are encountered perhaps for the first time as the child passes through varying developmental trajectories. Adolescents are often subject to circumstances over which both the clinician and client have little control. Although I do not imagine different principles, I recognize the enormous differences that must shape interventions. Among adolescents in particular, the navigation of autonomy and emerging interpersonal relationships are persistently high-stakes issues. "Who will I be in all this mix?" "How will I be understood, if at all?" Although I am not an expert on the treatment of adolescents, I have helped in the development of ACT for adolescents by consulting with those who specialize in that treatment.

The idea for this book began over dinner at a restaurant in Toronto. Sheri Turrell and Mary Bell had enlisted me on such consultation. Over a period of years, they had tried different ACT approaches with adolescents with varying success. Some components fell flat. Others were picked up enthusiastically by adolescents in both group and individual treatments. Little by little, these women crafted a flexible manual, one that retained the parts of ACT they found to be workable and left behind or modified what was not.

I suggested over that dinner that they turn their treatment manual into a book. They were stunned by the idea. Committing to a book is a frightening prospect. But from our many conversations I was certain they could write the book they'd wished they had when they started the journey.

We are a long way from definitive answers to the treatment of psychological difficulties. Many of our best-supported treatments leave half of those treated still suffering at long-term follow-up. And as I suggested earlier, our knowledge about the treatment of children almost always lags behind that of adults. This is a book written by and for clinicians who are interested in exploring the application of ACT to adolescents in individual and group treatment. It was developed through collaboration between Mary and Sheri and the adolescents they have served. These adolescents were not hand-selected, single-problem children. They were quite often children with multiple problems, coming from the most difficult of circumstances.

It is in the nature of community mental health that specialization is not an option. Readers will find in these pages a highly adaptable guide to the application of ACT to adolescents. Along with many, many treatment examples, Sheri and Mary provide a very nontechnical and user-friendly look at the basic processes that underlie ACT. I am sure they will join me in hoping that the readers of this book will help in the ongoing development of this important work.

With warmest regards from Oxford, Mississippi,

Kelly G. Wilson, PhD
Professor, University of Mississippi

Introduction

We are two clinical therapists who are passionate about the work we do with adolescents suffering from mental health issues. The clients we see are young people experiencing symptoms associated with anxiety, depression, suicidality, self-harm, substance abuse, eating disorders, and a high level of emotional dysregulation. We have dedicated our lives to helping adolescents with these difficulties, Sheri as a psychologist and Mary as a social worker. Doing this work matters to us a great deal. We expect that it matters to you, too. We don't need to tell you that not only is each of these adolescents a unique, special, precious human being, each is somebody's child—the most important person in a parent's world. We want to find the best possible ways to help them. We would like to share what we have tried and learned with you.

Before we met, neither of us was completely satisfied with the treatment modalities we were using. We had both come to a place in our lives where we wanted to provide something more helpful to our adolescent clients. We had each developed a mindfulness practice and had begun reading about acceptance and commitment therapy (ACT). The more we stepped into mindfulness and the more we understood about ACT, the more it became obvious to us that ACT could be a promising treatment modality for our clients. When Mary was hired at the clinic where Sheri was working, mindfulness and ACT came up quickly in our first conversation. They have been the focus of hundreds of hours of discussion since then.

This book is what resulted from voracious reading, attending workshops, questioning, debating, clinical work, and our ongoing, endless discussions about ACT. As our conversations unfolded, we realized we were not clear about how to actually practice ACT with our clients. The resources at our disposal were too technical and we couldn't figure out how to make the transition from theory to practice, or how to connect the concepts within a session or between sessions. Yet, at the same time, we knew this was going to be important, so we persevered.

Because ACT involves lots of experiential learning, mostly accomplished by "experiments" that are playful, we hoped our adolescent clients would be open to engaging with us. We asked them if they would be willing to experiment with us in exploring how ACT could benefit them. To our pleasant surprise, despite the huge burden of anxiety and depression most of them were carrying, they agreed. Our admiration for the courage of these young people is immense, as is our appreciation for their willingness to take a risk with us. It is only because of the unexpected openness with which they engaged in our experiments, and the refreshing honesty with which they let us know what happened for them, that we were able to learn what works and to offer it to you. We owe a huge debt of gratitude to these young people who showed up week after week and took steps into new ACT territory with us. It is our sincere hope that their contribution will make a difference for your clients.

When we began, we felt that we would learn faster and better if we could work together, so we stepped into the challenge of learning and delivering ACT as a group-based treatment. We created a guide, or manual, for our groups and ran pilot groups prior to embarking on a research endeavor connected to our adolescent "ACTion" group. Amid the group sessions were countless hours of debriefing, planning, supervision with ACT co-founder Kelly Wilson, and continued reading and workshops.

We began by following our guide rather rigidly, but learned to move through the processes with more fluidity as time went on. The ACTion group has now been running for five years and the feedback from the adolescents has exceeded our hopes. These experiences informed and expanded our practice with individual clients, and that practice has in turn grown exponentially. This book is a session-by-session guide for clinicians working with clients individually. At the end of each session, we provide suggestions to modify the content for use in a group format. There are advantages and disadvantages to ACT with individuals versus groups of adolescents. While some adolescents may be reluctant to share their personal experiences and need the safety and privacy of individual therapy, others may benefit from the learning that takes place when groups of adolescents are engaged in experiential exercises, and from the vicarious learning that happens when peers are sharing and working through ACT processes. Logistical issues will also influence your decision, including things such as space, time, available facilitators, and your clinical setting.

Why ACT for Adolescents?

The overarching task of the adolescent stage is ego development (Erikson, 1959), which presupposes successful transition of stages leading to autonomy and initiative. The shift to becoming autonomous is a huge step for a young person. Much as they want the freedoms and privileges of adult life, even "normal" adolescents often lack the confidence in themselves to navigate the world independently. They alternate between pushing away their parents as they move toward independence, and clinging to Mom and Dad for dear life (Wolfe, Jaffe, & Crooks, 2006). When they don't get the freedom they want or when their parents and other adult authorities appropriately begin to place more grown-up expectations on them, their response is likely to be a tantrum that looks a lot like the ones their parents remember from when they were two. There is a reason for this. A precipitous brain-cell pruning and a period of massive brain-cell growth happen during both the toddler stage and the early adolescent stage. As the adolescent brain grows, development of the amygdala results in a high level of emotionality. Because there is much less activity at this stage in the frontal lobes, adolescents have difficulty managing emotions: on the treacherous road to autonomy, they are largely driven by emotions (Jensen & Nutt, 2015).

While all this is happening and adolescents are beginning to take new, scary steps away from parents, they move toward their peers. They have a felt need to attach at a deeper level with peers in order to develop safe, new attachments that will enable them to move away from their parents' original safe base. New connections with peers serve as the "launch pad" for real autonomy. But this connection with peers is fraught with all kinds of challenges. Early to mid-adolescence for youths is a period of trying on lots of different identities and values in order to figure out who they are and what kind of person they want to be. Many connect first with one group at school and then with another—becoming a "jock," a "nerd," a "cool type," or a "goth." They wear the required uniform and hang out with others who are their mirror image one semester and migrate to another world the next semester, trying on different versions of "self" in the context of like-minded peers and figuring out which one fits. From the outside it may look very superficial. But those who work with adolescents know that under all these costumes are sincere young people who are really trying to sort out what is important to them and what will guide their way forward into adulthood and throughout life. We find that the primacy placed on values in ACT lines up perfectly with the urgency our young clients have to discover a sense of their own values and what matters.

In ACT case formulation, what would usually be described as "pathology" is traced back to "avoidance" in some form or another, except that in the ACT frame of reference, avoidance is considered a natural human response rather than a pathology. It is the default coping strategy we all use when there does not yet seem to be a better way to deal with something. Because of their brain wiring and life stage, our adolescent clients have a heightened sensitivity to the immediacy of avoiding hurt and rejection and very little experience with relatively more long-term solutions to life's problems. Avoidance is their primary strategy. Because ACT specifically targets avoidance, it has been a really good fit for our clients.

In individual therapy we work with adolescents who are referred for all sorts of struggles, including anxiety, depression, eating disorders, relationship problems, substance abuse, and self-harm. In our group-based therapy, the "ACTion" group, we usually have a diagnostically heterogeneous group, and this has worked well. Clients' struggles cross common domains and are irrevocably entwined in interpersonal dilemmas, a common thread that binds group members. The transdiagnostic applicability of ACT makes it useful for anyone whose struggles involve experiential avoidance, and particularly for adolescents, for whom values identification is so important.

Who Is This Book For?

We have written this book for mental health professionals who have experience in providing therapy to adolescents but who may be new to ACT or to using ACT with adolescents. We are hoping that the reader has already sought out basic knowledge of ACT, so our focus is not to provide an in-depth description of the fundamental ACT concepts but to present the best explanation we can give of how these concepts can be successfully adapted for use with adolescents.

We hope that our ideas and ways of seeing things will not only provide some concrete strategies for you, the clinician, but will also inspire your own creativity to develop strategies that are best suited for your own clients. This book is intended as a guide that we hope will be held lightly, used flexibly, and modified to suit you, the clinician, and whoever shows up in your office.

For new learners of ACT, we would like you to know that we feel your pain. For us, learning ACT has been a path with many twists and turns. It seemed simple and elegant to us when we first began to explore the concepts. But you may find, as we did, that as you learn more and try to incorporate ACT in your clinical work, you will hit a wall of confusion from time to time. What seems simple can become very messy and convoluted. More reading, training, and supervision will help, and you may also notice that ACT is starting to be helpful for your clients, but lots of rinse-and-repeat cycles of the above pattern may nevertheless be necessary. It now appears to us that learning to embody and practice ACT as a therapist is a bit like the "working through layers of the onion" process that is therapy itself. As a therapist, you can choose to take ACT as far and as deeply as you are comfortable with. The serendipitous discovery we made was that while asking our clients to notice when they were choosing actions that were in congruence with a valued way of living, we were reminded to do the same. It has not been possible to do this work without being challenged every day to live more consistently with our own values. It pushes us to be better therapists and, we hope, better people.

We hope that this book will be helpful to those beginning on this journey and we highly recommend that you seek out as much literature, training, and supervision as possible. Joining the Association for Contextual Behavioral Science (ACBS) will link you to invaluable learning and networking opportunities, and there may be a local chapter in your area.

General Description of This Book

This book is divided into two parts. Part I consists of "ACT Basics." Part II consists of a description of the initial assessment session and the treatment sessions that follow. In "ACT Basics" we provide an overview of the philosophical and theoretical bases of ACT and an explanation of the six core ACT processes—mindfulness, defusion, acceptance, self-as-context, values, and committed action—along with a short description of what each process entails. It is important to note that these processes are not techniques to be taught to clients, but rather, they are ongoing abilities we want to foster within our clients.

We finish "ACT Basics" with a description of the "matrix" and address the "therapist stance" of ACT. The latter refers to a way of "being" in relation to a client—in the room, in the moment—that makes possible the discoveries your client can make about choosing and living a meaningful life.

In the assessment session that begins part II, we have provided a way of gathering typical information that lends itself to ACT and the sessions that follow. Each of the subsequent session chapters describes a single therapy session, starting with content for working with an individual client and followed by modifications for group therapy. Because our original guide was connected to our group-based treatment delivered over ten weeks, each session focused on a single point in the ACT "hexaflex," representing one of the six processes. Although there are six processes, providing ten sessions for our groups allowed for the opportunity to spend more than one session on a given process as well as time for culminating experiential exercises and review. We used what we learned in facilitating group-based ACT to inform our work with individual clients, and vice versa. Descriptions of the content in each session include metaphors and experiential exercises, some of which we have created and many of which we have borrowed and adapted from the brilliant ACT pioneers.

Although we have presented the sessions (and the ACT processes) in a particular order, our hope is that clinicians will use the sessions in whatever order works for their own clients. As always when doing ACT, we go into a session prepared to focus on one of the ACT processes while remaining open to the possibility that clients will share material that requires us to gently shift to another process. The reader is encouraged to feel free to change the order of the sessions or to pull content from one session into another, according to client needs. In addition, it may turn out that what began as a single session focusing on one of the ACT processes will require more than one session in order for the client to really experience and discover what is there to be learned.

Throughout this book we have tried to present the overall flow and contents of each session in a consistent order. For example, we begin with a review of previous content and home practice, then move into mindfulness and new content. If your client benefits from some brief mindfulness right at the start of a session, then go ahead and incorporate that; we certainly have done this at times. We chose this order because we sometimes use mindfulness as a visualization exercise to experience a new concept or process and want to do so after reviewing prior concepts.

As familiarity with the model increases, these decisions about the order of sessions and the length of time spent on each process will seem more natural. Cues that the client is giving us about what he needs will become more obvious. Clinicians whose own practice is more oriented toward brief therapy may want to work through the processes more quickly, keeping more or less with the structured content of the sessions in this book. Conversely, those who provide more long-term therapy may want to expand their ACT work to a deeper level, continuing to work with present-moment material as it enters the therapeutic relationship.

Once you are familiar with the ACT processes, ACT can be integrated with other approaches that are theoretically compatible, including the "collaborative problem solving" model, some streams of psychoanalysis, attachment-based therapies, and mindfulness-based stress reduction. Within the ACT model, specific skills such as assertive communication and problem solving can be incorporated as needed.

If you are relatively new to ACT, we strongly encourage you to read the entire book before you start to work in an ACT way with clients, so you have the overall context of the work. New or not, it may help you to know ahead of time, for example, that session 9 focuses exclusively on self-compassion, so you may want to read session 9 before you start your work and incorporate pieces of that session earlier as appropriate.

A word or two about mindfulness is important before we continue. Throughout the book we provide meditation scripts for formal practice, as well as informal ways to help clients develop a sense of mindfulness. If you are new to mindfulness, we strongly encourage you to develop your own practice to some degree before taking this journey with your clients. It is often said that ACT is best learned from the inside out, and nowhere is this truer than with regards to mindfulness. Your own experience and practice will help you to process the experience with your client in a way that you just can't know how to do if you haven't spent time with it. Mindfulness, like the other ACT processes, is not "taught" through cognitive or intellectual exercises, it has to be experienced. We also suggest that you practice the meditations first, finding your own sense of the wording and the flow so that it does not sound too scripted and stiff when you are engaging with clients.

Fictional Clients

We have woven the experiences of several fictional clients into this book to illustrate concepts and session content. They are composites based on the very real qualities and circumstances of the many clients we've encountered in our work. We tried to include details and struggles that come up frequently, in the hopes they are representative for other clinicians. The names of these "clients" are also fictional.

Our adolescent clients are often immobilized at home, unable to attend school or socialize with their peers. They desperately want to feel better and to step back into their lives. But because they are teenagers, everything in their lives—their peer group, their parents' expectations, their school's academic demands—seems to be changing so fast that even as their symptoms decline, it's hard for them to find their way back in. They hold back and hide. They avoid.

The range of our fictional clients is typical of the adolescents we see in our practices, but it is by no means exhaustive. Our clinical experience is consistent with research that shows ACT to be helpful for people with obsessive-compulsive disorder (Twohig, Hayes, & Masuda, 2006; Twohig et al., 2010), social anxiety disorder (Dalrymple & Herbert, 2007), generalized anxiety disorder (Roemer & Orsillo, 2007; Roemer, Orsillo, & Salters-Pedneault, 2008; Wetherell et al., 2011), skin picking (Twohig, Hayes, & Masuda, 2006), and chronic pain (McCracken, MacKichan, & Eccleston, 2007).

Notes About Individual Therapy

Working with individual clients has its pros and cons compared to delivering ACT in a group format. As a clinician, you may already have your own criteria for determining individual versus group-based treatment, so here we offer only a few thoughts. For adolescents whose struggles require discretion and privacy, or for those who simply prefer it, approaching individual therapy from an ACT stance is very rewarding. Individual therapy may be more efficient, which is important if duration of therapy is an issue, and allows for more attention on processes that are relevant for a particular client. In addition, you can add parents to the sessions as needed; this helps to keep parents aligned and supportive of your work while promoting generalization of the ACT processes outside of sessions. At the same time, having only the therapist and the client in the session requires that therapists use their "self" in an authentic way and really be a part of what is happening. This means that experiential exercises need to be set up in such a way that you can take part along with your client, physically, emotionally, and in terms of disclosure when necessary, while keeping boundaries in mind.

Notes About Group Therapy

As clinicians, we are immensely gratified by what happens as adolescents move through the ACT model with a group of their peers. Recognition of the universality of their struggles is a powerful realization and normalizes their experience in a way that cannot be captured in individual therapy. For adolescents who are particularly isolated and in need of a shared experience, group-based ACT can be very impactful. But because the majority of the time in our ACTion group sessions is experiential in nature, rather than didactic, we have been hesitant to offer group-based ACT to clients who are fearful about participating in "experiments" or about speaking within a group setting.

We typically run our ACTion groups for ninety minutes each week over a ten-week period, with a follow-up session three months later. We run closed groups with a maximum of eight adolescents at a time, although when our clinic referrals have been high we have sometimes raised the limit to ten. When an adolescent misses a session we have tried to meet with him prior to the next session to "make up" the content with him, so that he arrives at the next session as aware as he can be of what transpired in terms of content and the group process. This strategy, however, is not without limitations. First, it is really impossible to catch up regarding the subtle nuanced interpersonal interactions that took place and that in many cases were very powerful, so our adolescent is limited to a less intensely "felt" sense of what happened. Because we refer back to experiential exercises repeatedly once they occur, we prefer closed groups so we don't have to repeat ourselves and explain things over and over again. We are very emphatic prior to the start of the ACTion group that attendance is of paramount importance.

We have offered a few open groups and find this to be tricky, but not impossible. As new clients arrive, you can repeat previous content by reintroducing concepts using different metaphors and experiments, which is possible because of the wealth of options available.

It has been helpful to run the groups with two clinicians for several reasons: to have a clinician available in case a group member is in crisis; to increase the likelihood of noticing subtle nuances or dynamics as they arise and that can be used to illustrate concepts in the moment; to ensure adherence to the ACT model; and to enhance clinician knowledge and skills while debriefing after group sessions and preparing the next session. Interestingly, it was our group work that gave us greater confidence and skill to work in an ACT way with individual clients, because we had the priceless gift of collegial feedback, debriefing, and teaching to stretch our comfort zone and grow.

Although there appears above to be a linear "flow" to the group content, there actually isn't! We have rarely, if ever, followed the same sequence exactly. We have tried to go with the needs of group members as they arise. When clients appear to be stuck in their "story" (conceptualized self), we gently shift to acceptance or defusion strategies, even if the session was supposed to be about values. When focusing on acceptance or defusion, we may begin to make reference to values if clients understand the concepts. As a clinician, please defer to your own judgment and expertise and hold our book lightly. Learning ACT has been an incremental experience for us as clinicians. We were much more linear in our approach when we began, gaining increased flexibility as our comfort and skill developed. We have written the book to be used "as is" if you are beginning your journey, knowing that if you are further on your way, you will make your own adaptations.

It is important for the clinician to arrive at her own "creative hopelessness" when a session is not going as expected. We have learned to loosen our grip on what we thought was a nicely planned session, and to embrace our own willingness to go with what shows up in the group. Don't let adherence to your own planning get in the way.

To enhance the learning and practice of mindfulness, we recorded audio tracks for the group. We provide members with the tracks after each session and ask group members to listen to them as part of their "home practice" for the week. The audio recordings are available online on the New Harbinger website: https://www.newhar binger.com/33575.

Kelly Wilson suggested we write "the book you wish you had had when you started all this," and that is what we have tried to do. We hope that our words will give clarity where it is needed, inspire new thoughts and ideas, and most of all, help as you as you forge ahead in your work with adolescents. They are some of our favorite people!

PART 1

ACT Basics

In this chapter we provide a very brief review of the theory behind acceptance and commitment therapy (ACT, pronounced as a single word) and the processes of ACT. For those who are familiar with ACT, it will serve as a quick review. For those new to ACT, we hope it will serve as an introduction. We highly recommend further reading, training, and supervision in order to more fully understand both the theory and the treatment model.

We begin this chapter with a brief description of the foundational underpinnings of ACT, which are, from the ground up, the philosophy of functional contextualism (FC), applied behavioral analysis (ABA), and relational frame theory (RFT). We then provide an outline of the six basic ACT processes within the context of the ACT hexaflex, a hexagram-shaped depiction with one of the six processes at each corner. We then move to a description of the matrix, a tool for "sorting" client information and helping clients move toward psychological flexibility. Finally, we provide a few thoughts about therapist stance to consider as you learn to embody ACT.

Acceptance and Commitment Therapy (ACT)

Traditionally, psychological suffering has been explained by a disease model that identifies specific illnesses (for example, social anxiety disorder) characterized by signs and symptoms (such as avoiding social situations) that can be treated and eliminated (Hayes, Strosahl, & Wilson, 2012). This focus has led to numerous therapeutic approaches that primarily seek to reduce symptoms. As the disease model comes under question, ACT offers a different paradigm in the form of a transdiagnostic model that posits experiential avoidance as a core process inherent across what we typically refer to as "disorders."

From an ACT perspective, suffering, whether in the form of "social anxiety," "depression," "OCD," or other traditional diagnoses, results not from the thoughts, feelings, memories, urges, or physical sensations that we experience, but from our responses to these internal, private "events." Clients often arrive at therapy having put great effort into "solving" thoughts and feelings they don't like by trying to get rid of them, in much the same way as they might try to get rid of unwanted experiences in their external world. As our clients struggle to control their private, internal events, they may attempt to suppress, avoid, or get rid of experiences that appear to "trigger" or cue the thoughts and feelings they don't want to have. Over the long term, however, these control strategies lead to a paradoxical increase in the frequency and intensity of these unwanted internal events. As clients try to control and avoid their ever-increasing thoughts and feelings, their lives become very narrow in focus, diminishing their chance of living in a way that's meaningful and fulfilling. ACT is essentially about changing our relationship with thoughts and feelings and other internal events so that we stop trying to get rid of things we can't get rid of; rather, we take our thoughts and feelings with us, in the context of pursuing a meaningful life.

As a clinician interested in the ACT approach, it is important for you to understand both the philosophical (functional contextualism) and theoretical (applied behavioral analysis and relational frame theory) underpinnings, which are described below. This will foster your ability to move through the ACT processes creatively and fluidly in a manner consistent with the foundations of the therapy. Clinicians new to ACT may approach sessions in a mechanistic or technical manner. This is not unexpected. However, as your familiarity increases, you will be better able to embody ACT not as a technology, but as a broad, flexible framework.

Functional Contextualism

The philosophy of functional contextualism (FC) underlies ABA, RFT, and ACT (Hayes, Strosahl, & Wilson, 2012). While we can't cover FC in its entirety, there are a few points that will be helpful as you move through the remainder of the theory portion of this book, and into the therapy.

From a functional contextualist perspective, predicting and influencing behavior is of key importance and is the goal of behavior analysis and therapy. Functional contextualists consider "behavior" as an act-in-context rather than breaking it down into units. In this sense, "behavior" includes overt motor behavior such as speaking or walking, as well as behavior on the inside, which refers to psychological "events"—what we "do" on the inside. Psychological events include, for example, things such as imagining, feeling, and sensing. While some therapies attempt to alter one of a client's "behaviors" by changing another of his "behaviors," such as trying to change his emotions by changing his cognitions through disputation or rational argument, this does not make sense from a contextualist perspective. For example, a client who reports depressed mood may also report co-occurring cognitions, such as, "I will never succeed." This co-occurrence may be more of a correlation than a cause-and-effect relationship and tells us nothing about how to change or influence either of these behaviors (feeling and thinking). It is possible that depressed mood influenced the development of the thought, but the reverse is also possible, so this does not get us very far. When the thought *I will never succeed* pops up, clients can become quite tangled in the thought and experience it within a context of literality, assuming that it is true and acting accordingly, perhaps by not taking risks when their success is not assured. Alternatively, the same thought experienced within a context of openness and curiosity may not influence a client's overt behavior, and he may be able to have the thought while doing something that matters to him. In this sense, psychological events are not inherently "bad" or problematic: what is problematic is the context in which they occur and the function they serve. Behaviors may serve to move us away from internal experience, or toward what matters: the important thing here is to understand the *function* of a behavior within its overall context, including interpersonal, intrapersonal, historical learning history, and situational factors.

A second important feature of functional contextualism is the emphasis on a pragmatic truth criterion (Hayes, Strosahl, & Wilson, 2012). Rather than asking clients to dispute the "truth" of their cognitions, the "truth" criterion for contextualists is the "workability" of client behavior. A behavior is "workable" or "true" if it leads clients in a direction that matters to them. To know if behavior "works," we help clients identify what matters to them and help them become aware of their behavior and the function of their behavior relative to their values. This is the "commitment" part of ACT and involves identifying and moving through life according to values, or what matters to each of us. We help clients to adopt a posture of openness and curiosity when they notice what is happening inside and to do so while moving toward what matters instead of away from their internal experiences. This is the "acceptance" part of ACT.

The goal in ACT is to predict and influence behavior, so that our clients can respond to their world, as it unfolds in a given moment, with greater flexibility instead of in ways that are rigid, repetitive, and problematic. Rather than suggesting that clients change their thoughts and feelings, we help them change the context in which their thoughts and feelings occur and to examine the function of their behavior. Keeping the function of behavior in mind, we turn next to a very brief summary of applied behavioral analysis, or ABA.

Applied Behavioral Analysis

When we consider client behavior in ACT, we examine the "function" of a client's behavior within that client's unique context. A typical functional analysis considers the antecedents of behavior (environmental factors, physical states such as hunger or fatigue, private experiences such as thoughts and feelings, and so on), the behavior itself (what we are analyzing from a functional perspective), and the consequences of behavior (the effect of the behavior), all of which can be denoted as "ABC." This will be important to keep in mind with ACT.

For example, let's consider a client, Joyce, who values relationships and a sense of connection with others. While at an outdoor party near the start of her school year, fifteen-year-old Joyce suddenly leaves and makes a fast retreat home. Her peers, unsure about what has just happened, can only guess as to the function of Joyce's behavior. Was she just swarmed by bees and running to escape being stung? Was she overcome by food poisoning and nausea and did she leave to avoid the embarrassment of public vomiting? They are not sure.

Joyce arrives at your therapy office the next day and tells you that while at the party (antecedent) she was flooded by thoughts (antecedent) that if people spoke to her and got to know her they would not like her, and by feelings of anxiety (antecedent). Joyce reacted to her thoughts and anxiety by leaving the party (behavior). When she got home, Joyce experienced a reduction in the intensity of her thoughts and of her feelings of anxiety (consequences), albeit only temporarily. Soon after, her anxiety intensified as she worried about how to explain her behavior to her peers, and she now feels a sense of shame and regret for missing the party (more consequences). Her behavior also took her away from the sense of connection with others, which matters to her (more consequences). In this sense, Joyce's behavior is functioning to avoid psychological events, but it is not "workable" because it took her away from what mattered. This is an example of behavior that is negatively reinforced in that an aversive stimulus (internal event) has been removed. Because the behavior was reinforced, it is likely to happen again. The same thoughts and feelings, if experienced within a context of openness and curiosity, might have allowed Joyce to approach her thoughts as just something her mind was doing at the time, and to notice by observing others' actual behavior whether or not they were rejecting her. This would open up possibilities for Joyce to discover alternative ways of responding and she might move toward a sense of connection. This would be an example of behavior that is positively reinforced through the presentation of something pleasant (in this case, connecting with peers). The sense of connection would serve as a motivator or reinforcing stimulus, making the behavior likely to occur again in the future. In ACT, we want to bring behavior under positive reinforcement, where acting according to what matters, according to values, is intrinsically reinforcing.

Through discussion with Joyce, you learn that she often leaves social situations for the same reasons she described in this circumstance. However, Joyce has never been overtly rejected by peers, so her behavior cannot be explained through contingencies of reinforcement and punishment. Before we proceed to relational frame theory, we need to understand behavior such as Joyce's that has a repetitive quality to it and not only moves clients away from what matters, but also brings with it additional consequences. Joyce's behavior was influenced not by contingencies in her environment, but by verbal contingencies, or "rules" that *describe* a contingency (for example, *if* people get to know me, *then* they won't like me). Joyce's behavior is an example of what we call "rule-governed behavior," which occurs in the absence of direct learning. Rule-governed behavior is an important type of human learning that can be both beneficial and problematic.

Rule-Governed Behavior

Our clients often arrive at therapy with deeply entrenched ideas about themselves, others, and the world around them—ideas that guide their behavior in a variety of unhelpful ways, such as Joyce's, outlined previously. These same clients may engage in persistent, inflexible behavior that to others appears to make matters worse. For example, an adolescent, Johnny, reports an intense fear of failure, even though he has never failed at anything. If Johnny merely imagines failure, he notices emotions, physical sensations, memories, and urges consistent with the experience of failure, even though it is not happening to him at that moment. Johnny might then avoid studying, which would likely reduce these unwanted internal events, but would do little to move him toward being a successful student.

Johnny's aversive reaction to the word "failure" can't be explained by traditional respondent or operant conditioning, since there is nothing in his history to suggest direct learning of an aversive relationship to the word "failure." The role of language seems relevant for our clients who suffer with thoughts and feelings connected to events that have happened in the past or might happen in the future, but are not happening to them in the moment. When clients use language to speak of worries about the future, for example, they *feel* anxious. In this example, Johnny's behavior was not directed by experience with direct learning and reinforcement contingencies, but by verbal "rules" that specify a contingency or relationship between failure and physical sensations and emotions. We refer to the resulting behavior as "rule-governed behavior."

Language, as a symbolic communication, is central to human development. And it is a more effective means of communication than grunts or physical gestures. Young children learn to use language to name objects, ask for what they need, and share their experiences with others. As children get older, language allows them to engage in problem solving, to learn, and to participate in a more complex and sophisticated society based on shared knowledge.

As you will see further expanded below, over time language allows human beings to develop increasingly complex networks of relationships between spoken words, objects, written words, and internal events (memories, thoughts, urges, emotions, physical feelings) that do not rely on direct training. This is the rule-governed behavior mentioned above, which allows us to learn and adapt quickly and efficiently.

Our ability to verbally specify the relations between events without experience allows us to respond safely to potentially dangerous circumstances without having to experience the actual dangerous consequences. For example, if a child is told, "Look both ways before you cross the street so you don't get hit by a car," he will likely obey because the two events (looking both ways and not getting hit by a car) have been put in a verbal relation of cause and effect. Using verbal rules, we can also regulate future behavior, such as when an adolescent is told, "If you do your homework you will get good grades." The adolescent may follow this rule without any learning history of failure, and thus avoid bad grades.

Language, however, is a two-sided coin and can also serve as a recipe for suffering. Using language, our minds can relate anything to anything. As a result, we can experience emotions and suffering when the emotions are cued not by present-moment circumstances but by a memory, a tone of voice, physical sensations, or other internal events. The suffering we experience on the inside does not feel good and we try to get rid of it through various avoidance and suppression strategies. This is the paradox of suffering: as we try to get rid of or avoid what's inside, the strategies we employ enter into existing relational networks and the cues that are associated with suffering increase.

Moreover, when behavior falls under the control of verbal "rules," we tend not to alter the rule in the presence of conflicting or discrepant experience. For example, an adolescent who tends to procrastinate with schoolwork, or not do it at all, may find himself failing several subjects at school. Despite the serious impact of his repetitive behavior (not studying), the behavior persists. This adolescent may be following a rule such as, "If I study and fail others will think I'm stupid." When faced with the fact that he has never studied and failed and is asked by his therapist to dispute his rule, he replies, "But it happens to other kids and it *could* happen to me." This rule is, in essence, untestable and following this rule is resulting in failure, which he may see as: "Better to not study and fail than study and fail; this way, I'm not stupid." The debate could continue, and likely get nowhere between the adolescent and his therapist. From an ACT perspective, it is about "workability," so there is not much point in debating the rules behind rule-governed behavior.

Furthermore, rules generally are not followed when doing so results in aversive consequences. So why does the aforementioned adolescent continue to avoid studying when this results in failure? Within his context, his behavior is reinforced by its function, which is to reduce aversive internal events (in this case, anxiety).

To recap, rule-governed behavior is that which is under control of verbal rules or specifications, in the absence of direct experience with the environment. Rule-governed behavior is not very sensitive to changes in the environment, meaning we may not change the rule, or our behavior, in the face of conflicting experience. We see this in our clients, who describe engaging in repetitive behavior, such as drug or alcohol use, that seem to make things worse in the long run. Clients often describe such behavior as a "habit," or say something like, "I know that avoiding school makes me more anxious, but I do it anyway," or "I just assume people don't like me and I pull away from them, even if they haven't done anything." Rule following often leads to experiential avoidance and this can take our clients far away from what matters: their values. Much of ACT is about aligning clients with their values as a sort of compass, to undermine rule-governed behavior.

Zettle and Hayes (1982) described several categories of rule-following behavior: pliance, tracking, and augmentals, each of which is characterized by different reinforcement histories. There has been a great deal written about rule-governed behavior in ACT texts, based on substantial empirical research. We provide here a very basic description of pliance, tracking, and augmenting, so that you the clinician can get a feel for "rules." We discuss normally developing rule-governed behavior first, and problematic rule-governed behavior after the RFT section. Later on in the book we will explain how to work with inflexible rules and rule following that show up clinically. For a fuller explanation, we suggest that you read Hayes, Strosahl, & Wilson (2012), Törneke (2010), or McHugh & Stewart (2012). If you are interested in the empirical literature, many professional databases contain relevant articles, and the website for the Association for Contextual Behavioral Science (ACBS) offers online access to resources: http://contextualscience.org.

Pliance

Pliance is a form of rule-governed behavior that is under the control of socially mediated consequences (Zettle & Hayes, 1982; Zettle, 2007), that is, consequences under the control of a particular speaker. We learn pliance with a speaker's rules over time and from multiple examples, reinforced by the person stating the rule, often a parent (McHugh & Stewart, 2012; Törneke, 2010). To put this more simply, we do as we are told because of the consequences delivered by another! As children, if we are told to do something, or not to do it, because a particular consequence will or will not follow, and we obey in order to please our parent or avoid punishment, this is pliance. When children are repeatedly told, "You need to do homework," and do so in order to gain the parent's approval, this is pliance. An adolescent who found that staying up past his bedtime met with parental disapproval is engaging in pliance when he makes sure he is tucked in on time to avoid punishment. Rule following of this sort is important in the development of socially appropriate behavior in children.

Tracking

The second type of rule-governed behavior, *tracking*, develops after pliance is established. "Tracking" a rule refers to following a verbal rule that develops from a historical link between the rules and natural contingencies. The child who once followed the rule, "Do your homework," in order to receive parental approval was engaging in pliance. Over time this same child may be told, "Do your homework and you will get good marks at school." If he is "tracking," he will do his homework not for parental approval, but because he has experienced the natural consequences of following or not following the rule, in terms of his academic success. As another example, consider the adolescent who is already pliant with the rule, "Take a shower when you get home." After coming home from a soccer game, covered in mud, he is then told to "take a shower," which he does. After showering, he eventually figures out, on his own, that he is less dirty, not scratching so much, and feels more refreshed. In this instance, he is making observations based on his five senses of the natural consequences of his own behavior, without any additional social consequences. Contact with the natural contingencies or consequences determines if the rule is or is not followed in the future.

Augmentals

Whereas pliance and tracking involve social and natural consequences, respectively, an augmental is a type of rule that alters the reinforcing nature (aversive, or pleasurable and approachable) of an event (keep in mind that this refers to internal and external events, or behavior) based on what is said about the event (Törneke, Luciano, & Valdivia Salas, 2008). Augmentals are considered a sophisticated form of rule-governed behavior because they establish control based not only on the relations between stimuli, but also the abstract consequences that have not yet been experienced. For example, consider the adolescent who studies because he is following the verbal rule, "Study hard and you will get a good job when you grow up." He is following the rule in the absence of a learning history that has established getting a good job as a reinforcing consequence. Augmenting, although related to pliance and tracking, works a bit differently in that it is connected to both, and appears to augment or depotentiate consequences.

This will all become clearer once you understand something about RFT, which comes next. Afterwards, we extend RFT into the clinical realm and use examples to illustrate how pliance, tracking, and augmentals can be problematic.

Relational Frame Theory

When we began our ACT journey, we spent time getting comfortable within and between the ACT processes. Eventually, however, we realized that an understanding of RFT would be helpful: our curiosity and the values of being active learners and supporters to our clients eventually won out, and we dug into the trenches of RFT. (In ACT we try to keep sight not only of the client's values but also of our own.) How *combinatorial entailment* (explained below) was going to connect to our adolescent clients who were asking for help with fears about failure and abandonment by friends wasn't immediately clear. We persevered, however, and again found ourselves in one of those rinse-and-repeat cycles of incremental learning: we figured it out, bit by bit. We provide here a streamlined version to demonstrate the clinical relevance we were looking for when we started. However, in our effort to be succinct and clear, details may not be included that might expand your knowledge and practice. For comprehensive reading about RFT, please refer to the books and articles in the References (Hayes, Strosahl, & Wilson, 2012; McHugh & Stewart, 2012; Törneke, 2010).

Because RFT can be confusing, we want to clarify some terms before we continue. What is "connected" through relational framing is "behavior" or "events" (we use the two terms interchangeably). What is meant by behavior is anything that people do. This includes not only overt motor behavior (walking and talking, for instance) but also behaviors that are internal and private. Internal, private events or behavior includes remembering, hearing, smelling, tasting, sensing, feeling, and imagining, for example. Dr. Robyn Walser summarized it nicely during a consultation: "Behavior is that which occurs inside the skin, and outside," and, "What is inside can relate to what is also inside or to what is outside, and what is outside can relate to what is outside or inside" (personal communication, September 11, 2015). When we refer to "stimuli," we are referring to anything that clients respond to. In this sense, stimuli can be cognitions, feelings, sounds, smells, tastes, sensations, memories, urges, gestures, tones of voice, spoken words, written words, and features of the environment.

How humans form relations between stimuli (or events) is complex and not adequately explained by traditional models of learning through mechanisms such as respondent and operant conditioning. RFT is a functional contextual theory based on derived relational responding, a process that appears to be uniquely human. Early on, as children acquire language, they relate stimuli based on nonarbitrary features, namely those that are part of their five senses experience. Relating refers to behavior in response to one stimulus based on its relationship to another stimulus. Various ways of relating are directly trained and reinforced. Once nonarbitrary relating is established, through experience and reinforcement, children develop the ability to engage in relational framing, a term used to denote a type of relating that is based on arbitrary, or socially established, features of stimuli (Törneke, 2010). To be clear, the term "relating" is used in reference to our use of language to connect nonarbitrary stimuli, while "relational framing" is used in reference to relating arbitrary stimuli. Derived relational responding is defined as a learned behavior that consists of mutual entailment, combinatorial entailment, and transformation of stimulus function (Hayes, Strosahl, & Wilson, 2012), each of which is described below. Relational framing has two main features. The first is the relational context, which determines how events are related (for example, comparison, temporality, cause and effect). The second is the functional context, which refers to the psychological impact of the relating (Hayes, Levin, Plumb-Vilardaga, Villatte, & Pistorello, 2013). RFT explains both nonproblematic and problematic rule-governed behavior, the latter of which is defined by a lack of workability.

Nonarbitrary Relating

Getting back to the five senses experience mentioned in the previous section, when children begin to use language, they relate objects according to what they can see, hear, touch, taste, and smell. The three main properties of this relating, mutual entailment, combinatorial entailment, and transformation of stimulus function, are described below.

Mutual Entailment

Early on, children are taught that a particular object can be referred to by a particular word, and vice versa. When they produce the word that refers to an object their caregiver is holding, for example, they are praised or reinforced. The same thing happens if they produce the object that a parent has asked for. With experience and reinforcement, children learn the bidirectionality of relationships between spoken words, objects, and written words. As they get older, children only need to be taught a relationship in one direction, such as, "This cold, yummy stuff is ice cream," and they will derive a second relationship, that the spoken word "ice cream" refers to the cold, yummy stuff, without direct training. We can say that the child has learned a relation of coordination, or sameness, between the spoken word and the object, such that they stand for the same thing. We will use two additional examples to illustrate these concepts.

For our first example, imagine that after repeatedly being shown a dog while parents say, "This is a dog," to their child, the child learns to utter something that sounds like "dog" when she sees the furry, four-legged creature that licks her, sometimes barks, and smells like the outdoors. In response, parents reinforce the utterance by praising their child, "Great, yes, this is a dog." In this example, the words "this is" provide a context in which the child learns that the spoken word and the object refer to the same thing. They have entered into a relation of coordination in which the verbal stimulus (the words) functions as equivalent to the object, so they stand for the same thing. So when we say "dog" the child will orient toward the family pet. When relations between the object and the spoken word (or the written word, for that matter) are trained in one direction, and the reverse relationship is derived without direct training, we call this mutual entailment. This happens first based on nonarbitrary features of the stimuli, those that we experience with our five senses, and it happens over multiple learning trials.

Combinatorial Entailment

Once mutual entailment is established, children learn combinatorial entailment, which involves training two relationships and deriving four untrained relationships, resulting in a total of six relationships.

Expanding on the previous example, when a child is taught that the spoken word "dog" is coordinated with the actual family pet, one trained relationship and one derived relationship emerge, as explained above. Once this is established, the child is later taught that the spoken word "dog" is coordinated with the written word D-O-G, and she then derives the reverse, that the written word D-O-G is coordinated with the spoken word "dog." Furthermore, she will derive two additional relationships, for a total of four: she will derive that the family pet, the object, is the same as the written word D-O-G, and the reverse, that the written word is the same as the pet.

Training of relations takes place with reinforcement and over multiple exemplars of a particular type of relation (for example, "bigger than"), in which events relate to one another based on their nonarbitrary features. The number of relations that can be derived are not restricted to six, but are limitless, as networks expand and connect to other networks over the course of development. These expanding networks allow us to learn vast amounts of information without direct experience, which makes our ability to manage in the world much more efficient. Once a child learns to relate and derive, he does so automatically when encountering new stimuli.

Transformation of Stimulus Function

Over time and many, many examples, through mutual entailment and combinatorial entailment, the relationships between an object, the spoken word, and the written word enter a relation of coordination, as described above. This relationship ultimately extends to include the internal private "events" associated with the stimulus, such as memories, sights, sounds, smells, sensory feelings, and taste. Once the relations are established, the function of a given stimulus will transfer to other stimuli within the relational network, such as the spoken word, the written word, and our internal behaviors. What does this mean? If the "stimulus" is the word "dog," and dogs are related with pleasant memories, emotions, experiences, or physical feelings, upon hearing "dog" a child will orient towards the animal. Conversely, if the stimulus "dog" is associated with unpleasant thoughts, emotions, experiences, or physical feelings, the child will perhaps run away when she hears the word, even if she hasn't seen the animal yet. In this same way, the spoken word "dog" and the written word D-O-G will also evoke internal events with all of their nonarbitrary features (for example, furry, smelly, soft to touch, can be heard barking), and will evoke the same emotional responses. Once spoken words, letters on a page, objects, both real and as events in our minds, all stand for the same thing, the emotional experience and characteristics of the object or its verbal referent (or "stimulus") also appear when we hear or read the word or imagine the object. In this sense, the function of the word takes on the function of the real object, with "function" referring to the effect the stimulus has on us, or what we do (approach or avoid) in response to the stimulus. This is transformation of stimulus function.

Over time, the child will generalize the concept of "dog" to include different types of four-legged creatures, so that Australian shepherds, poodles, Chihuahuas, and Rottweilers, for example, are each referred to as "dog," and are responded to similarly.

Nonarbitrary relating becomes more complex with time and experience, as new relations are added into existing networks. When the same child who found dogs pleasant learns that "dog" is the same as "poochie," thoughts, emotions, and memories that were connected to "dog" now transfer to "poochie," and elicit the behavior of approaching something called a "poochie."

For our second example, if repeatedly shown a crinkly brown paper thing that is open at one end while parents say "bag," a child learns to relate the spoken word to the object; they stand for each other. Through mutual and combinatorial entailment, the child will learn and derive relationships such that the spoken word, written word, and object are all representing the same thing. Over time, internal "events" associated with "bag" will also enter the relationship. If a child has only known pleasant experiences of "bag," for instance, that it is a crinkly brown paper thing containing candy from the bulk bins at the candy store, the child might have thoughts associated with "bag" such as, *Chocolate, my favorite!* or emotions such as excitement and happiness, and physical sensations that are pleasant, like a warm feeling in his tummy, when he sees a bag or hears mommy say, "Daddy brought a bag home." However, if a child has experienced "bag" as a crinkly brown paper thing containing bugs that the bully across the street scared him with, the child would likely have unpleasant thoughts, feelings, and physical sensations associated with "bag"—thoughts such as *I can't defend myself*, feelings of fear, and the corresponding physical sensations, such as shivering, fast heart rate, and an urge to run, that are related to those memories.

Once a child knows that a "bag" is the same as a "sack," the thoughts, feelings, and physical sensations associated with "bag" quickly enter into a relationship with "sack" through the *transformation of stimulus function*. Now think about a child who has had the frightening experience with "bag," and imagine the potential for affective and visceral responses when, later on, the child hears something like "They gave him the sack." This statement could suddenly connect to intense feelings of fear and all the sensations that go with fear. Because of relational responding, "getting the sack" is something to be very afraid of, and avoided. This relational responding may later influence behavior when the child, as an adolescent, desperately tries to avoid "getting the sack" at his part-time job by being overly compliant and constantly seeking reassurance that he won't get fired.

What is transferred between stimuli is their ability to function as something that one wants to approach or wants to avoid. For humans, what this means is that when an object is in a relation of coordination, equivalence, or sameness, for example, with emotions we don't want to have, emotions we prefer to avoid, then we try to avoid the object, and even the internal events associated with the object. Through transformation of stimulus function, a child's internal, private behavior associated with a stimulus—thoughts, emotions, physical sensations, memories, and urges that are evoked by the object—are transferred to the spoken and written word. This explains why our clients are hesitant to talk about what makes them anxious. Thinking about and talking about what makes them anxious makes them *feel* anxious!

Types of Relations Between Stimuli

RFT describes several types of stimulus *relations*: *coordination* ("same as," "similar," and "like"), *temporal* ("before" and "after"), *causal* ("if/then," "because of"), *comparison* and *evaluation* ("better than," "bigger than," "faster than," and "prettier than"), *deictic* ("I/you," "now/then," and "here/there"), *opposite* ("love and hate"), *hierarchical* ("a part of/includes"), and *spatial* ("near/far") relations (Hayes, 2005). These words tell us about the relational context of the stimuli, which means they tell us how the verbal stimuli are related. In this way, children learn that "a nickel is bigger than a dime," based solely on the physical properties of the coins. They may also learn things like "this bag has more candy than that bag," based on the number of candies in the bags. Once our use of words, of language, establishes relationships based on nonarbitrary (five senses experience) features, children learn to establish arbitrary relations between stimuli, based on properties that are not based on our five senses experience, even for stimuli with which they have no previous experience.

Arbitrarily Applied Relational Responding: Everything Relates to Everything

Once relational responding has been established based on five senses experience, or nonarbitrary features of stimuli, we expand our learning to include the relating of arbitrary stimuli, those that are socially established contextual cues. When asked, "What is bigger, a dime or a nickel?" a small child might compare the two based on physical size (a nonarbitrary relation) and respond, "A nickel." A more experienced child, having learned the socially established, arbitrary values of the coins, would respond, "A dime." Adolescents learn that earning an "A" in school is better than earning a "B." There are no formal, nonarbitrary properties of "A" and "B" to establish this relation. What brings the stimuli together is the language that provides the relational context (in this case, "better than"), which is socially prescribed and arbitrary.

Arbitrarily applied relational responding (AARR), or relational framing, refers to verbal behavior that relates stimuli based on arbitrary features. In this sense, virtually any feature of the environment can serve as an arbitrary contextual cue, and therefore things that were rewarding in previous experiences can become aversive, and vice versa. Relational frames develop throughout our lives, influenced by training and reinforcement contingencies, and form complex networks in which everything relates to everything, somehow. Once a child learns to relate stimuli in a particular frame, such as coordination, he can relationally frame any new stimuli he encounters in the same way.

As a child grows and enters adolescence and then adulthood, relational frames continue to grow and networks expand and connect. Frames of comparison and evaluation, important in childhood as we form our sense of who we are, continue to be important in adolescents as our clients try to make sure they "measure up" to peers (more on this in session 4). We find ourselves worried that we are not "as pretty as" or "as smart as" someone else, and reassurance and rational debate seem to do little to reduce these fears.

If our adolescent client hears that someone "is like a dog," her interpretation will depend on which socially established characteristics of "dog" she has experienced, including, but not limited to, someone who is sweet and friendly, morally reprehensible, unattractive, or sneaky. These relations are arbitrary, based on social convention, and their usage has been reinforced. None of the arbitrary qualities is based on what we can hear, taste, touch, see, or smell with regard to "dog."

Let's consider an example that ties RFT together with rule-governed behavior. A child, within the context of a particular learning, social, and cultural history, may be told early on to "do homework" and do so to gain verbal praise or reinforcement: this is pliance. Later on, this child, now an adolescent, is doing homework because he has tracked the natural consequences: he does well at school. Through mutual and combinatorial entailment, he relationally frames doing homework to doing well at school (cause and effect), and doing well as coordinated with being successful, for example. As relations are established, derived relations enter the picture and expand the network of associations with doing well. This may include feelings of pride and excitement, imaginings about his future, and nonverbal cues from his teachers—perhaps tones of voice or mannerisms. All of these events are appealing, and in this sense his behavior of doing his work is positively reinforced. Along the way, he may study under the control of an augmental, or verbal rule, such as, "If I do my homework, then I will get accepted to college and get a good job." This adolescent has learned to relationally frame "if this, then that," and is applying the frame to novel stimuli of college and a good job, in the absence of direct experience with either. The augmental is a verbal rule that specifies not only the "if/then" relation, but also the consequences. Augmenting, in this case, is motiving the adolescent to study because the consequence of getting a good job is put into an existing relational network that is pleasurable and establishes this possible consequence as a reinforcement. This is possible because of the relational frames this adolescent has established.

Over time and with experience, some relations may weaken in intensity if they have not been reinforced, and they may or may not intensify again at a later time. But once our minds have made connections between things, they do not unlearn them. Take, for example, an adolescent with a fear of roller coasters. Just hearing about them would evoke feelings of nausea and an urge to run away. At some point later in time, this adolescent found himself standing in front of a roller coaster while on a date and decided to impress his date by going on the ride. If his behavior was reinforced, by a kiss perhaps, the roller coaster might begin to evoke feelings of excitement and pleasure, as did the kiss. That's not to say that thoughts about the roller coaster, such as *I'm going to die*, and feelings of nausea are not still there and won't pop up again, but they may lessen in intensity. Now what if this adolescent hears that his friend vomited on a roller coaster? Prior relations may intensify, and the roller coaster could become a feared object again, equated with nausea, vomiting, and social ridicule.

A clinically relevant and important consequence of derived relational framing is the tendency for humans to maintain consistency, to make "sense" from the relations. You may have encountered clients for whom cognitive disputation becomes a frustrating exercise, and you the clinician are outsmarted at every turn. Take, for example, a client who tells you, "You don't really like me, you're just nice to me 'cause my parents pay you." Should you attempt to point out moments when this was not the case, or ask your client to identify such moments, you may then hear, "Yeah, but you don't like me, so you must be faking it, so now I can't trust you." In this example, and many others like it, clients' minds will turn things around so that their relational network, or "story," remains consistent.

If you find this section complicated, please just try to remember that because of language and our human ability to derive relations without direct training, everything connects to everything. Arbitrary contextual cues in the external environment, such as gestures, facial expressions, time of day, scent, and tone of voice, as well as internal cues, such as memories, urges, physical sensations, emotions, and thoughts, enter into relational networks with one another, and these elicit approach or avoidance behavior. Just as we try to avoid situations external to us that we perceive as threatening, we try to avoid our own private behavior that has acquired aversive functions through transformation of stimulus function. Clients' avoidance strategies and disputation efforts can expand their relational networks and further their tendency toward avoidance of internal behavior. This creates a vicious cycle in which life revolves around avoidance at the expense of a meaningful life. We return now to pliance, tracking, and augmenting to pull together rule-governed behavior, RFT, and the struggles our clients bring to therapy.

Extending RFT into the Clinical Realm

To facilitate our integration of RFT with rule-governed behavior, we will consider problematic pliance, tracking, and augmenting that can occur once an individual is able to relationally frame.

As children learn to relate stimuli arbitrarily, pliance can become more complex. For example, an adolescent who is told, "You got such a great mark on your exam, I love you," may put doing well and being loved into a relational frame of coordination or causality, such that she has to "do well on exams in order to be loved." Over time, being loved coordinates with self worth, and doing well also coordinates with self worth through combinatorial entailment. By transformation of stimulus function, doing well becomes desirable. Put more simply, the ideas of doing well, being loved, and feeling worthy all become connected, and thinking of one will evoke the others. In addition, if one idea is desirable, such as doing well, then being loved and feeling worthy are also desirable. Doing poorly, however, may be in a frame of opposition with doing well, and through combinatorial entailment, will also be in a frame of opposition with being loved. The derived rule, "If I do badly I am unlovable," will evoke fear and she will do all she can to avoid doing badly. Because of transformation of stimulus function, fear is evoked even though she has never done poorly or felt unloved. In other words, she has developed a response to her world despite no direct experience with the contingencies. As a result, this adolescent may strive to do well at everything she attempts, not because the activity matters to her, but to gain the love and self worth that she desires.

Take, for example, the teen who is told by his mother, "Don't be rude to your father or he will get upset." If this enters a frame of temporality or causality, the relations may be expanded so that any behavior preceding Dad getting upset is in a frame of coordination with being rude. This behavior may, over time, include things such as voicing an opinion, arguing, or expressing anxiety, all of which are avoided in order to prevent Dad from becoming upset. The relations may increase in complexity as this teen now remains quiet and passive in social circumstances in an effort to avoid upsetting anyone at all.

The type of pliance described above can be problematic when it becomes generalized and life revolves around gaining approval or preventing disapproval from others, something that is not necessarily under the adolescent's control. Adolescents fused with the rule "Be nice to everyone and they will like me" may be traditionally characterized as "people pleasers" or "passive," and may ignore their own needs and preferences as they prioritize the wants of others. This sort of adolescent may arrive at therapy already entrenched in unsatisfactory or even abusive relationships.

Tracking can also be problematic when rule following is based on tracking short-term and not long-term consequences. Take, for example, the adolescent who follows the rule, "People who know me well won't like me and I will feel sad and rejected." As she follows this rule, she may track the short-term consequence of not feeling sad and rejected by avoiding intimate relationships. However, by not tracking the long-term consequences of avoiding intimate relationships, of feeling lonely and rejected, she remains stuck. Over time, tracking short-term consequences and not long-term ones can be problematic and lead to self-defeating behavior.

While augmenting can be helpful to motivate individuals toward distant goals, it can also be problematic. Augmentals can interact with pliance and tracking in ways that decrease the individual's sensitivity to contingencies and have him following rules regardless of changing consequences. We now share with you the story of one of our fictional clients, whom we will call Marilyn. She is a seventeen-year-old in her last year of high school. She lives with her mother, father, and younger sibling. Her mother works full time and describes herself as anxious and as a "helicopter parent," worrying a great deal about Marilyn being safe and happy. At the first sign of distress in Marilyn, her mother tells her how to "fix it" and "get rid of" her feelings. Marilyn has learned that she can distract herself with the computer and by watching television when she feels any sense of sadness, anger, upset, or distress, and thus, "get rid of" her anxiety. Marilyn's father works full time and is less hovering than his wife. He manages his emotions by "tuning out" and his family says that his face "has no feelings." Within the context of her family, Marilyn has learned that emotions are bad and scary, and can't be tolerated. She arrived at her therapist's office highly anxious, feeling afraid of failing, of disappointing others, of her future, and ultimately, of being rejected. She has learned to avoid these unpleasant thoughts and feelings by distracting herself and tuning out, but that is creating an endless cycle that has impacted her ability to study, her academic achievement, her school attendance, and her friendships.

Marilyn presented with the strongly held belief that failure means she is a "loser," and she can not tolerate even the idea of being a loser. We may or may not ever figure out how this came to be for Marilyn, but we can work with the material regardless. However, to use her fears as an example of how RFT works, let's consider how this may have developed, keeping in mind that this is not the *only* way it could have happened.

As Marilyn went through school, she and her academically able friends achieved well. At a young age Marilyn studied out of pliance with parental requests and for the reinforcing quality of their praise. As she got older, she came in contact with, or tracked, the natural consequences of studying, which for her was academic success.

Marilyn established a perspective of herself as "smart" through deictic frames of "I/here/now." After establishing the ability to relationally frame abstract events, Marilyn often scoffed in a derogatory tone at students who did not do as well as she did, and who spent lunch time with the teacher to receive extra help—students who, via a frame of comparison, were "losers." Over time and with experience, Marilyn established more arbitrary relations to the word "loser," which came to enter into a frame of coordination with the word based on her experience in her social world. The idea of "losers" now included those who dropped out of school, smoked, took drugs, and had no real friends and no hope for the future. When she referred to peers who failed as "losers," her academically able peers responded approvingly, thus reinforcing her behavior and the connections.

Putting this in RFT terms, through mutual entailment, the word "loser," acting as a verbal stimulus, entered into a bidirectional relational frame of coordination (or "sameness") with the students she considered to be "losers." The network expanded when, through combinatorial entailment, Marilyn derived frames of coordination between the word "loser" and memories of people she considered losers, and the word "failure" and the memories of these students failing tests, a relational frame of causation between failing tests and being a "loser," and a frame of opposition between "being a loser" and "being smart," the latter referring to how she was known to herself and her peers. When Marilyn thought of her peers who were described as "losers," she felt a sense of anxiety and dread connected to the very idea of being like a "loser," even though her expanded understanding of "loser" was never her own experience.

When her teacher uttered the words "math test," this contextual stimulus served as an antecedent, cuing her relational network around failure. Perhaps the idea of taking the test was framed temporally with failing, and the word "fail," as a verbal stimulus, was in a frame of coordination with external behavior (that is, studying and taking the test) as well as internal behavior, such as feelings of anxiety and physical sensations of nausea. As a result of tracking the short-term consequences, Marilyn avoided studying and engaged in distraction (behavior) to reduce the intensity of her internal behavior or events (short-term consequence). In doing so, she did not have the opportunity to track the possible long-term consequences of her behavior, such as failing the test and feeling ashamed, or passing the test and feeling proud. Private events such as memories, thoughts, emotions, and physical feelings connected to failing and being a loser are now aversive to Marilyn. As such, she remains stuck in a loop of avoiding studying despite her fear of failing. Negative reinforcement, or the removal of aversive feelings and physical sensations, however, is not entirely responsible for her "loop" of avoidance. Marilyn's behavior is an example of rule-governed behavior—in this case, an augmental, specifying, "If I fail, then I am a loser." In this sense, her behavior is under the control of an augmental, which is akin to an assumption and, through relational networks, is influencing the ability of a new event (for example, a math test) to be aversive by the relationship specified in the verbal rule. Although Marilyn has never failed, the idea is in a network with other aversive stimuli, and through framing and transformation of function an aversive function is derived. As networks expand, Marilyn may fear not only math tests, but other tests, exams, and anything that might relate to being a "failure," such as not saying the right thing, not answering questions correctly, looking at someone the wrong way, or dressing the wrong way. Just thinking about the possibility of doing these things may evoke anxiety and dread. Through RFT, we can see how networks form, connecting to more and more networks and influencing behavior in ways that don't seem to make rational sense, but are based on verbal rules that do not necessarily reflect the way the world works.

Although all the processes outlined above, such as pliance, tracking, augmenting, and relational framing, are normally developing skills, Marilyn's inability to discriminate the usefulness, or workability, of her rule following in terms of attaining what matters to her is trapping her in perpetual avoidance. She has not learned to discriminate between the "I" located "here/now" (deictic framing) as the context in which internal events occur and the events themselves as something that is "there/then." As a result, Marilyn is trying to avoid private events. Unfortunately, humans are very limited in their ability to control private events, so her efforts won't be very successful.

Although augmenting can add flexibility to behavior, and allow adolescents to pursue distant goals, insensitivity to direct contingencies increases and is the basis for experiential avoidance and pathology. How this all relates to one's sense of self is important for adolescents and is discussed next.

RFT and "Story"

Through *relational framing, we can connect anything to anything, with networks growing over time.* In this way a highly complex narrative about the "self" can be created, developed, and perpetuated as we move through the world and learn about who we are. From a young age, children begin to explain, predict, and rationalize their behavior. These descriptions of who they are, through relational framing, become organized into a complex network that we refer to as "self-as-content," or their "story." This story not only describes past behavior, but may guide future behavior and as such, is an important part of the work we do with adolescents.

Important relational frames in the area of "self" and "story" include the deictic, comparative, and evaluative ones. Deictic framing is closely tied to perspective taking and allows one to learn about oneself in relation to others and the world: I-You, Here-There, and Now-Then. Deictic framing is established within a social context involving countless experiences of "I versus You," for example, which are comparative and evaluative by nature (McHugh & Stewart, 2012). Over time, we experience our sense of who we are as being equivalent to what our mind tells us about ourselves; we become fused with our "story" and behave accordingly. If our mind tells us that we are "losers" and that studying is pointless because being "losers" means we will fail, we put the books away and the thoughts settle down—for a while. Furthermore, the anxiety associated with an upcoming test that we will certainly fail is also temporarily disrupted when we close the book. Avoidance is highly reinforcing and almost invariably leads to suffering.

In our work with adolescents we make these "stories" of "self" transparent. All the various elements of the adolescents' stories about the self can be drawn on paper in the form of what we call a "Word Web." The Word Webs our clients draw reveal their intricate, delicate, and sticky webs of cognitions. As you will read in later chapters, we bring a bit of RFT into our sessions so clients really "get" the idea that everything connects to everything, and pulls everything into their stories. This allows us to help the adolescents gain some compassion and acceptance of their stories as well as some distance and defusion at the same time. We work with the story experientially to give them "in the moment" opportunities to accept and defuse, and to change direction so they orient toward what matters.

The ACT Processes

As you would expect from the name, ACT involves two things: acceptance and commitment. The acceptance part of ACT refers to the ongoing ability to foster a context of acceptance of unwanted private experience (thoughts, feelings, physical sensations, memories, and urges). The commitment part refers to committing to what matters in our lives. When our clients are better able to accept and commit, we refer to this as psychological flexibility, which denotes the idea that they can more often respond to their present moment without relying on inflexible, rigid, rule-governed behavior.

ACT is not about "getting rid of" thoughts and feelings; it is about accepting what is inside while moving ahead with what matters. In working through the ACT processes toward committed actions, clients will need to be willing to have whatever private experiences arise inside. This willingness to accept whatever private experiences show up is a prerequisite to taking committed actions. There will likely be two kinds of private experiences: those evoked by clients' current circumstances (sometimes referred to as "clean" emotions), and those evoked by clients' attempts to get rid of what they don't want to experience (sometimes referred to as "dirty" emotions). As clients stop struggling to get rid of what's inside (which usually just makes it more intense), they will still have the discomfort that arises in response to their present circumstance, the "clean" emotions: none of us can get rid of that! This leaves them having to adapt to situations that evoke sadness, anxiety, or some other emotions, but likely at a more tolerable intensity.

The next section describes the therapeutic processes from the standpoint of psychological flexibility. The processes are often depicted as a six-sided shape, commonly referred to as a "hexaflex," which can be found in many ACT texts. We begin with defusion and acceptance, which are located on the left side of the hexaflex; then we move to the center points of mindfulness, or contact with the present moment, and self-as-context; and then we move to values and committed action on the right side.

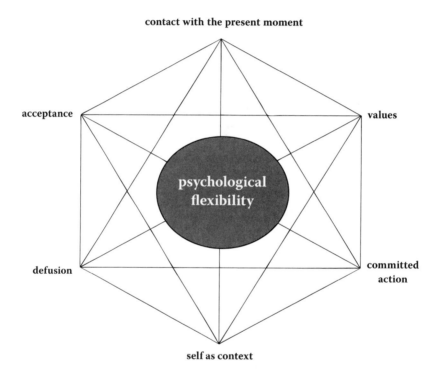

Defusion

Defusion addresses the problem of fusion, of clinging too closely to thoughts and operating as if they were literal facts. ACT fosters the ability to take thoughts less literally and to see all private experiences for what they are—simply thoughts, feelings, physical sensations, or urges that are momentarily passing through our awareness. Defusion focuses primarily on the verbal part of these experiences. It stresses that thoughts are just thoughts, rather than literal truths by which we have to live. In this sense, we hope to change the context in which thoughts and other internal events occur.

Acceptance

"Acceptance"—which we use interchangeably with "allowing"—refers to the ability to "allow" unwanted private events or behavior (thoughts, feelings, physical sensations, memories, urges, and so on), to simply let them be present until they pass rather than trying to push them away, push them down, or avoid doing things that bring them up. The process of acceptance focuses primarily on the affective part of these experiences, and ACT facilitates an exploration of feelings with an open curiosity and a sense of self-compassion.

Mindfulness

Mindfulness practice helps clients return to the present moment, gently distancing themselves from relational networks. Mindfulness is the practice of bringing attention on purpose to the here and now, without judgment about how things were or are going to be or how they are now.

Self-as-Context

This process involves the development of an alternate observing perspective, the "observing self." This means learning to stand "outside" oneself and observe "me-here-now" with compassion for one's self. This ability to stand back and see the self from "outside" is what makes defusion and acceptance possible. Self-as-context is in contrast to "self-as-content," or the conceptualized self ("story"), which is the network of descriptions and evaluations we each hold about ourselves that develops over time as we frame behaviors.

Values

The identification of one's core values creates a kind of compass in ACT. Identification of values makes it possible for people to take actions that go outside or beyond the restricted repertoire of rule-governed behavior. Clients are encouraged to discern what they truly and fundamentally value and to begin to envision what life would look like if their behavior were consistent with their values. Values are what create motivation for change in ACT. They can serve as augmentals that provide the forward momentum.

Committed Actions

Committed actions are the concrete steps, often uncomfortable ones, that clients begin to take in ACT in the service of living life according to their values. These actions, or behaviors, are almost sure to bring up a mental replay of unwanted private experiences that the clients have been trying to avoid. Taking these steps requires mindfulness, acceptance, and defusion from internal events.

The matrix, described next, is a very helpful tool for you and your client to better understand how fusion and experiential avoidance are functioning, and to develop a frame of opposition between fusion and avoidance, with values and committed action.

The Matrix

There is a visual option for working with clients within the frame of the ACT processes called the matrix. This framework can be visualized diagrammatically as a grid with four quadrants and a circle where they intersect, labeled "Me Noticing," to represent the client, who is doing the work of noticing (Polk & Schoendorff, 2014).

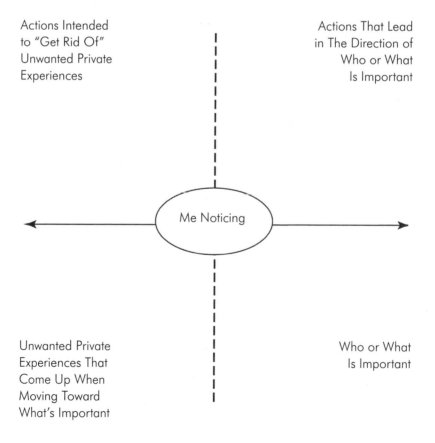

Actions Intended to "Get Rid Of" Unwanted Private Experiences

Actions That Lead in The Direction of Who or What Is Important

Me Noticing

Unwanted Private Experiences That Come Up When Moving Toward What's Important

Who or What Is Important

Drawing a horizontal line across a piece of paper, we locate "outside" information above the line, on the top half of the page (that is, information derived from the real world via our five senses that can be observed both by the self and by others), and "inside" information (private experiences, symbolic, verbal, "story" information that can only be noticed by the self) on the bottom half. Then, drawing a vertical line, we can locate moving "toward values" on the right side of the line and moving "away from what we don't like to have inside" on the left side. Working with this simple four-quadrant framework, the therapist can ask questions which help clients recognize which of their actions are in the service of *experiential avoidance* and which are in the service of living according to their values. At the center point of the two axes is "Me Noticing" (mindful awareness). As a client describes a problem, the clinician can ask questions that help the client to notice which actions actually take him toward values and which are about avoidance of thoughts and feelings. In matrix work this process is called "sorting." The clinician simply sets the framework for the client with the matrix, allowing the client to learn independently. The client "sorts" who or what is important (lower right quadrant), which actions lead in that direction (upper right quadrant), what unwanted private experiences (that is, thoughts and feelings) come up in the process of moving toward what is important (lower left quadrant), and what actions he engages in to "get rid of" the unwanted experiences (upper left quadrant). For the "sorting" process, a matrix can be drawn on a piece of paper or on an office whiteboard. Information can be recorded in the appropriate quadrants, written either by the client or by the clinician acting as scribe. This matrix format is incorporated into all the work we do.

Therapist Stance

We include a few quick notes regarding therapist stance in case it differs from your usual way of being with clients. From the first session onwards, we encourage the use of language that facilitates defusion, such as "So, you are having thoughts that others won't like you," or "I'm having the thought that I'm talking too much." This overtly models defusion; clients get to see a demonstration of the inner process involved in treating thoughts just as thoughts and not facts. You will see that some use has been made of self-disclosure in the above example. This can be very helpful in working with ACT, but only for the purpose of letting clients see that unwanted inner experience is universal, and never to highlight the therapist's own issues. So, "I had the thought just now that you might think my office is messy," opens up your own private experience to the client, whereas "I was devastated last night because my partner told me he wants to separate," would unnecessarily also open up your life issues.

With clients, try to drop into your own empathy, not just in the form of a cognitive understanding of a client's struggle, but as an emotional experience that you actually share with her, verbally or nonverbally. Letting her see that you also have the desire to control thoughts, feelings, physical sensations, and urges is key, as is normalizing her use (and your own) of control strategies. Clients feel accompanied and supported enough to risk new behaviors when you don't hide that we are all in this soup together.

In order to induce a response-to-real-world opportunity for learning, we find it helpful to *ask* clients if they are willing to *experiment* with experiential exercises in session, and in home practice outside of session, as opposed to being directive. When clients are engaged in the moment, they will make sense of their behavior based on values and in-the-moment experience ("tracking"), not necessarily on pliance, as described earlier.

Therapists new to ACT may feel inclined to resort to reassurance, cognitive disputation, or relaxation training, especially when they aren't sure how to proceed in the moment. This is something to be aware of when working in the spirit of ACT. If you let clients experiment freely, they have an opportunity to learn to respond flexibly to their real circumstances. And the fundamental criterion for making choices is, of course, whether a choice is workable, whether it would take your client toward her own values or away from thoughts and feelings she does not like (experiential avoidance). In light of this, the emphasis in sessions is essentially on values-driven behavior and not on changing or getting rid of thoughts and feelings. For some therapists this could require an "unlearning" of sorts.

As we just mentioned, ACT does not involve cognitive disputation or relaxation training. What you will find in the sessions that follow is an emphasis on using metaphors and experiential exercises, along with some didactic teaching. Through metaphor, networks of relations are coordinated, and through transformation of stimulus function, values-based behavior can become more likely. Experiential exercises allow clients to become physically engaged in metaphors, which may provide a new contextual cue to derive frames of coordination and increase the likelihood of values-based behavior (Dahl, Plumb, Stewart, & Lundgren, 2009).

To model the flexibility that you want your client to develop, it is important to be mindfully present and to operate in response to the minute-to-minute real-world behavioral information that your client is giving you in session. Working consistently with the philosophy of functional contextualism, we need to leave our own assumptions at the door and adopt a stance of open curiosity about what is workable for a given client.

Finally, to be an ACT therapist is to embody ACT from the inside: the processes and experiences are not just for your client, they are also for you, the therapist. This is why ACT trainings and workshops are so experiential. When we as therapists are not in the moment with our client, but are stuck in self-as-content, when we avoid emotions that come into the room, when we struggle to accept our clients' reality and their choices, and when we act against our values—we are not embodying or practicing ACT.

Conclusion

To sum this section up: we can relationally frame behavior that takes place within our skin (thinking, sensing, feeling, and imagining) to behavior outside our skin (overt motor behavior) through arbitrarily applied relational framing. How each of us frames behaviors will be influenced by our unique and complex learning histories. As we go through our day, various cues in our environment will trigger behaviors and the related networks. For example, if we once heard a harsh tone of voice while being rebuffed for something we did, we may, out of awareness, enter these two behaviors (tone of voice and being rebuffed) into a frame of coordination. Years later, upon hearing a harsh tone of voice from someone else, we expect to be rebuffed and react by withdrawing from the other person. This entire sequence of initial learning, or relational framing, and our reaction some time later, can all take place quickly, automatically, and out of awareness. Because everything connects to everything, ACT does not involve cognitive disputation or other efforts to "get rid of" what is inside. Rather, the focus is on awareness and allowing, workability, and values-based behavior.

PART 2

The Sessions

Session 1

The Assessment

Now that we have looked at some theoretical and technical issues, you are ready to begin, starting with an assessment. The following is a description of how your first session could look and what you might want to be keeping in mind as you begin. We have included a description of measures we typically administer in case that suits your purposes.

Although the focus is on assessment, the language used and the stance you take set the stage for the rest of the ACT journey. We outline our assessment with individual clients first and then describe modifications for group-based ACT. Throughout this book, modifications will only be described that depart from the content in the earlier description of individual therapy. When there is no mention of some topic in the description of group modifications, you can assume it is the same as in the individual therapy.

To provide a context for this session and the next, we will return to our fictional client, Marilyn, who you will remember was suffering from a need to be perfect in order to feel secure that others would love her.

Focus of This Session

Many of the adolescents we have worked with struggle with severe anxiety, depression, and shame. Many have engaged in self-harm or suicide attempts. Personality characteristics that may be difficult to manage are commonplace. ACT emphasizes the importance of a nonjudgmental stance in the therapist, with empathy and acceptance of any strategies that patients have already tried. This could not be more essential than when working with adolescents. In this session in particular, as adolescents talk about their coping strategies, they are likely expecting us to point out the negative impact of their efforts, to argue, or to challenge them. By *really* putting ourselves in our patients' shoes, we can provide a very different experience and help the adolescents to feel truly *heard* and *understood*.

Right from the beginning in this first session, we use defusing language such as "I'm having the thought that..." and rephrase the adolescents' disclosures with "You are having the feeling of, or the thought that..."

Assessment of Individual Client

In this section we cover topics such as the focus of the session, who to have in the room during the assessment, and how to listen in an ACT way, with ACT ears. We begin with the assessment in the context of individual therapy, and provide details of modifications for a group format at the end of the chapter.

In the first session our main focus is to create confusion! Parents often arrive with a request for their child to be "fixed" and for help in "getting rid of" anxiety or other emotions and thoughts. Ending the assessment session with some confusion helps develop the "creative hopelessness" outlined in the next chapter.

Conduct the assessment as you normally would, whether it be a semistructured diagnostic assessment or a more client-centered assessment. Feel free to use your own approach. We gather typical demographic information and then use the majority of the time to really get into the life of the adolescent. We don't ask different questions or ask questions differently, but rather, we *listen differently* to the responses, having the hexaflex and the matrix in our minds.

More specifically, as we gather information, we sort it into the quadrants of the matrix. Sometimes we create a matrix in the assessment; other times we hold the matrix in mind, using it to formulate information and guide our feedback at the end of the assessment, and perhaps as a sorting tool for later sessions. This includes what is important to the adolescent (lower right), what thoughts, emotions, physical feelings, and urges she tries to avoid (lower left), and what avoidance strategies she uses to avoid (top left). In addition, we want to be sure to ask what the adolescent has done in the past—things that matter to her, despite the intense thoughts and emotions (top right) that threaten to derail her efforts. We also ask what our client would like to be able to do (top right), but "can't" because of thoughts and feelings that get in her way (lower left), and the avoidance strategies she uses to manage (top left). As you work through this material with your client, the futility of avoidance strategies starts to become evident, which may result in a mix of emotions for your client and her parents. Clinicians should use their own judgment in deciding how much of the material to elicit and share if parents are present, whether the material is organized in a matrix or not. This is the beginning of creative hopelessness and opens the door for the idea that there may be another option to dealing with aversive thoughts and feelings. Thinking in terms of the ACT processes and how the elements are interacting will help later on in the session and beyond.

Who Is in the Room?

Generally speaking, we prefer to have parents in the room and involved at the beginning to get multiple perspectives, and to see the larger, family context in which the adolescent is living. If this isn't possible, we may opt to have the adolescent in for half the session and the parents in for the other half. Explaining ACT to parents has helped to get their support for the process later on when symptoms don't go away as fast as they might like. It also provides an opportunity to share the ACT perspective that their teen isn't "broken" and in need of "strategies" to "fix" her, which gently introduces the concept of acceptance to parents. We find that the idea of ACT, although initially easy for parents to embrace, usually turns out not to be quite what they expect from a therapist, so it is better for parents to hear an initial explanation from the therapist rather than put the adolescent in the position of trying to explain why she spent a session with a clear plastic sheet in front of her face, talking about DOTS, or doing other seemingly nonsensical activities in which ACT therapists are likely to engage them.

Listening with ACT Ears

What do we listen for? The adolescents and their parents are often eager to talk about the symptoms and the impact they are having on the adolescent's life and that of the parents and family. By listening with ACT ears we refer to our ongoing internal arranging of the material presented to us within the ACT framework, which will support cohesion across sessions as the full "story" emerges. The six processes describing a psychologically inflexible condition are as follows, with the terms referring to psychological flexibility in parentheses: cognitive fusion (defusion), experiential avoidance (acceptance), inflexible attention (mindfulness), attachment to conceptualized self or "story" version of self (self as context/observing self), lack of clarity about what matters (values), unworkable action (committed action/doing what matters).

Cognitive Fusion

Adolescents will quickly tell you what they are fused with as soon as you ask, "What brings you here today?" They may begin with more surface level thoughts such as *I'm anxious, I'll never pass chemistry, I have no future*, or *My classmates think I'm boring*. This is perfectly fine for the beginning of therapy and may be the only level you ever need to explore. More deeply rooted thoughts and beliefs may surface as trust is built and therapy progresses, especially if your client engages in long-term therapy. (ACT can be done as brief therapy with specific targets, or longer term as needed, with the work deepening over time.) Other common examples of cognitive fusion include: *School is boring, I won't get into college, I have to get rid of my depression/anxiety/anger,* and *People are stupid. They aren't worth my time.* For Marilyn, it's thoughts such as *I'm going to fail high school and my parents will be disappointed in me,* and *If I fail I will have no friends.*

Many of the adolescents we work with have suffered an interpersonal trauma of sorts, ranging from rejection, bullying, or repeated invalidation to active abuse or neglect. They often arrive at therapy with their walls up and are very guarded. When clients articulate statements such as "Other people are stupid," "Everyone will just let me down," or "Everyone is weird, why bother," it is important to keep our stance of curiosity and empathy, mindful of our own cognitive fusion, accepting of our own emotional responses, and not engage in a debate or provide reassurance. If your adolescent client has had adults tell him he is wrong or try to "fix" his thoughts or the situations he is in, he doesn't need you to do more of this. We should keep in mind that humans are social creatures, that we need our "tribe" and that this particular stance of defensiveness may have developed as a means of protection and of avoiding rejection, although it is likely now getting in our client's way. This will all make its way into later sessions, however, so there is no need to address it overtly now. As Kelly Wilson has said to us many times, "What you value makes you vulnerable." If adolescents are trying to keep a wall up between themselves and their interpersonal world, they are likely avoiding the vulnerability that comes with human connection, which is likely something they value. Again, don't rush to get there right away, and notice any urges of your own to argue or share this wisdom with them. Allow them the opportunity to move toward this in their own way over time.

In later sessions you will see that we don't work for very long with individual cognitions or thoughts. We try to help the adolescent discover his broader "story" and defuse from the entire story. You can begin to role-model defusion during this initial session by using phrases such as "So, you are having lots of thoughts that people will not like you or you will fail," or move it one step farther from the individual with a statement such as "So, you are noticing yourself having thoughts about failing." We often reflect on our use of this phrasing with adolescents, sometimes in the first session, with a statement like "Have you noticed that I tend to say 'You are having' a great deal?" We often leave this to the end of the session when we set the stage for what ACT is all about, so that our unusual way of talking will have a context.

Experiential Avoidance

Much like cognitive fusion, strategies the adolescent is using to avoid internal events such as thoughts, emotions, physical sensations, and urges make themselves known quite quickly. Experiential avoidance is on the left side of the hexaflex, along with cognitive fusion, because the two are not mutually exclusive and function together to help clients avoid the stuff inside they find distressing. Adolescents avoid not only what's inside, but also the external events that may serve as a "trigger" or cue for unwanted internal events, such as social gatherings, school tests, and family functions. Avoiding what doesn't feel good is a natural human reaction, and it works: feelings and thoughts we don't like are temporarily reduced, so avoidance is negatively reinforced. However, when used in excess and in ways that limit our lives and impact our sense of fulfillment, experiential avoidance can have devastating effects.

We often frame experiential avoidance within the framework of DOTS, adapted from Russ Harris's "Join the DOTS" approach (2009). The letters stand for: Distracting, Opting Out (avoidance), Time Travel (thinking into the past and the future), and Self-Harm. Adolescents tell us about commonly used distractions such as hours spent on social media (Facebook and Twitter, for example), playing with their cell phones, sleeping, or listening to music. They tell us about events or people they avoid (parties or other social functions, school, studying, family gatherings, and so on) and strategies they use interpersonally to avoid being rejected (such as excessively helping others, always presenting themselves as happy, or never asserting their own opinion). They describe moments of rumination during which they worry about the future or wish they could change the past. They also report using strategies that may be harmful, such as cutting or burning themselves, excessive shopping, or engaging in compulsive sexual activities. Simple questions like "When you feel anxious, or have thoughts of no one liking you, how do you handle that?" or "How do you get rid of thoughts and feelings you don't want, even for a little while?" can elicit DOTS quite easily. Clients often won't endorse self-harm strategies immediately, and we have found it helpful to simply ask, "Many teens use drugs or alcohol, or harm themselves to feel better; have you tried any of these ways to cope with difficult thoughts and feelings?"

Marilyn was intent on avoiding emotions of anxiety and dread, and physical sensations connected to her anxiety. When she so much as thought about academic tasks or social events, her anxiety increased and she looked for ways to get rid of her feelings. Through the lens of RFT, this makes sense. Imagining tests, homework, and social events is connected, through relational framing and transformation of stimulus function, to aversive emotions and physical sensations, which results in avoidant behavior and a reduction in anxiety. This behavior led to a short-term reduction in her anxiety, but the anxiety and dread returned when tests remained to be written, and the threat of a call from the school about her missed classes was always present in her mind. So in the long term Marilyn's avoidance was not leading to feeling "better," as she put it.

Inflexible Attention

Although we may not assess this process directly and it is less obvious than the others, we can get a sense of how aware the client is by noting what drives her behavior, what thoughts and feelings she notices. Mindfulness is not only about present-moment awareness, it's about curiosity, openness, and as we say to the adolescents, "being on the lookout for judgment." Statements like "I know this will sound stupid" or "I'm probably wrong about this" will give you an idea of the adolescent's inner dialogue and his "story," to which you can return later on.

Some adolescents lack vocabulary and language for their own emotional states, and may truly struggle to put words to their inner experience. Others say, "I don't know" when asked about thoughts, and some, we have discovered, really don't know because they are engaged in avoidance strategies. Their minds are so busy distracting, maybe even dissociating, that they really aren't aware of thoughts in the moment. When this happens, we go with their response, and offer a guess about the prevalence of avoidance in that moment, with questions like, "For many people I work with, their mind just goes somewhere else really fast, or goes all foggy before they can catch what they were thinking of, do you think your mind might do this?"

Self-as-Content

Self-as-content and its more flexible counterpart, self-as-context, are terms we rarely use with anyone but each other, and with colleagues when we engage in discussion or teaching. We like to describe it simply, and this is where "story" comes in. Self-as-content refers to the amalgamation of messages we have been given about ourselves or give ourselves, about our identity, both good and bad. Russ Harris does a great job of clarifying this term in *ACT Made Simple* (2009). We talk about self-as-content as "story." We all have a layer of our "self" that we share with others when we meet them for the first time: our name, our profession, and our interests, with variations depending on the social context. We can add our perceptions of our strengths, weaknesses, roles in life, and judgments, as they arise. Some of who we are (or who we think we are) comes from our experience. Some of it is bestowed on us as we grow up, both directly and indirectly. Often, adolescents won't know where the judgment or self-descriptions have come from, but they tell us, "I know, in my head, that my parents love me, but I still feel like they don't unless I'm being perfect," or "I might get straight A's and have friends and stuff, but I still feel totally unlovable." This is where RFT offers us lots that will find its way into later sessions, but at this stage we keep an ear out for judgments with which the adolescent is fused and that are part of his "story." For example, judgments such as "I'm stupid," "I'm boring," and "I'm a failure," can form the backdrop of a client's story, and through relational framing, connect to pretty much everything in her life.

Judgments we think of as more "positive" may be trickier, but may cause just as much distress. An adolescent who carries as part of her identity the judgment "I am the smart one" may be content with this judgment if it leads to appropriate studying and effort. This judgment may become less workable when it is gripped tightly and framed causally with not needing to study, or as part of a rule, such as, "Smart people do well even if they don't study." This may lead to rule-governed behavior of not studying, which may result in academic failure. Many adolescents say they have been told repeatedly how intelligent and clever they are, so when they come up against an academic demand that feels difficult, they may hesitate to ask for help if they are holding "the smart one" identity tightly and don't want to "lose face"; or they may assume they have been lied to about their intellect and are, in fact, stupid. It is pointless to argue with them about this when they arrive in your office holding their test with a bright red "D" displayed on the top. This is often followed by "How can I be smart if I got a D?"—and at a deeper level, opens the door for *No one will love me if I'm not smart.*

Lack of Clarity About What Matters and Unworkable Action

Adolescence is a developmentally rich phase for the identification of values. Many adolescents are trying on different ways of being in the world and figuring out who they are and what really matters to them. Sometimes, however, they are so caught up in their identity of "sick" or "ill," with emotions that are so overwhelming, they haven't thought much about values. In later sessions we will talk about eliciting values through more direct means, but for now, be aware they may show up less directly. Values may be hidden where the emotions are most intense. However, as you are listening for values, ask yourself whether it's really a value you are hearing about or whether perhaps it's a rule (for example, "I *should* pay more attention in class"). Also, ask yourself about values as qualities that belong to the adolescent versus those that belong to parents, who may be trying to pass their own values on to their adolescent (for example, "He should care more about being involved and joining clubs at school"). It is not unusual for adolescents with attentional difficulties, for example, to tell us they value the very behavior they struggle to engage in and are often reprimanded over, such as the need for them to "pay attention," to "be more organized," and to "be a better listener."

We have found it helpful to ask about what matters in moments when emotions are intense, keeping in mind, once again, that values and vulnerabilities are on two sides of the same coin. For example, when an adolescent expresses frustration regarding how horrible one of her teachers is, we may respond, "Wow, sounds like math class would be much better if your teacher wasn't so bad." If the adolescent agrees, this opens the door to further discussion about math specifically, and school more generally, in terms of what matters. If school, for example, didn't matter, then school not going well would not matter. There would be no intense reaction. Intense affect generally suggests that there is something that matters and that our success with this "important something" is at risk. For this reason, we like to spend time where anger and frustration show up, or any other intense affect for that matter.

Often the adolescent's life has become narrow in sphere and there is not much time devoted to things that matter and promote fulfillment. Asking the question, "Was there ever a time you did something you wanted to do even though you were anxious or sad?" followed by "Hmm, I wonder what made doing that so important?" can start to give hints about what matters. Most adolescents can recall something, and for those who cannot we suggest coming to the initial session as a possible example. If the adolescent agrees that coming was difficult, gentle inquiry may open up values either in this session or later on, and help him to see that he can do one thing even when his mind tells him to do another. In working with Marilyn, the therapist found values emerging as she spoke about doing something even though she was anxious:

T (Therapist): So, would coming to this appointment today be an example of doing something even though you weren't feeling confident? You mentioned feeling kind of scared to come; you weren't sure what it would be like, but you are here.

M (Marilyn): Yeah, my parents forced me to come. I didn't really have a choice, so here I am.

T: You have told me about how you get out of writing tests and going to parties when you are too anxious, so I am curious, could you have gotten out of this appointment if you really wanted to, if you put your mind to it?

M: I guess so (laughing), I could have had a stomachache, I'm good at those. (DOTS.)

T: What stopped you? (Looking for hidden values and personal meaning.)

M: I think my parents will be really angry and I can't take the sad look on their faces when I back out of stuff. They have tried everything to help make my anxiety go away, but it's too hard. I can't control it and neither can they. No one can, so now they just get frustrated and yell at me when I can't do stuff. It's not like I'm having fun. I've gone from being an A student to practically a dropout, so I feel totally awful and guilty, which makes it worse, and my friends have stopped calling me. But who needs them anyway? (*Marilyn may be identifying the domains of education and relationships as important.*)

T: You don't like to have feelings of anger between you and your parents, and not being able to go to school sounds like it really frustrates you. And you feel let down and rejected by friends.

M: Yeah, my life totally sucks, this is not what my life was supposed to look like in high school.

T: Sounds like your relationship with your parents is important to you, and your relationship with your friends used to be? (*Could easily have asked about DOTS at this point, regarding strategies she uses to get rid of guilt and upset, but it's a nice moment to get at values, so the therapist stayed here.*)

M: Yeah, my family is really important. Friends, we'll see.

T: And coming here might help with your relationship with your family?

M: Yeah, I'm hoping it will help.

T: So you brought your feelings of anxiety and thoughts of how hopeless this all seems with you to this appointment! Wow, I wonder what this says about you as a family member, about what matters to you?

M: I want my parents to know that I love them. I want to be normal.

T: Sounds like being connected with your parents matters to you.

M: Yeah, I guess it does…a lot.

T: What would you do if you were normal? (*Wondering if there are additional values or important domains hidden within this statement.*)

M: I would probably go back to school, and be with my ex-friends at dance class. I used to dance competitively, but I got so nervous about screwing up that I stopped going, I would go back if I wasn't anxious anymore. (*Here, Marilyn gives us a sense of fusion and "rules," because she can't do things until anxiety is gone.*)

T: What did you enjoy about dancing? (*Going to dance class is a "goal,"
            and the therapist is still curious about the underlying values.*)

M: I like to be physically active, and I like the way I get to express myself
            when I dance. Oh, and I also really liked the other girls in my group.
            We got along well and were really supportive of each other. I do miss
            them. They must think it's weird that I just stopped going. (*We now
            get more of a sense of what matters for Marilyn, what qualities are
            important from within, and she is expanding her values within the domain
            of relationships.*)

During the assessment, the matrix may be helpful in sorting information. The
values of "being connected" and "being supportive" can be put in the lower right
quadrant of the matrix and "attending the initial session" can go in the upper right.
Thoughts your client is fused with, including her "story," as well as feelings she avoids
can go in the lower left quadrant, while strategies she uses to avoid thoughts and feelings go in the upper left. During this initial session you may or may not go into detail
about what the quadrants mean at any great length, aside from telling clients "It's my
way of sorting what you have said, we'll look at it more when you come back next
time."

Pulling It All Together and Setting the Stage

Once you have finished your assessment, it's time to set the stage for treatment.
Our pitch to Marilyn and her parents might go something like this:

*I want to pull together everything you have told me so far. It seems, Marilyn,
that you have been trying really hard to get rid of thoughts and feelings that don't
feel good, which makes sense. Why wouldn't you try to get rid of stuff that feels
awful? You have tried distracting yourself for hours on the Internet, and you
avoid going to school and having contact with friends because your anxiety is
telling you that you will fail and be rejected. But even though you have tried
really hard to make the thoughts and feelings go away, they are still here. And to
top it all off, while all of this is going on, you are missing out on the social world
at school, you aren't being the student you would like to be, and you aren't feeling
connected to your parents. So instead of having yourself do more of what you
have been doing, avoiding situations and distracting yourself from thoughts and
feelings, what if you get to stop doing that?*

This will inevitably be met with varying degrees of confused expressions, and we
might ask, "If fighting this stuff isn't working, what else is there?"

You may get responses like "I could give up," to which we reply, "Yes, you could," and leave that dangling, allowing the opportunity for more ideas to flow into the room.

Many adolescents will come up with the idea: "I guess I can just stop fighting," to which we can respond, "And do what matters while bringing all the thoughts and feelings you have with you." This was the case for Marilyn, who attended her therapy appointments despite feeling scared. We may add at this point something like: "Can you hear that white noise machine outside my office? What if we can work together to help you treat thoughts that get in the way of what matters like white noise? So that they are there, in the background, but they aren't the most noticeable thing and they aren't in charge?" This idea sets the stage nicely for many adolescents. You can use any other comparable elements you have in your environment—a clock, a calendar, a computer screen—in this way, for the impact it can have at this moment.

Other ways of framing ACT with adolescents include references to their own environment. Given Marilyn's experience with dance, we might ask, "What if we can look at the thoughts and feelings that get in your way the same way your audience members might look at other things on the stage during a performance, like the lighting or curtains? They aren't center stage, with all the attention, but they are still there."

Sometimes we tell adolescents we are working from a model called "acceptance and commitment therapy." Other times we don't label it in any way, we just outline the philosophy as "working together to help you put your attention where you want it to be, which takes practice, so that you can do more of what matters in your life and not spend time trying to get rid of thoughts and feelings that won't go away." In both cases we let adolescents know that "I will include in our sessions different activities that might help you put your attention where you want it to be, as well as different ways of practicing mindfulness, or noticing. That's what will help you notice what's up, so you can do things differently."

We typically define mindfulness to our clients as "being present (in the moment), on purpose, without judgment," which is similar to Jon Kabat-Zinn's definition, "paying attention in a particular way, on purpose in the present moment, nonjudgmentally" (1990). Another way to phrase this is: "Mindfulness is a way to train yourself and your mind to put your attention where it is needed in any given moment."

The introduction of mindfulness may bring up concerns around why we aren't offering traditional CBT (cognitive behavior therapy). We've had therapy-savvy parents who demand we send their teen home with self-monitoring sheets and a deep-breathing protocol, and who question why we aren't going to "fix" their teen by getting rid of his emotions and thoughts. At this point we patiently repeat our summary and gently ask about the parents' perspective of how helpful past strategies have been.

Sometimes concerns arise about possible religious connotations and content, or fears that mindfulness is part of something "new age." To respond to these questions we say something like this: "Mindfulness is a part of many traditional practices, but we use it without any philosophical or religious meaning attached." We may repeat here the idea that mindfulness is about training our ability to notice and pay attention. Sometimes families have had previous experience or knowledge of something called "mindfulness" that is loaded with negative associations, so it can be important to talk about this with them to address their fears and avoid future undermining. We are happy to add that there is research supporting both ACT and mindfulness as effective practices, and we offer them the URL for the Association for Contextual Behavioral Science (ACBS).

Research Protocol and Questionnaires

If you use standardized questionnaires or want to include some ACT-specific measures in your work, this is a good session in which to have the adolescent complete them, either at the beginning or end of the session. Below we discuss several measures in keeping with our research protocol. (The ACT-specific measures are available to members of the Association for Contextual Behavioral Science.) We've learned over time, however, that most adolescents benefit from discussion about trying to identify values and distinguish them from rules, so we often leave values identification until a later session, when we can devote more time to exploring what really matters. Our research battery includes:

1. "Child Acceptance and Mindfulness Measure" (CAMM-10) (Greco, Baer, & Smith, 2011). This is a ten-item questionnaire that measures mindfulness, or the extent to which adolescents observe internal experiences, act with awareness, and accept their internal experiences without judgment.

2. "Avoidance and Fusion Questionnaire for Youth" (AFQ-Y8) (Greco, Lambert, & Baer, 2008). This is an eight-item questionnaire designed to measure psychological inflexibility as related to cognitive fusion and experiential avoidance.

3. "Values Assessment Rating Form" (Harris, 2008). This is an adaptation of the Valued Living Questionnaire (Wilson, Sandoz, Kitchens, & Roberts, 2010) and is available from http://www.thehappinesstrap.com. This questionnaire is laid out as a table and asks respondents to rate, from 1 to 10, ten life domains (work, education, family, and so on) with respect to how important that domain is to them, and how consistently they are living according

to their values within that domain. Respondents are also asked to rank order the ten domains in order of how important each is to work on.

4. "Self-Compassion Scale—Short Form" (SCS-SF) (Raes, Pommier, Neff, & Van Gucht, 2011). This is a twelve-item questionnaire that asks participants to rate how frequently they behave in ways that suggest self-kindness, self-judgment, common humanity, isolation, mindfulness, and over-identification. We use the full score, because this is more reliable than subscale scores with the short version. Clinicians can access the SCS-SF through Dr. Neff's website, http://www.self-compassion.org, where clients can also access the questionnaire online.

5. "Multidimensional Anxiety Scale for Children" (MASC) (March, Parker, Sullivan, Stallings, & Conners, 1997). This is a thirty-nine-item self-report instrument that assesses the major dimensions of anxiety and is sensitive to treatment-induced changes in symptom level and type.

6. "Children's Depression Inventory—2nd Edition" (CDI-2) (Kovacs, 2011). This is a twenty-seven-item self-report measure that taps into symptoms of depression and asks respondents to choose from among three choices for each item.

Assignment of Home Practice

We typically do not assign home practice work at the end of the assessment.

Modifications for Group Work

The first "session" with potential group members is an assessment of sorts, but not conducted in a group format.

Screening Potential Group Members

We have tried several methods for screening adolescents referred to our group by clinicians in the outpatient, hospital-based clinic to which we are connected. Our preferred method is to first review a client's chart to make sure that the adolescent meets our inclusion criteria for group-based ACT and then to meet with each adolescent and a parent for a brief time. We conduct a "screening" as opposed to an assessment because the adolescents referred to our group have already had a comprehensive mental health assessment within our clinic. During this screening meeting we ask about the nature of the adolescent's struggles, what she has tried so far to get rid of thoughts and feelings, and whether it is working for her or not. During this screening session we also try to determine if the adolescent will be able to participate in a group-based treatment more broadly, and in experiential exercises more specifically. Parents' input is helpful at this time to identify any potential barriers to attendance that the adolescent may not have thought of, and parents' interest tends to parlay into good attendance.

Setting the Stage

We introduce ACT (including its mindfulness component) explicitly as the therapeutic basis of our "ACTion" group, in much the same words as we provided in the section on individual therapy. We have found that the sense of safety and community in the group is severely impacted when an adolescent misses a session, so we place high importance on regular attendance. If you use questionnaires, this is a good time to have them completed.

Additional Information

Contact numbers of facilitators are provided at the end of the screening session, as is a single sheet with the session dates and times. Families are informed that they will receive a reminder call a few days before the first session.

Conclusion

Now that the assessment is finished and you have set the stage, the information you gleaned about what your client avoids and how she avoids it, together with what you learned about what she values, will be essential in beginning the first therapy session, which is described next.

Session 2

Creative Hopelessness

The first therapy session builds on the assessment and introduces concepts such as DOTS and the matrix to support a developing sense of creative hopelessness in your client. *Creative hopelessness* is the ACT term for a client's realization that the strategies she's using to avoid her thoughts and feelings aren't working—which opens the door to new possibilities, new ways of being with thoughts and feelings. As she goes through the experiential exercises with you, she may notice some hopelessness related to current coping strategies and leave, potentially, with a sense that something new may be around the corner.

Focus of This Session

We have already opened the door for creative hopelessness during the assessment session, so we approach this session as the first therapy session and include some discussion, experiential exercises, and metaphors focusing on mindfulness, the inner events or behaviors (thoughts, emotions, physical sensations, and urges) humans try to get rid of, and the evolution of the human mind. We introduce the concept of the illusion of control, through which clients discover their own sense of creative hopelessness. Introducing or integrating the matrix in this first therapy session allows an opportunity for clients to deepen the work on noticing their behavior, both inside and outside, and the workability of their behavior. What follows in this chapter is a suggested "flow" for the content of this session, first with individual clients, and then in a group format.

Creative Hopelessness with Individual Clients

In this session you really want to get as much of an idea as you can about your client's perspective—about her struggles and what she wants most out of life. Normalizing the experience of her mind getting in her way when she tries to approach something that matters may create some relief. When there are only two of you in the room, she will be watching your every response, so approaching her with a genuine attitude of acceptance, understanding, and curiosity will go far to creating therapeutic trust.

When clients arrive for help, they have often engaged in numerous strategies to make unpleasant thoughts and feelings go away. We empathize with this effort. After all, who wants to feel sadness, guilt, shame, anxiety, or worthlessness? Unfortunately, such efforts usually don't last long, and in many cases clients tell us "it makes things worse." They get "tangled up in even more thoughts" as they try various strategies to get rid of thoughts and feelings. In addition, their efforts to get rid of thoughts and emotions usually impact their ability to be the type of person they want to be and their ability to do what matters.

We have had many clients tell us that the very idea of letting go of trying to control what's inside saddens them, because they want to get rid of it. At the same time, this new idea of letting go may feel like a relief because they know the old way isn't working and they are exhausted from trying. This conundrum is the essence of creative hopelessness: if what you are doing is not "working" and thoughts and feelings won't go away and stay away, stop trying. In ACT, what "works" is what takes us toward valued living, not what gets rid of unwanted thoughts and feelings. The criterion for making this decision is not about being "right" or "wrong" based on "true" or "untrue" thoughts. The criterion is *workability*. An action is *workable* if it leads someone in the direction that she wants for her life. This is the benchmark to which we return over and over again in ACT.

What Stuck?

By asking your client "what stuck" from the assessment session, you will gain a sense of what was memorable or thought provoking for her. This is a good time to reintroduce metaphors that were brought up during the assessment that can be used to move unhelpful thoughts and emotions into the background, such as white noise, lighting, or the curtain on the stage, or other ideas that fit the client. We always ask "what stuck" at the beginning of every session to hear about influential ideas that "jumped out" at our clients and to gauge their understanding of the material.

Review of Home Practice

If you assigned home practice at the end of the assessment, you may want to review your client's progress prior to embarking on mindfulness and the introduction of new concepts. If you did not assign home practice at the assessment session, then there is nothing to review, although you may want to check in with your client regarding the assessment and give her a chance to share any thoughts or questions.

Mindfulness

A brief mindfulness meditation to start the working part of the session will help to establish this as a routine, and the conversation that follows often provides a good starting point for the session. Before proceeding, however, a brief description of mindfulness is helpful. You can initiate this, for example, by asking your client if she ever gets so caught up in her head that she misses the moment, misses what someone said, or arrives somewhere with no recollection of passing certain landmarks. Her response to one or more of these examples will likely be yes. This opens the door for a discussion of mindfulness versus mindlessness. The former is defined as "paying attention on purpose, in the present moment without judgment" (Kabat-Zinn, 1994). Mindlessness, in contrast, is the experience of being so caught up in our heads or in our emotions that we don't notice what is happening. Ask your client if she has had moments of mindfulness during your session so far, and share your own as appropriate!

You can offer a brief explanation of the benefits of mindfulness, including the fact that noticing what is going on around us with our five senses allows us to "respond" to what is actually happening, instead of "reacting" to what our mind tells us is happening.

An important part of the definition of mindfulness is the phrase "without judgment." Although we cover this in more detail in later sessions, raising the idea of "judgments" versus "facts" can be helpful and will likely bear repeating. For now, it may suffice to ask your client to notice what happens when she gets caught up in "sticky" thoughts such as *I am a failure*, as opposed to *I got 52% on my math test*. Many clients notice an appreciable difference in the way they feel physically after each statement, and many notice that the former hooks them into more derogatory thoughts and into their "story."

Simple exercises are good for beginning mindfulness practice. Ask your client to focus on one thing, such as a sound or an object, while you, the clinician, guide him through the likely event of his mind wandering off, noticing that, and bringing it gently back to the focus. This will add to his experience of his mind as something that is just doing its normal job. Sharing this experience with a kind and gentle clinician will start to build self-compassion in many adolescents. We introduce formal mindfulness practice early on to support self-compassion and acceptance, and add in informal practices as we deem appropriate. In this book, we begin informal practices in session 4, but you may want to begin sooner.

Next, we provide two examples of mindfulness exercises. The two exercises, as well as many that follow in later sessions, can be done with eyes open, for those clients who are uncomfortable sitting with eyes closed. However, engaging in mindfulness with eyes closed may deepen the experience and we recommend it whenever possible. You can allow your client to sit as she is, or suggest a more formal stance by asking her to sit with arms and legs uncrossed, feet flat on the floor, in a tall and upright posture. You can stress that mindfulness is about being alert, awake, and noticing what is happening, and not about relaxation, although she may feel that way at times. This may be an important notion to clarify if your client has had previous therapy that included relaxation training. Having this posture can help to develop a sense of being grounded and centered in practice, and literally *embodies* a confident and open frame of mind. But if you find bringing attention to posture becomes a distraction, omit it. It can be addressed at a later time.

You may want to use either a singing bowl or chimes to begin and end mindfulness meditations. We let our clients know ahead of time that we will ring the chimes once to start a meditation, and twice to finish. We add the instruction that the first of the two rings is to shift attention back to the present moment with awareness of sounds in and around the office and any other relevant sensory experiences, and the second signals the end of the exercise and time to open our eyes.

With some mindfulness exercises you may want your client to remain silent and use your questions to guide his experiences. At other times, you may want your client to report his inner experience as you go along to ensure he is alert, involved, and "on task," or to know what his feelings look like, for example, so you can incorporate his description into the remaining portion of an exercise. It may help to let your client know which you prefer ahead of time. To avoid repetition, we assume you will incorporate these points into the exercises that follow, and in a manner that suits you, so we don't repeat them with each mindfulness script.

Mindfulness of an Object

Place a small object on a desk or table near your client. It could be a vase or other decorative object or something common and functional like a pencil sharpener or a tissue box. Ask her to simply observe it, as if she had never seen such an object before. Ask that she try to see simply what is there, not more and not less, and to notice if thoughts, especially judgments, or any emotions come up and get in the way of just seeing what is there. You may have to explain that judgments are thoughts that categorize the qualities of something as either positive or negative, good or bad, and so on. This meditation might go something like this:

See if you can just sit and take in the object as if you had never seen it before—as if no one had ever seen it before. Try to just take it in, noticing what is there. Notice every detail. (Pause.) As you look, you may notice that your mind is giving you thoughts about the object. Your mind might give you thoughts about other things the object reminds you of. When your mind is giving you thoughts, see if you can just kindly and gently detach from these thoughts and return your attention to the actual object—just what is actually there. (Pause.) See if you can experience only what your five senses bring you of the object. Notice when your mind is bringing you something else, and kindly and gently detach and return to the object itself. (Pause.) You might notice especially that your mind may bring you thoughts about what you like about it or don't like about the object—what you think is good or bad, useful or not. Just be aware of these judgments, and kindly and gently return to the object itself. (Pause.) And now you can bring your attention back to the rest of the room.

In debriefing this exercise, ask what your client noticed about the object, and be prepared to hear whatever it may have been. Model not judging by being careful to accept whatever observations she may have had. Then ask about any thoughts or other internal reactions she may have noticed herself having while observing the object and treat your client's responses without judging. You can share your own observations of the object and of your internal processes as well. Use this as an opportunity for your client to begin to notice her internal processes in the moment. If she denies having any thoughts or reactions to the object, don't push for any, normalize the fact that sometimes we notice them and sometimes we don't, being careful not to imply that she should have noticed something. Just model by sharing your own noticing. That will help her to notice her own internal events. Normalize these events, including the judgments, as the usual processes of the human mind. Discuss the principles of mindfulness and the benefit of learning to notice what is present, both external and internal.

Mindfulness of Sound

Another exercise you can choose to do with your client is a "Mindfulness of Sound" exercise. The basic one involves just asking your client to sit quietly and listen carefully to any sounds that are audible. You can do this very informally, simply asking your client to bring all her attention to her sense of sound and to listen to whatever can be heard, or more formally as described earlier. For this practice, a script may be something like the following:

Close your eyes if you are comfortable doing so, or if not, just lower your eyes so that you are looking at the floor just beyond your feet. Let your gaze go soft, if your eyes are open, so that you are not looking at anything in particular. Bring all your attention to listening. Pay full attention to anything you can hear, whether in this room, outside it, or outside the building. (Pause.) Just notice what sounds are there. (Pause.) See if you can pick out the nearest sound you can hear—something that is very close to you. (Pause.) Now see if you can hear the sound that is the farthest away. (Pause.) Now you can open your eyes and bring your attention back into the room.

Alternate Mindfulness of Sound

To do this exercise, it is helpful to have a mindfulness bell or singing bowl, either of which, when rung, will give you an elongated ringing sound with a slow fade-away. If you do not have either of these, a glass, especially a fine glass or crystal one with a stem, held by the base, when stuck lightly with the handle of a spoon or fork, will give you a shorter but similar ring sound. (Just be careful!) Alternatively, you could search out a mindfulness bell or meditation bell app on your phone to use: we have used an app called "Mindfulness Bell" for this purpose. Give your client the following instructions and engage in the exercise with her:

I'm going to ring this bell and you will notice that the ringing sound goes on for a long time and then slowly fades out. (You can demonstrate with your bell.) I'd like to ask you to listen to the bell, and as you are listening, hold your hand up and keep it up until you have heard the very end of the sound. Listen very closely, because the sound will get quieter and quieter. Don't put your hand down until you absolutely can't hear any sound at all. Keep your hand up as long as you can hear the very end of the ring. I will put my hand down when I can't hear the ring any longer, which may or may not be the same time that you put your hand down.

You can repeat the exercise a few times to allow for mindfulness practice. You can debrief afterward by asking if there were any thoughts or reactions inside that got in the way of hearing. This brief exercise may elicit thoughts of comparison and judgment for your client. She may have noticed her mind telling her that she did it "wrong" if her hand went down either before or after yours, or that she "is not good enough" at the task if her hand went down first. Handle these in the same way as for "Mindfulness of an Object," making sure that you normalize her experience of the exercise, including any comparing or judging that may have come up.

The Matrix

As we mentioned, the matrix can be a very helpful way to organize and work with information the client has provided. It is easily created in session by dividing a piece of paper, oriented horizontally, into four quadrants, with a circle in the center where the points join. As a reminder, the lower half of the matrix, below the horizontal line, refers to internal events. On the left of the vertical line, the internal events refer to thoughts, emotions, physical feelings, and urges we want to get rid of and avoid, while on the lower right, the internal events refer to values: who and what matters to your client. The material in the lower left quadrant will eventually grow to become the "story" that we speak of. Above the horizontal line, we list observable behaviors, or things that both we and others know of our behavior from our five senses (often described as "five senses experiencing"). On the upper left go the things we do to get rid of the thoughts and feelings we don't want. On the upper right go values-consistent behaviors. The circle in the middle is the person who is noticing it all; we ask our clients to write "Me Noticing" in the center after asking our client, "Who is it that notices the thoughts and feelings in the lower left?" and "Who is noticing when what matters shows up inside, like on the lower right?" and finally, "Who is it that notices what comes up inside as you try to do the sorts of things in the upper right, and when you engage in strategies in the upper left to make the lower left go away?"

For more detailed information, you may want to read *The ACT Matrix* (2014) by Kevin Polk and Benjamin Schoendorff. Before you and your client try to fill in the matrix, the approach below may be helpful, as may the description that follows of DOTS, which we've found helpful in conceptualizing and normalizing coping strategies that go in the upper left quadrant.

Filling in the Matrix

Asking clients what they noticed during the earlier mindfulness meditation may give you some material to sort within the matrix. We have found that the left side is much easier for many of our clients to complete, but you can start in any quadrant. They appreciate us getting familiar with the internal events that get in their way, and our acceptance of the avoidance strategies they have used, so we don't rush to the right if they start on the left. Like Marilyn, they may let us know that the meditation was accompanied by thoughts like, *I was worried I wasn't doing it right*, *This is stupid, it won't help me*, and *I started thinking about how mad my parents will be if I can't do this*. Each and every one of these comments can be a starting point, and we write them in the lower left quadrant of the matrix. You can follow this up by asking, "What did you do to manage your feelings during the meditation?" as a way of adding to the upper left quadrant. If they aren't sure, we change the context by asking what they do to manage those thoughts and feelings when they arise outside of session, as they likely have in the past, with questions like: "So, outside of this session, when you aren't sure you are doing something correctly, what thoughts and feelings come up with that and how did you deal with them?" Asking about what they have tried to avoid during the previous week and how they avoided it will also help to start filling in the upper and lower left quadrants.

While you may not want to spend much time caught up with your client in her "story" (lower left quadrant), moving too fast may leave her feeling unheard and dismissed. When this is the case, she may pull back to her story repeatedly, so don't rush her at this stage. Approaching your client with curiosity and compassion will help you to understand her story and avoidance behavior. Having a clear understanding of these will be useful down the road, so time here is a worthwhile investment.

Once you have an idea of the inner events that your client struggles to experience, and how she copes when they arise, you can move to the right-hand side. There are many ways to approach the right side; we start simply and expand on it in later sessions. Start by asking your client who it is that matters to her and put these names in the lower right quadrant. Asking what her behavior would look like when she is treating these people (or things) as though they matter will give you material for the upper right quadrant. Ask your client what she has lost out on or stopped doing, or where her unwanted thoughts and feelings, as well as her coping strategies, make her daily life tough. This will start to give you material about what it is she wants to do in life, which is material for the upper right quadrant. As you and your client notice qualities about her that seem important, write these in the lower right quadrant. You will collect more information about the right side in sessions 3 and 4, which focus on values.

You may like the acronym DOTS, described below, as a way of organizing material in the upper left quadrant, and it is especially helpful when clients arrive at therapy with a long list of avoidance strategies. DOTS is also a fun way to talk about avoidance and control strategies; it seems to normalize the very existence of control strategies.

DOTS

DOTS are an adolescent-friendly way to identify, understand, and organize avoidance strategies—the things we do to get rid of what's inside that we don't like. When we begin to talk about DOTS, we engage our client using the matrix and write the letters vertically on the left side of the upper left quadrant. We can start a new matrix, bring out a matrix already started for our client, or use a flip chart or white board. We adapted the acronym slightly from Russ Harris (2009) so that the letters in DOTS stand for distracting, opting out (avoiding), time travel (thinking about the past or future), and self-harm. You can simply ask your client what she does to get rid of unwanted thoughts, emotions, physical feelings, and urges when they arise. The DOTS are not mutually exclusive, and many responses can be written in more than one row. The chart below shows some common examples of DOTS that clients have shared with us.

D	Distraction	Daydreaming, doing homework in a compulsive or perfectionistic way, being too busy, compulsions related to OCD, playing video games, using a cell phone or pretending to use a phone, cleaning, watching movies or television shows
O	Opting Out	Avoiding by not turning up—often relates to social contact, school attendance, and homework or exams, as well as behavior for the purpose of avoiding possible rejection and other thoughts and feelings
T	Time Travel	Ruminating in the form of "wishing" we could change the past or worrying about what may happen in the future
S	Self-Harm	Sleeping, eating, or exercising too much or not enough, cutting or burning oneself, suicide attempt, regretted shopping or sexual activity, drug and alcohol use, smoking

After identifying which DOTS they use, you can ask your client to evaluate short-term and long-term benefits and costs associated with DOTS. We do this by asking, "Does it work?" and most of the time the answer is yes, DOTS work to get rid of unwanted inside stuff. This is a moment when it is important to be aware of your own beliefs about DOTS and to be compassionate so that you don't convey a judgmental attitude toward clients and their choices. To get at long-term consequences, you only have to ask, "How long does it work for?" or "Do your DOTS ever stop working?" Above and to the right of the DOTS, still within the upper left quadrant of the matrix, it is helpful to make two columns, one for short-term and one for long-term effects, and ask your client to put a checkmark next to DOTS that work, and an "X" next to those that do not, for the short-term and the long-term.

Once your client identifies her DOTS and has a few things in each quadrant, you can start a discussion about the quadrants and how the contents impact each other. For example, asking how the use of DOTS impacts values and valued living may reveal that DOTS get in her way of doing what matters; we cover this more in session 3. Explorations such as this will help your client to derive relations that, over time and with practice, will transform stimulus function, such that DOTS become more aversive, while values and valued living become more rewarding. For example, the use of DOTS may enter in a frame of opposition with values and a frame of temporality may emerge between DOTS and long-term consequences. Through transformation of stimulus functions, DOTS may acquire more of an aversive function, as something to be avoided. As you talk about values and what behavior might emerge from values, derived relations will emerge through hierarchical framing and through transformation of stimulus functions: values-based behavior will become more appealing. As clients move toward what matters, their behavior will be under the control of positive reinforcement, as opposed to behavior that is controlled by negative reinforcement: the removal of aversive stimuli (lower left quadrant).

DOTS with Paddles

With credit to our colleague, Erin Lipsitt, we created "paddles" that consist of yellow cardboard circles, about eight inches in diameter, with a popsicle stick taped to the back so they can be held up in sessions. Clients can be asked to hold up their yellow paddle when they catch themselves using DOTS in session. You as the clinician will of course have your own paddle and will role-model for your client. Subtle behaviors such as changing topics when emotions start to intensify may be a DOT and you can use the paddle to identify present-moment use of DOTS. These paddles can be given out at the start of each session, or whenever you think they will be helpful, with clients who seem to engage with the paddle.

When using the matrix, you may have a conversation that goes something like this one with our previous fictional client, Marilyn.

M:	My week was okay. Kind of boring because I stayed home all week.
T:	How come you stayed home?
M:	I had a test at school and I couldn't study, I didn't want to look stupid by flunking, and I couldn't get my mind to shut up, I just kept thinking about the test, about the future, about failing. In some weird way I thought all that thinking would help, but it didn't. Then I got more anxious and went to bed all day. At the end of it all, I still hadn't studied, so I stayed home. My mind was racing too much, and I didn't want to look stupid by flunking, so I stayed home. (*Upper and lower left.*)
T:	So you had the thought that you would fail and that you would look stupid if you did?
M:	Yeah.
T:	And you noticed that you felt anxious. What feelings came up with these thoughts?
M:	I felt really nauseous. I hate that. (*She is identifying lower left.*)

T: What did you do to manage all of this? How did you cope? (*Eliciting DOTS.*)

M: I watched TV for a while, then went on my computer and after a few hours I felt better because I hadn't thought of school. (*Distraction, upper left, with the short-term benefit.*)

T: So distracting yourself helped. How did you feel once you stopped watching TV and using the computer? (*Eliciting her perspective of long-term outcome.*)

M: Awful, because then it came back to me that I still have to take the test, and the other kids in my class will know I missed it, they will think I'm such an idiot, which I am. I'm nowhere near as smart as them and now it's way more complicated. Oh, and I have another test this week, so the work piles up and then sometimes I have to skip class to finish the work, which makes it worse. This always happens to me. (*She has identified a long-term cost of using DOTS.*)

T: You sound so frustrated and upset, school seems to really matter to you. (*Being curious to see if she can go toward the right side of the matrix.*)

M: Yeah, it does, I wish it didn't. I've never been as smart as everyone else, they all must think I'm really stupid, especially my teachers.

T: If you could be the kind of student you want to be, what would that look like in terms of behavior? What would I see you doing if I were a fly on the wall? (*Eliciting upper right information, values-consistent behavior.*)

M: I would study, I would not be watching TV or be on my computer. Maybe I'd even ask my teachers for help, because there's lots I don't understand. (*Upper right.*)

This would be a perfectly reasonable moment to move to values and help Marilyn identify what matters to her in the domain of being a student, and would give us information for the lower right quadrant. We will touch on it lightly here, since values are discussed in more depth in later sessions, and then move to evolutionary material and some experiential activities.

T: If you were able to notice your urge to distract yourself and chose to study instead, or to ask teachers for help, what qualities in you would that be showing? What does that behavior say in terms of what matters to you as a student?

M: It says I am committed to learning and I care about my education. I'm actually a really curious student, I'm interested in learning, but I don't think it shows and I've forgotten how that feels lately.

T: So when you are feeling nauseated and are caught up in worries about failing (*pointing to lower left*), you watch TV, use the computer, and sometimes skip class (*pointing to upper left*). How does this work for being the type of student you want to be (*pointing to lower right*), committed and caring about your education, and studying (*pointing to upper right*)?

M: It doesn't work at all.

T: What would interested, determined, and committed look like in terms of behavior? What would I see you doing if I were a fly on the wall? (*Eliciting upper right information, values-consistent behavior.*)

M: I would study or ask teachers for help. But this is too hard, my brain just keeps thinking the same thing all the time.

T: Can we spend a few minutes talking about the human brain and see what you think?

Now that your client has an idea that her DOTS, while normal and somewhat useful, may also be getting in her way, some experiential exercises and an understanding of her brain as just doing its job may be helpful.

The Acetate

We developed an experiential exercise, "The Acetate," by adapting Russ Harris's "Hands as Thoughts" metaphor (Harris, 2009) when we first started this work. We've used it ever since, because it provides a powerful defusion/acceptance experience that can be referenced again and again throughout your work with clients. Here's how it works: First, see if you can find a box of clear acetate transparency sheets, the old-fashioned kind that were used with overhead projector systems. If you're old enough to have experience with these, the nostalgia effect when you see them is almost guaranteed, whether it be pleasant memories or the vision of your scowling fourth-grade teacher!

The Setup

Because the transparencies are expensive, you may not want to use a whole sheet for your client's acetate. If you hold a single sheet in portrait orientation (not landscape) and cut it horizontally in thirds, you will wind up with three clear plastic sheets that are each about 8½ by 3½ inches. We find that one of these will be big enough. If you are unable to find overhead transparencies, you can use any other kind of clear plastic sheet that can be written on with a felt pen and that is stiff enough to hold up in one hand without bending. If you use a permanent marker pen, your client's acetate can be kept for use in future sessions, but if you want to reuse the acetate, you could use a dry-erase marker and let your client photograph the finished piece with her phone, or with yours (with permission), for future reference.

Ask your client to write any frequent thoughts, feelings, physical sensations, urges, and so on, that tend to get in her way, on the transparency. Ask her to write as big or as small as she needs to pretty much cover the sheet of plastic with felt-pen writing. If there doesn't seem to be enough to cover a whole sheet, ask your client to write the thoughts and feelings in larger letters so that the sheet is completely covered. What ends up written on the acetate should be consistent with information in the lower left quadrant of your client's matrix; it is the inner events she hopes to get rid of. Because this is individual therapy, you need your own acetate! We recommend having one already prepared for general use that can be adjusted to a given client, always keeping boundaries regarding disclosure in mind. Our acetates have general thoughts such as "I'm stupid," and emotions such as "anxious" and "angry" written on them.

Observing Through the Acetate

Now ask your client to hold the sheet in front of her face so that she is looking through the words on the acetate in order to see you. Make sure the acetate is right at her eye level so that she is looking through it and not over or under it, and as close or as far as she needs it in order to read what she has written. We instruct clients to hold the acetate with their hands up, thumbs on the side closest to them, and fingers spread out behind the acetate. There are several ways to use the acetate in the first therapy session and they can be repeated in later sessions as needed. Reminding your client to keep the acetate in front of her eyes, ask her to look around your office and just see what is there, what she can notice. Be careful here: many clients will look under, over, or beside their acetate; it is important that their arms move with their heads, so the acetate is always in front of their eyes. Spend a few moments inquiring about what this was like. If your client does not have much by way of observations, have her look around the room without the acetate, then again with it, and ask what she notices in terms of the two experiences. What generally comes up is that clients notice that things aren't so clear when the acetate is in front of them, and many will notice that they became fused with what is written on the acetate and weren't really able to notice much at all; they were in their heads.

Conversing Through the Acetate

If your client can notice a difference in the quality of looking at your office with and without the acetate, this next experiment will make a more powerful statement. Ask your client to carry on a conversation with you while you each hold your acetate in place in front of your eyes. After a few exchanges, ask how it feels to be talking and interacting in this way. Your client may say it is strange or uncomfortable and hard to do. Sometimes adolescents are very aware of the actual words written on the acetate and find these disturbing to try and communicate through. Many become fused and, as with the previous exercise, spend the time in their heads. Sometimes they just notice there is an obstruction of their eye contact with you while talking, and find this annoying. In all these cases, they are usually able to notice that the words on the acetate are a problem for them in trying to do something else (communicate with you), and they may even notice that they communicate better when they focus on you rather than on the writing. You can heighten this insight by asking them to try keeping the acetate in place while attempting to do a task, such as writing something on a piece of paper, doing a little math exercise, or, better still, doing some small thing that would be important to them in moving toward their values. This exercise usually provides an opportunity for them to learn experientially that the "stuff" in their heads literally gets in the way of life. If your client doesn't seem to make this discovery, you can ask questions like, "Is it easier to do things with the acetate there or not there?" and "Does having this in the way remind you of anything that happens to you in your everyday life outside this room?" Once you have established the connection, you can refer to "the acetate" as a metaphor for how the actual "stuff" in their heads gets in the way for them.

When Clients Prefer the Acetate

Occasionally we have had clients report that they enjoy interacting through the acetate, because it reduces eye contact and (at least to some degree) their interpersonal anxiety! When this happens, it has been helpful to engage in discussions about the quality of the interaction, visual cues from their conversation partner that they may miss, and the impact of this on the conversation and the quality of the relationship. If values related to relationships have already been identified, any value that remotely resembles being "connected" with others can be brought up now, as a way to ask, "Is engaging with others while you are stuck in your head leading you toward being connected?" Many adolescents have reported that they interact with others just as they did in this exercise, caught up in their heads; and they may wonder if their peers have noticed that they aren't really "present" in those interactions.

Defusing from the Acetate

Once we have finished experiencing the office and each other through the acetate, we ask clients to continue holding it up in front of their eyes while we ask this final question, which is meant to promote defusion and acceptance of the stuff inside. We ask a question that goes something like this:

Before we finish with the acetate, I invite you to try one last thing with me. You mentioned that looking through the acetate gets in the way of seeing what and who is there with you, and of feeling connected to me as we were talking. For the sake of this exercise, let's assume the acetate is super-glued to our hands, we can't let go of it at all. What can we do to move it out of our way, so it isn't front and center anymore?

At this point, clients may move the acetate up and over their heads, and if they do, we say something like, "Great, you got it out from in front of your eyes, are you willing to hold it there for the rest of the session?" Most clients will say no, since it is physically uncomfortable, and they are likely already feeling some fatigue from holding their hands in front of their face. We suggest they try other options until they find a place where their acetate can come to rest. This involves two competing processes: figuring out where they can put their acetate (since it's super-glued to their hands) and, at the same time, doing what matters, in this case, engaging in the session with the therapist. Clients inevitably come to the idea of moving their hands so that they settle in their lap, along with the acetate. We then ask them to notice what it is like for them to talk with us without the acetate in front of their faces, just sitting in their laps instead. Later, throughout the course of therapy, you can revisit this defusion experience repeatedly by asking your client to try and "treat thoughts like the acetate."

Our Mind's Job

When we get to this point with clients, it helps to have a discussion about why our minds torment us so much by staying stuck on aversive thoughts and experiences. Essentially, we want to engage our client in a discussion about the workings of the human mind. There are several points to be made in this regard. Each is open to discussion and some are accompanied by experiential activities. We hope that by the end of this discussion we have helped our clients to make some space for the idea that they are not broken or abnormal, or in need of fixing, but rather, that they are the owner of a normal human mind, and in need of some compassion, defusion, and acceptance. While we have picked up many helpful tidbits from readings and workshops over the years, Shawn Smith's book *The User's Guide to the Human Mind* (2011) has been particularly helpful in terms of providing simple, easy-to-use explanations.

The Comparison Machine

We begin with several points about the mind and what it does, generally speaking. This can begin with a simple question posed to our client: "What is the mind for? What does it do?" Along with other functions that the client suggests in response to this question, we can add that our minds solve problems, plan, remember, create images, and engage in abstract reasoning. We can also point out that they protect us by ensuring our survival and sending out danger signals when we are threatened. Thousands of years ago, our minds were busy keeping us alive by ensuring that we had access to tribemates, food, shelter, and a mate, which in turn protected us from the dangers of the world, mostly from being eaten!

We continue describing how this plays out: today, we humans live in a world that has evolved in many ways and the dangers aren't the same as they once were, but our primitive brain is still concerned with making sure we aren't abandoned by the tribe and put at risk of becoming something's lunch.

Adolescent clients' worst fear is being rejected, ostracized, and ultimately left alone or abandoned. This makes sense when we recall that, in addition to a normal human need to be part of a tribe, adolescents especially need the "tribe" of their peers in which they can develop their identity and achieve autonomy from parents. The level of fear of abandonment that adolescents experience is not logical or rational, and many arrive at ACT having already tried to dispute, argue, and debate with their minds. Many realize on an intellectual level that giving a class presentation, despite the many opportunities for embarrassment, is not really as dangerous as being kicked out of a tribe or swimming with a hungry shark, in terms of their survival. But we aren't dealing with rationality. We are dealing with a frightened mind that is determined to keep us safe and will do anything to achieve this.

So how does our mind ensure that we stay in the tribe, ensure that we aren't abandoned? We may continue with something like this: "So, without your tribe, you will get eaten, which makes having a tribe very important," or "What could you do to make sure you are a valued part of your tribe, so they don't think you are slacking and kick you out?"

We are getting toward the idea that to ensure that we remain valued tribe members, our minds get caught up in comparing our performance to that of our tribemates, so we will be alerted to shortcomings and can adjust accordingly before we are noticed.

We can end with: "So our human minds are still functioning as if we are in a tribe, comparing us to everyone else to make sure we don't get kicked out of the tribe." We can ask their thoughts on the matter at this point: can they entertain the possibility that maybe they have a normal human brain? Even if they aren't totally convinced, we've opened space for them to consider this idea. This may contribute to a shift in how your client perceives his thoughts, moving from a place where his thoughts define who he is to a more defused place, where he can observe the workings of his mind as normal and something to be curious about, from a distance.

The Fix-It Machine

Another job of our very normal human brain is to fix things, and brains do this well. Problem solving and creating are all about the brain fixing what isn't quite working in our world. We can separate this into inside and outside stuff (LeJeune, 2007), where *inside* refers to our thoughts and feelings and *outside* refers to stuff in our five senses world. Our brain helps us figure out how to "fix" or "get rid of" stuff in our outside world that we don't like. For example, if our clients don't like the song playing on their phone, they can change it and "get rid of" the offensive music, and if they don't like what they are wearing, they can fix it, or get rid of it, by changing their outfit. If they aren't prepared for a test, they can study, skip the test, or make other arrangements to take the test. If your client detests the liver he is served for dinner, he can smother it in ketchup or slip it to the family dog, and voilà, he has "gotten rid of it." We ask our clients for examples of things in their outside world that they can fix, and ask how they go about it.

We explain that our brain also tries to apply this strategy to inside stuff as well, so that when we don't like the thoughts and emotions that are popping up inside, it generates ways for us to "get rid of" them, and this works—at least for a while. Client behavior such as hiding schoolbooks under coats or desks so as to avoid the anxious thoughts and feelings attached to homework is one example of the "fix-it machine," in which some tactic designed to solve problems on the outside is applied to inside stuff. We stress at some point in this conversation that using avoidance solutions (upper left) for thoughts and feelings may be okay if used occasionally: many people do it, and it's fine if the solutions don't make matters worse. However, when these avoidance strategies become inflexible ways of managing things that we can't actually control, and get in the way of our valued living, our brain may not be helping us by staying in "fix-it" mode.

Our mind also sets up rules in terms of problem solving and prioritizing, which is helpful for struggles that involve the external world: we can't get to school because it snowed and the car is stuck, and we "have to get to school." Our mind figures out that to get to school, we must first get rid of the obstacle, in this case, snow, which we can do by shoveling. But this tendency can also work against us when our mind sets up rules involving the internal world, such as: *I can't be happy until my sadness is gone*, or *I can't go to parties with friends until my anxiety is gone*, or *I can't do what matters until I lose five pounds*. In the latter examples, sadness, anxiety, and weight are not as easy to "get rid of" as snow on our driveway, and in fact getting rid of them does not guarantee the desired outcome. These are, in fact, examples of rule-governed behavior.

At the end of this discussion we hope the client is left with the idea that brains that compare a lot are normal. Brains that try to fix things are normal. When our thoughts and feelings are unpleasant, we try to make them go away or "fix" them on the inside in much the same way we try to get rid of things or "fix" things in the outside world. When we attempt to get rid of what's inside, however, we use experiential avoidance, strategies that can be categorized as DOTS. Yet most of us, even with some degree of understanding and acceptance, will want our normal brain to be quiet. This is natural. When our thoughts and feelings are unpleasant, we try to fix the situation with DOTS. Our DOTS get in our way and usually make the thoughts and feelings worse, creating an endless loop of unpleasant inner experiences and actions that are aimed at avoiding thoughts and feelings but that actually just make them worse. So what is the alternative? Now that your client understands that his mind is normal and is just trying to be helpful, it's time to finish off the session with some fun experiential exercises to really *feel* the point that trying to control what is inside is a futile endeavor.

Illusion of Control

"So, you may in fact have a very normal human brain. It's just doing its job and we may not want to fire it." This brings us to the "illusion of control," a phrase used to describe our tendency to believe we can control the stuff inside in the same way we can make outside problems go away. At this point, we engage our clients in experiential activities (which we refer to as "experiments") and metaphors, focused on the futility of control efforts exerted against cognitions and emotions. Below we have outlined a smorgasbord of the metaphors and experiments that we typically engage our clients in. Feel free to choose what you believe will resonate with your client. If you are familiar with ACT, you may already know some of these, as we've adapted a few of them from other ACT texts (like Harris, 2009); others emerged in session.

Purple Gorilla

For this activity, we give clients a pen and a sheet of paper and ask them to divide the paper in half. We then ask them to close their eyes and picture "a purple gorilla, on roller skates, wearing a tutu." Then we tell them to open their eyes again, and ask them to purposefully *not* think about the gorilla from the time we say "start" until we say "stop," but if they do, we ask them to put a tick mark in the top half of the paper. We give them one or two minutes for this. Once this is done, we let them know that this time, they are allowed to think of the gorilla. We still want them to put a tick mark, this time on the lower half of the paper, if they think of the gorilla, but they are under no pressure *not* to think of it. Once the time is up, ask your client to compare the total number of tick marks in each half of the paper. Many, but not all, will report thinking about the gorilla more frequently when instructed not to, which we reflect back to them with a summary statement like: "So, when you tried *not* to think of something, you thought of it more. Is this familiar?" We are hoping they get at the idea that thought suppression doesn't work. In fact it often backfires and makes the thought more frequent. This realization can be combined with other elements of creative hopelessness.

I Want Candy

That last idea, that thought suppression may actually intensify thoughts, can be played with using the idea of a child in a grocery store who wants candy while the parent is ignoring him. Especially for adolescents who babysit or spend time with kids, this may seem a familiar scenario to ask about: "Have you ever seen a child in a grocery store who wants the candy by the cash register, and is trying to get his parents' attention to tell them that? If they aren't paying him any attention, what does he do?" Most will answer that the child will "yell louder," "have a tantrum," or something similar. The client may take away that, like this child, the mind does not like to be ignored, and will work harder to get what it wants.

Cutting Off Your Leg (Well, Not Really)

Ask your client if he can make one of his legs go totally numb, so he can't feel it at all. Some clients will tell us they can do it; regardless, we further clarify that we want them to make their leg so numb that if we were to try and cut if off with a knife, they would not feel it. At this point, clients tell us it's an impossible task. We end by asking, "Why can't you do it?" hoping they will realize for themselves that they can't control physical sensations.

Beach Ball

It can also be fun to liken how we try to manage thoughts to trying to hold a large beach ball under water. This connects easily to several ACT processes. It can be done as an eyes-open discussion or an eyes-closed visualization. We are partial to the latter and might do it like this:

Is there a place with water, a lake, an ocean, a pool, somewhere you enjoy? Imagine yourself there now, noticing what is around you, the water, any trees, maybe a cottage, the sound of birds, and the warmth of the sun. Notice who might be there with you. What would you be doing? Imagine that a beach ball floating in the water makes its way to you and bumps you on the arm. You notice the beach ball and are irritated by it, so you hold it down under the water with all your strength. It's a huge beach ball, and a lot of pressure is required to hold it under. While you are holding the ball under water, what else can you do? How can you be with the other things you had been noticing?

Most clients will reply that their activity will be curtailed by their efforts to hold down the ball. Then we can ask, "When your arms finally get too tired to hold it down, and you let go, what happens?" The common response is, "It flies up." Now we can reply with, "Wow, that's much more noticeable than when it just floated along and gently nudged your arm." Next we ask our client to visualize being in the water, doing what matters. We ask if he can picture the ball bumping into him, gently, and ask if he can imagine doing something differently this time, so he can continue with whatever he was doing in the water. If necessary, ask your client to imagine just acknowledging the ball's presence, allowing it some space to just float around, and then going back to what he was doing. This can also be used as a defusion exercise in later sessions, so you can use it now and repeat it later, or leave it until later.

Falling in Love

In this activity, we are trying to help clients question whether it is reasonable to expect themselves to be able to control their emotions. We give them the following scenario:

Let's pretend that I have a million dollars, and I am going to give it to you if you can fall in love with the next person who walks through my door. (Clients may indicate they can do this initially, and often smile about how easy this would be. The smile tends to fade as you continue.) *However, what you have to know is that this person has not bathed for years, hasn't brushed his or her teeth either, and is extremely mean-spirited, selfish, and nasty.*

The client's response has usually turned to revulsion by now, and no one has ever answered yes when we ask, "Well, can you do it? Can you fall genuinely, authentically, in love with this person?" They reply with statements like "No way!" and we ask, "Why not?" With very little processing required, the futility of trying to control affect is now clearly understood.

Thoughts Are Inevitable

You can demonstrate the idea that thoughts will occur no matter what, that it's our behavior that is optional, by asking your client if his mind fills in anything when you say "Mary had a little...," "A, B, C...," "A penny saved is a penny...," showing that thoughts automatically occur. You can use any familiar saying or nursery rhyme for this purpose if your client would not recognize these ones. We might explain: "Through life experience, we have learned these sayings, so now when our mind is prompted with the beginning, we automatically generate the ending. Throughout life, your mind is programmed to generate certain thoughts, including thoughts about your self, your anxiety, and so on."

Back to the Matrix

Bringing out the matrix again can be helpful for summarizing what we have done so far, pointing out to clients that they can't control thoughts and feelings—as seen in the gorilla and falling-in-love experiments, for example—and that efforts to do so mirror what goes on in the upper left quadrant of their matrix. Asking if they have had any greater luck controlling those thoughts and emotions will quickly yield a no from most clients. If they are still tied to control efforts, reviewing DOTS and their short-term and long-term costs and benefits once again is helpful. Once your client gets it that trying to control cognitions and emotions is futile, you are ready to ask the question pivotal to creative hopelessness: "If control doesn't work, if you can't get rid of the stuff inside, then what?" Many clients will come to the idea of *I can stop trying*, but they aren't really sure what that would look like in their day-to-day lives. This is the creative part that comes with the hopelessness.

The Tissue Box

We always have a tissue box handy and have found it can be very useful for all sorts of experiential activities and for helping clients make choices on their matrix. Start by reminding your client that the stuff in the lower left is not going anywhere, and that when he engages in DOTS it impacts being the person he has indicated on the lower right that he wants to be and his ability to do things that matter, located in the upper right. You have just established this, so there shouldn't be any disagreement at this point. Then, tell him he has two choices. First, cover the entire right side of the matrix with the tissue box, and offer him the option of spending his life engaged on the left, dipping into the stuff in the lower quadrant that he doesn't want, and then getting caught up in DOTS to try and get rid of it. This first choice represents behavior under control of negative reinforcement. For the second option, cover just the upper left, offering the idea that since the lower left isn't going anywhere, he can have the lower left quadrant plus the two quadrants on the right. The majority of clients will choose option two, which is behavior under the influence of positive reinforcement. For those who choose the first option, don't fight it. Let them have it. There may be more you don't know that is keeping them stuck there.

Now that some degree of creative hopelessness may be settling in, a brief eyes-closed mindfulness exercise called "Quicksand" can help to open up a felt sense of allowing what is inside as an alternative to avoidance and control strategies. We focus more on allowing in session 5.

Quicksand Metaphor

This metaphor is credited to Steven C. Hayes (2005). It can fit nicely here in this session and clinicians can refer back to it in later sessions as a way to think about stopping the struggle with what's inside. The quicksand metaphor can be done as a brief eyes-closed activity, or eyes can be left open. It supports the idea of letting go of the struggle with what's inside, a struggle we can't win. It involves saying something like the following:

Imagine yourself walking along a path. It doesn't matter where or what it looks like, just let your imagination give you the image…and then imagine suddenly your next step lands you in quicksand… Try to picture yourself in this moment and try to notice what you would do."

You can ask your client to open his eyes and describe to you what he noticed himself doing. Most clients tell us they would "freak out" or try to "swim" and are pretty sure they would sink—which they would! We agree with them that they would sink and add just the simple explanation that "moving your legs up and down as if walking creates a vacuum that pulls you down." If you would like a more detailed scientific explanation of why this is, there are some great sites on the Internet, and if you want to add visual aids to your session, Bear Grylls has several great videos on YouTube; our favorite is at https://www.youtube.com/watch?v=JHCW_bqWLTo.

Once your client gets the idea that fighting the quicksand by trying to get out will sink him, you can engage him in a second way of thinking about being caught in quicksand, like this:

Close your eyes again and imagine yourself in the quicksand. Just for a moment, allow yourself to struggle, see "you" struggling and feel yourself sinking. (Pause.) Then imagine gently tipping your upper body forward, so you are lying with your chest down on the quicksand, and spreading your arms out to the side. Then try to pull one leg and then the other, to lift them up and spread out so you now look like a starfish. And just imagine yourself floating on top of the quicksand. If you start to panic and find yourself upright and sinking again, try to notice that happening, and gently get back into the starfish position. Now if you were really in quicksand, you would want to be in this position and "monkey crawl" to the shore. The key is to move into the experience, accepting it for what it is. You can't change it by moving your limbs quickly. Wishing you weren't in quicksand won't help either. Accept that you are stuck in quicksand. Allow your thoughts and feelings, knowing you can't control them, and respond to the present moment by moving slowly, purposefully, toward the shore as you lean into the quicksand.

Some clients engage in visualization exercises easily, others not, and it can vary from session to session. We can get a lot of mileage out of the quicksand metaphor later by referring back to the question, "Can you treat this like quicksand?"

The "Story"

Before drawing the session to a close, we give the lower left quadrant a bit more attention by labeling the contents as "story." When we were first learning ACT, Kelly Wilson often spoke of the "storied up version" of oneself. This phrase certainly influenced our work. We let clients know that we realize they aren't struggling to stave off just a single thought or feeling. We want to make sure they know we have an appreciation for the sheer volume of inner events they are experiencing—enough to easily fill a whole book that could be known as "the story about me," which they have been reading from all their lives.

If your client has engaged in other therapies, especially more traditional CBT, she may be in the habit of engaging in cognitive disputation with one thought after another. Many of our clients tell us that they get even more caught up in their heads when trying to dispute their thoughts because there are so many of them. RFT helps us understand this, and we'll share some grasp of it with our clients in a later session. Still others tell us that, although they know intellectually that the thoughts aren't true, they still "feel" as though they are, and so this knowledge doesn't seem to relieve their distress.

Feel free to share the hexaflex with your clients if you believe they might benefit from the added visual "map" or explanation of the journey you are taking together. Regardless of what you decide, it is important that ACT is something that is mostly experienced, not talked about, beyond this basic explanation; otherwise it becomes too much of an intellectual exercise. You don't need to infuse your client with all the technical terms. For example, with our clients we usually refer to defusion as "unsticking." You can provide visual details of the hexaflex either in traditional form or drawn with the adolescent in the center, perhaps in a circle, with each of the processes indicated around the center. You can discuss how typical life scenarios unfold, with a person's energy going into avoidance and getting trapped by fusion, using examples they have already shared. Allow your client to notice the short-term benefits and long-term costs of DOTS. Then explain the processes. The adolescents themselves often realize that until they *notice* what they are actually doing in any given moment, they aren't very likely to do things differently. You can walk them through the scenario(s) again, emphasizing mindful awareness of the present, defusion, and acceptance, and ask what options might emerge, pointing out the difference between reacting with avoidance versus responding with a conscious choice coming from awareness. This is a good time to stress the centrality of mindfulness as a place to begin to change what they have been doing, a way to practice "noticing." Mindfulness can be described as a way of training our brains to notice what is going on, in real time, and to let it all still go on but with awareness of it a bit more in the background, the way we hear the "white noise" mentioned earlier. From this place clients can more freely choose to go toward what matters to them. In order for them to practice noticing, ask if they are willing to try something daily, for as many days as they can, before their next session, emphasizing that there are many ways to practice and enhance mindfulness.

We end the session with a mindfulness exercise and provide sample transcripts below.

Mindfulness

We have provided two mindfulness transcripts below for you to choose from: "Mindfulness of Breath" and "Mindful Writing." Choose whichever you prefer, or use both, depending on what feels right in the moment.

Mindfulness of Breath

This meditation is pretty standard and would go something like this:

Bring your attention now to your breath. See if you can just focus on your breath as it enters and leaves through your nostrils at the tip of your nose, as if there were nothing else in the world to notice. (Pause.) Bring your full attention to the air entering and leaving at the tip of your nose. (Pause.) See if you can notice what you experience with each breath. You might notice one breath is shorter or one longer. It's okay if they are different, just let your body do the breathing. Each breath might be different. (Pause.) Do you notice any difference in the temperature of the air as it enters your nose and as it leaves your nose? (Pause.) See if you can stay with the actual experience of the breath. If you notice that your mind is giving you thoughts while you are trying to pay attention to your breath, just kindly and gently detach your attention from the thoughts and return it to your breath. (Pause.) You might have thoughts about your breathing—whether it's right or wrong—just notice those thoughts, and kindly and gently detach from them and return to just paying attention to your breath itself. (Pause.) You might have thoughts about things that have nothing to do with being here now—like thoughts about what you're going to do later today, or what someone said earlier today. Just notice these thoughts and kindly and gently detach, and return your attention to the breath. (Pause.) Now see if you can focus only on each breath at the tip of your nose just at the moment it finishes leaving your nose. (Pause.) Bring your full attention to your out-breath just at that moment it ends and before a new breath comes in. (Pause.) Keep watching for that very end moment of each out-breath. (Pause.)

Afterwards, process this experience. Usually adolescents will say that they found it "relaxing." We validate whatever feelings are observed, but usually point out that when doing a mindfulness practice, there may be times when it is experienced as "relaxing" and times when the same thing is experienced as quite stressful. We can never anticipate how calm or how turbulent our minds will be. We stress the importance of staying with the experience, whatever it is, with an attitude of curiosity and openness.

Mindful Writing

This is an eyes-open exercise that may be a little less threatening for someone new to mindfulness. Give your client paper and a pen and ask her to start writing whatever comes into her mind, without stopping or lifting the pen away from the paper. You can let her know that she can start when you say, "Start writing," and stop when you have timed a two- or three-minute time interval and say, "Stop writing." Or alternatively you can set a timer for two or three minutes and ask her to start when you say "Go," and stop when the timer goes off. Ask your client not to think before she writes, but to just keep her pen moving and put down what her mind gives her as if she were a court reporter faithfully transcribing every word being spoken. It is important to stress that she will not be asked to share what she is writing, and best for you to stay far enough away that she is assured that she has privacy. The idea here is for the client to experience noticing thoughts in real time as they arise.

Debrief after she has stopped writing by asking what she noticed about the experience. You can model acceptance for your client here by taking an open, curious, nonjudgmental stance toward her experience and the content of her writing. This will support her in approaching her own experience and the content of her own mind with an attitude of acceptance. It isn't necessary to ask about the content of the writing, but if your client is willing to share it, that's fine. The important part to highlight is the actual experience of just noticing thoughts, whatever they might be. Often someone doing this exercise will find she can't write as fast as the thoughts are coming. You can normalize this observation if it is made and ask what she thinks that could mean about the number of thoughts going through our minds all the time. This will open the door for later conversations about thoughts and other private events. Sometimes clients struggle with this exercise, telling us, "I'm not thinking of anything." We gently reply, "That was a thought and you can write it down."

Assignment of Home Practice

We don't like to call the work between sessions "homework" since many of our clients are struggling academically and the very word "homework" conjures up all sorts of allergic reactions. Calling it "home practice" is a thinly veiled disguise, but one they are happier to go with. We don't ask clients to fill in paperwork unless it helps them. If they like, we can provide a paper version of a template for them to fill in, or have them take a photo of one with their phone. Many clients like to use the calendar of their phone to set reminders for themselves to practice. We allow time at the end of sessions for them to do this.

At the end of this session, we ask them if they would be willing to try "noticing" over the week, and here we are referring to noticing with one or more of their five senses (taste, smell, sight, hearing, or touch), and noticing when they are using DOTS.

There are many ways clients can practice noticing, and we give two options here. First, have the adolescent identify an activity he does every day, and ask if he is willing to slow down his pace and try to notice, with one or two senses, things he has never noticed, or things he has forgotten during that activity. We suggest activities like brushing teeth, showering, washing hair, eating, or walking to the bus stop if the client can't think of anything. Alternatively, he may be willing to set a daily alarm in his phone, and when the alarm goes off, to notice his experience in the moment, using his senses.

With respect to DOTS, we ask adolescents to try and notice their use of DOTS over the next week, stressing the fact that they may not notice they engaged in DOTS until after the fact, and that noticing in "real time" will become more likely as their mindfulness practice progresses. We let them know we will ask about DOTS, as well as the short-term and long-term benefits and costs of engaging in them when we meet next. There is a handout at the end of the chapter that you can provide to clients; many opt to make notes in their cell phone or not at all.

Modifications for Group Work

As mentioned previously, in the group therapy section we will only outline ways in which group therapy diverges from individual therapy. We always start off the first group session with introductions and an icebreaker exercise, and then proceed as with an individual client, with the modifications outlined below. We chat about group rules and engage in the "Skittles" game before proceeding to the content. Approaching content, we begin with "What Stuck," as we did for individual clients, followed by mindfulness, DOTS, the matrix, "The Acetate," our mind's job, and the illusion of control.

Group Rules

We like to generate these as a group. Confidentiality is our main rule, and so we ask each group member to commit to it, especially if they know anyone else in the group, if two or more group members attend the same school, or if they have friends in common. Despite our clients coming from a large catchment area, we have run into circumstances in which clients are somehow connected, in ways we can't always discover during screening meetings. Depending on the nature of their relationship or connection, it may or may not be problematic to have all parties remain in what often develops into a very intimate group. We try to keep the rules to a minimum and add others as necessary throughout the sessions.

Next we proceed to a fun icebreaker, within an ACT context.

Skittles Game

This can take up to forty minutes, depending on the size of the group and the willingness or ability of participants to share. Some group members will be vague, some will disclose a lot more. It has proven to be a good bonding tool, and begins to elicit fusion and personal struggles, so we take our time with this activity.

The "Skittles" game goes something like this: Fill a bowl with multicolored Skittles candies. (You can also use colored marbles if you don't have the candy handy or any other type of multicolored candies.) Pass it around with a spoon, and ask each group member (and each facilitator) to take four to six Skittles, ensuring that at least one is red and one is purple. (You can designate different colors instead of these two, but the point is that each group member needs to take at least one of each of the designated colors). Watching how the adolescents put their Skittles down in front of them can sometimes be revealing of personal struggles. (We give them a paper tissue or paper towel.)

Only after everyone has his or her Skittles, we hang up a previously created poster (or flip chart sheet) with the following list:

Orange—Country I would like to visit.

Yellow—Favorite food.

Green—Someone I would like to invite to dinner.

Red—Thoughts or feelings that get in the way of what I want to do.

Purple—Something I was able to do even though I was feeling anxious or sad or angry.

Then we say something like this:

Now that you all have your Skittles, here is what we are going to do. When it's your turn, you will share something about yourself that goes with or corresponds to the color of your Skittles. So if you have an orange one, you will tell us the name of a country you would like to visit. Yellow means you tell us a favorite food, green, you tell us about someone, alive or dead, that you would like to invite to dinner. Red is to tell us a thought or emotion you try to get rid of and one way you have tried to do this. And purple, you tell us something you have done even though you were too anxious, sad, angry, or any other emotion, to do it. Once you have had your turn, feel free to eat your Skittles if you want to. We (the facilitators) are going to do this as well. Would anyone like to start?

If there are no volunteers, one of the facilitators starts and then we reopen the option for volunteers. We try to space out the facilitators between adolescents. Sometimes a reminder that "If you really hate talking in groups, you could go now and use the fact you have done that as the answer to your purple Skittle." Someone usually goes for this option, and eventually they each take a turn. Group members often share beyond the minimum required, and we model this as facilitators. For example, with the red skittle, we might say something like, "Even though we are clinicians here, we still worry about doing a good job and being helpful enough, and we handle this by overpreparing and reading too much. And sometimes we're a bit silly when we're nervous."

We don't tend to process much during the "Skittles" game, but as we listen with ACT ears, group members inevitably share something of their "stories" (self-as-content), including judgments about themselves and expectations about others and about relationships. These are important to note and worth a brief discussion as the "Skittles" session is debriefed. The information that has been shared can be used to begin setting a conversational tone of acceptance and defusion, and can also be woven back in during later sessions as examples of commonly experienced private events.

What Stuck?

We always begin a session by asking what stuck from the previous session. In this case, we are asking about what they remember or what made an impact during the screening meeting. It is a good refresher for those who were distracted at times and missed something, and provides a context for this session. We fill in the missing bits.

Mindfulness Meditation

The two mindfulness practices described for use in an individual session, "Mindfulness of an Object" and "Mindfulness of Sound," can easily be done as a group practice as well. In the debrief, hearing from others about their experience of practicing mindfulness and noticing thoughts can be very helpful, because it underscores how normal it is for all of us to struggle with what our minds are giving us. This can be reinforced if the therapist uses defusing language like "the stuff our human minds give us," "so you had the thought that…," "and then you noticed you were having the thought that…" In "Mindful Writing," for example, it is not uncommon for group members to get caught up with thoughts such as *I'm not writing as much as he is*, and *I'm not doing this as well as others*. If they are able to share these thoughts, it provides helpful material to use later on regarding the illusion of control and our mind's job as a comparison machine.

DOTS

We explain and work through DOTS as in individual therapy. However, when working with groups, there is peer pressure to be harnessed in some circumstances. Sometimes a group member will describe long-term benefits of DOTS, such as, "I got to stay home from school and my anxiety was gone" (referring to school avoidance).

Other group members may challenge this, with questions like, "Yeah, but don't you still have work to do?" If other group members don't challenge the use of DOTS, we can do so with a stance of gentle curiosity. We try to hold almost everything gently, including both use and nonuse of DOTS, so we stress that there are moments when DOTS may actually be helpful or necessary; it's when we rely on them as our sole means of reacting to the world that they are problematic.

The Matrix

Sometimes concepts flow faster within a group, sometimes slower, depending on the group. To ease a group of adolescents into the idea of values and how they fit with DOTS, we often give each member a blank matrix and have them fill it in regarding their role as a group member. This has the advantage of bringing interpersonal struggles and DOTS to the surface, which can impact group dynamics in many ways. Once it is in the public domain, it makes it easier for you, as a group facilitator, to ask people something like, "Is doodling now, during group, a DOT?" in the moment, to increase members' capacity for noticing.

We often start with the lower right quadrant, asking what type of group member each person wants to be (lower right), what those qualities would look like to the rest of us (upper right), what thoughts and feelings are likely to come up and get them stuck (lower left), and how will they deal with those (upper left). Once we have the left side of the matrix filled out, at least partly, that information can be used as the basis for "The Acetate," which we do next.

The Acetate

"The Acetate" is done as it was with an individual client. However, when it comes to conversing through the acetate, we ask that group members, holding their acetate in front of them, stand up, walk around the room, and ask three questions to each of three people, and then report back to the group about the experience. While processing the experience, we ask that group members continue to hold the acetate at eye level, which results in significant fatigue and makes the additional point that looking through one's "story" is exhausting. As facilitators, we take part in this as well. After engaging group members in moving their acetate somewhere so that it is not front and center, but still stuck to their hands, and dealing with any other processing that comes up, we continue while group members sit with their acetate in their laps. We then work through "our mind's job" and proceed to "illusion of control," as we did with our individual client.

Illusion of Control

Illusion of control can be way more fun in a group! We have numerous activities to choose from and tend to pick just a few, making sure that we always include one targeting cognitions and another targeting emotions. The ones described in the section above on individual therapy work nicely in a group setting. The "falling in love" scenario, for example, usually provokes great discussions and creates camaraderie among group members. The advantage of engaging with groups around the illusion of control is that if a group member hangs on to his control agenda and keeps insisting that he can have control of private events, peers usually exert subtle pressure to question this belief. We have outlined two additional exercises in this group section, since they are fun in this context and can add more to a sense of group cohesion. You can also use them with individual clients if you like.

Delete a Memory

You can begin by saying, "Take a moment to remember something from earlier today, perhaps a snapshot in your mind of coming to group today. Great. Now forget it. Delete it from your memory." If anyone says they can do this, ask what it is that they deleted. If they can tell you, that shows that it isn't gone! What often results from this quick exercise is a discussion about how nervous group members were prior to the start of the session, as many tried to delete a memory of being in the waiting room of our clinic, or a memory related to their journey on the way to the session; this allows facilitators an opportunity to pull together upper left and lower left material!

Don't Salivate

Give each group member a slice of lemon and ask them to hold it up to their nose, but insist that they don't salivate. Be prepared to define "salivate," because many adolescents don't seem to know that it refers to your mouth getting watery. They can then lick the lemon, bite the lemon, eat the lemon, but no salivating allowed! The majority of adolescents will find that they can't avoid salivating. This gives you the opportunity to explore with them what this lemon experiment shows us: we don't have control over our body and its physiological responses. Here you try to elicit their thoughts about other physiological responses that are difficult to control, such as a pounding heart and sweaty brow they may experience when anxious, turning red when embarrassed, or even the act of digestion (it just happens).

Mindfulness

Group members are asked to sit with arms and legs uncrossed, feet flat on the floor. This exercise is done preferably with eyes closed, but if any group members are uncomfortable closing their eyes, it can also be done with eyes lowered to the floor directly beyond the feet and gaze soft, so that the attention is inward rather than outward. Occasionally we find adolescents in the group who really struggle with a sense of safety during mindfulness meditations and cannot tolerate the vulnerability this engenders. One solution we found helpful was to have group members each turn their chair so it faced away from the table and each other, leaving everyone facing the wall, giving a greater sense of privacy. We have also positioned those group members who struggle next to facilitators for an added sense of security. Regardless of how everyone is seated, group members are asked to bring their attention to their breath using the same script as for individual therapy.

End Remarks

Before we bring the session to an end, we like to wrap it up with some closing remarks, such as:

> *So, thanks to our minds, we will all suffer at some point. While they try to keep us safe, they get all caught up in comparing and give us "extra" thoughts and feelings that make it difficult to cope at times. And, it seems we all agree that trying to control them is not working most of the time.*

We also write the following question on the flip chart: "Which of these statements do you think is a reasonable goal: Learning to feel BETTER, or Learning to FEEL better?" This question can be used to lead to a discussion of the function of emotions:

> *Perhaps emotions are important. Do you think they might be trying to tell us something?* (Try to elicit the function of various emotions from the group, having some examples ready if you need them.) *Perhaps if we feel our sadness, it's because we need to slow down, to mourn a loss, or get back on our feet after failure. Anger might be propelling us to fight against injustice, or threats, or might tell us we have been treated unfairly. Shame may be a signal that we need to stop doing something that might bring disapproval. Fear might be telling us there is danger ahead and we should avoid it to stay safe.*

This part of the discussion can bring up topics such as grief, loss, death of friends by suicide, and bullying, among others. The group members may or may not need much in terms of clinician facilitation to pull together what we have been talking about and generate the idea, for example, that to grieve means *feeling* your sadness, and that grieving allows you to move forward with the person you are grieving still in your life somehow (framing pictures, sharing memories, internalizing that person in some way, and so on), whereas avoiding the grief does not allow this.

Assignment of Home Practice

We provide a folder containing a summary sheet of what we covered and a self-monitoring sheet to fill out over the week. (Copies of the self-monitoring sheet are available at the website for this book, http://www.newharbinger.com/33575.) Working with these, group members notice their use of DOTS, along with their short-term benefits and long-term costs. Alternately, we encourage adolescents to make notes in their phones if they prefer. We ask them to try and notice DOTS, even if it's long after they engaged in them. We also ask them if they would be willing to engage in noticing, as we do with individual clients.

Participants are encouraged to return to the next session despite possibly feeling confused and unsure about where this is going. This confusion can be normalized, and an expectation stated that things will seem clearer after a few sessions.

Conclusion

At the end of this session you want your client to leave with a sense that his DOTS are normal, that everyone uses them to some degree and that you, as his clinician, can understand the benefit of his efforts thus far. The experiential exercises and mindfulness meditations will set the stage for the remaining sessions. Assigning "noticing" as home practice will help your client begin to work with the ACT processes.

DOTS… Are They "WORKING?"		
What strategies have you tried to control, avoid, fight with, change, or get rid of unwanted internal stuff or symptoms? (DOTS—distraction, opting out, time travel, and self-harm)	Short term: Did thoughts go away? Did you manage to get rid of unwanted internal events such as urges, emotions, or physical feelings?	Long term: Did stuff inside (thoughts, feelings, physical feelings, urges) come back? Did they worsen or increase?	What was the impact of using DOTS?

Session 3

Identifying Values

Values give us a sense of direction in life, a sense of who we want to be and what matters to us. Helping your client to identify her values will be of immense importance in moving forward, and understanding how DOTS get in the way of valued living can be quite eye opening. In this session and the next, the focus is on the right-hand side of both the hexaflex and the matrix.

Focus of This Session

In this session we have one central focus: helping our clients identify their own values, while learning to differentiate between values and goals, and values and "rules." If you want clients to complete values-based measures for research or clinical purposes, we suggest doing so at the end of this session, once they understand what values are and can identify their own. For a more detailed description of values, we suggest the text by J. C. Dahl and her colleagues (2009).

Fictional Client: Erol

Here we will introduce another of our fictional clients, Erol, whom you will see in this session and the next. Erol is a fourteen-year-old boy in ninth grade, his first year of high school, who suffers from severe socially based anxiety. He had lived in another country with his grandparents until age thirteen and came to join his mother the year prior to starting high school. He is extremely conscious of the ways in which he perceives himself to be different from his peers, including his accent, appearance, and family constellation. Erol is angry with his mother for emigrating and leaving him at age four with his very traditional grandparents. Emotionally, he feels abandoned by his mother, despite an intellectual understanding that she did this to make a better life for him. He doesn't feel as though he can trust his mother or anyone else and is convinced that peers will reject him or physically hurt him. Erol was not attending school and was afraid to be seen anywhere in the community that might be frequented by his peers. He reported recurrent, intrusive thoughts that he believed caused him anxiety. To quiet his mind, Erol engaged in ritualistic behavior and played video games.

Relational frame theory can help us to understand Erol's struggles. Memories of being eight years old, bullied by older boys when he was back in his country of origin, continue to impact him. Those bullies had chased him, knocked him down and punched him, then laughed at him and taunted him because he was "slow" and couldn't run away fast enough. The word "slow" stuck to him. He began to think of himself as "slow," and through relational framing and transformation of stimulus function, learned that "slow" was the same as "weak" and "unlikable," and the opposite of "successful." Erol learned to be scared of being "slow" because his mind associated this in a frame of causation with being bullied and physically assaulted. His confidence decreased and his anxiety increased. He worried that he was also learning "slower" than his classmates at school (frame of comparison). He would think a long time before answering a teacher's question, in case his answer was wrong, and he interpreted the teacher's facial expression when this happened to mean that the teacher was mad at him for being "slow." Erol was so anxious about being "slow" that he avoided attending his classes. As time went on, his behavior was driven by his desire to avoid unpleasant internal events and circumstances that might cue these events. The next year he changed schools. His new teacher, who could see his lack of confidence, encouraged him to play soccer, "just for fun," in very informal games at recess. Erol discovered to his surprise that he was good at soccer. His teammates called him "Speedy" and often kicked the ball to him. His confidence grew again and the idea that he was "slow" began to recede as it was framed in opposition with "Speedy" and all of the relations derived from being called "Speedy."

At thirteen, when he emigrated to his new country, Erol had trouble speaking the language. The teacher who was assigned to help him with this transition offered a not uncommon recommendation that he "speak slowly" in his new language. He didn't want to speak slowly because it seemed to him that that must mean he was "slow" again, which meant he was again weak, unlikeable, and ultimately would be unsuccessful. He was anxious and scared that being "slow" would mean rejection and harm. Every time he spoke and heard a difference between his pace or accent and the way his new classmates spoke, he became more self-conscious and was convinced he sounded "slow." He began to hate the sound of his own voice. When he looked in the mirror and saw the dejected expression looking back at him, he thought he also looked "slow," and he increasingly saw himself as dull and unappealing. He began to avoid socializing with his peers. As you will see, connecting with values was very motivating for Erol since it encouraged him to reach out to his peers.

We have found that adolescents are very willing participants in the discovery of their values. What we really want to understand in this session is our client: who he is, what and who matters to him, what is important, what he wants to stand for, and what qualities in him make a day feel fulfilling regardless of what that day looks like. We want to engage his sense of curiosity, discontent, and discovery, as he plays with the idea of who he wants to be and what matters, beyond his long-standing ideas about who he "should be." Values, rather than symptom reduction, become the motivating force in ACT and provide a sense of direction for the adolescent's life. Once values are identified, they are expanded on and woven throughout every session.

When we started on our ACT journey, we felt a sense of relief once we arrived at the "values" point on the hexaflex. We thought it would be straightforward, easier than other processes. Our clients, however, taught us that this was going to be more of a challenge than we expected!

Sometimes we find that our clients' values are hidden behind walls of anger, sadness, loss, frustration, anxiety, and any other intense emotion you can name. If your adolescent clients are intensely fused with thoughts and highly avoidant of emotions, values may at first be quite elusive. Talking about what matters puts them in touch with something they may have lost in life, or something they may have never had and deeply wish for. Either scenario will evoke strong emotions that clients want to avoid. (Thanks to relational framing, now we get this!) Sensing that pain is near, they will avoid talking about what matters. For other adolescents, their lives may be so narrow in focus that they really have lost touch with what matters, or their sense of identity may be diffuse or fragmented, such that they never actually developed a sense of who they are.

If you are at a loss with clients who struggle with values, try what we do when we don't know what to do: use the current moment! Why did your client come to therapy in the first place? The answer to this question may lead gently into values. If values are scary, we will often start with our client's values related to who she is in the room with us, and stay there, not expanding values outside of the therapeutic relationship until she is ready. Another approach, when sometimes adolescents identify values that seem a bit "surface level," is to just begin there with them, kind of like dipping our toes into very cold water or a very hot bath. Going gently and slowly is okay.

Here are some examples with Erol:

T (Therapist): So, you've told me about what you don't like in your life, what you want to get rid of. What is there that you do want? What do you think is really important to you?

E (Erol):	(Looks uncomfortable. Looks down.) I don't know.
T:	What was your reason for wanting to come into therapy? (Using present moment to try to elicit values.)
E:	My mom told me I had to come.
T:	Was that your only reason?
E:	No, I guess not.
T:	Any reason that's your own?
E:	Well, I knew it was important to my mom.
T:	And that's important to you?
E:	I don't want my mom to be unhappy. She's had a lot of people make her unhappy.
T:	So you want to do things that make your mom happy. But does that say something about how you see yourself with other people, not just your mom, that you were thinking about how coming here would affect her? (Trying to elicit values.)
E:	Maybe. I guess I want to be kind of a nice person… That sounds dumb.
T:	No, not at all. What would that mean to you, to be a nice person? (Trying to make "nice" a bit clearer.)
E:	Well, I guess it would mean thinking about other people, and how they are feeling and trying to do things that help them instead of making things worse. I'd like to be able to help in some way—to be kind.
T:	So, do you think being kind might be important to you?
E:	Yeah, it really is a big part of me.
T:	Do you think kindness is important enough to you that you can use it as kind of a compass when you're making decisions about what you want to do?
E:	(Pause.) I guess.

Or, here is another way it might have gone:

T: What do you think is important enough in your life that you would
       want to keep it in mind when you were making decisions about what
       to do? Sort of like a guide for where you want to go?

E: (*Pause, looking uncomfortable.*) I don't know.

T: Anything you can think of at all that is an important part of who
       you are?

E: (*Long silence, looking uncomfortable.*) No.

T: So, here we are in this room together. Who is it that you would most
       want to be, here in the room with me, what qualities within yourself
       matter to you? (*Trying to elicit values.*)

E: (*Long pause. Shrugs.*) I guess not to waste your time.

T: What would that mean about what's important to you as a person, in
       general, if you don't want to waste my time when you're here with
       me?

E: (*Pause.*) I guess I'd like to be kind of a positive person—kind of like
       someone who makes things better for other people instead of making
       them worse.

T: So being someone who tries to make things better for other people is
       important about who you are?

E: Yeah.

T: Would "kindness" express what you mean, or does a different
       describing word fit better for you?

E: No, kindness works, that's how I want to see myself, being kind.

T: I wonder if kindness might be a sort of compass for you? Or a GPS?
       Something that guides your behavior when you are deciding what to
       do?

E: Yeah, I guess. I'd like to try and be sort of kind to other people.

For clients who are really struggling, and when it feels like a battle is about to
erupt between you, notice your own fusion about working from the right side of the
hexaflex or the matrix. Allow for your own feelings and thoughts, and make room for

93

the idea that your client has a different agenda in mind. If your client can't talk about what matters, he may be stuck on the left side of the matrix. Here you might shift to defusion and acceptance (his, but maybe also yours) and then return to values when appropriate.

E: But that's just an idea that everybody has—that you should be kind to other people. That doesn't mean it's really my value. That it's something I should live by. How do I know what I should live by? (*Voice sounds a bit defensive.*)

T: Sometimes it's kind of hard to talk about what really matters to us. (*Thinking: It's pretty hard for me to be here right now with you because you're sounding so scared. I have to breathe.*) Is it kind of hard for you, especially when you're not sure, like right now?

E: Yeah. (*Silence. Then, when therapist doesn't respond immediately...*) I'm kind of pissed off right now.

T: That's not surprising. Good noticing! Good for noticing that you're feeling sort of pissed off. I'm asking you some really hard questions. And you are having a "pissed off" feeling. Any thoughts that go with that feeling? (*Therapist is using language to begin defusion.*)

E: Yeah. I'm thinking, *Why is she asking me all this?*

T: Can you just let that "pissed off" feeling be there, and that thought too—*Why is she asking me all this?*—and watch and see what happens as we continue talking?

E: Now I'm feeling kind of disappointed in myself. Like I should be able to answer the question.

T: Okay. And can you just let that one be there, too, and see what happens, just in case we can get somewhere that's helpful?

E: (*Smiling.*) I guess I'm kind of pissed off because I don't want to screw this up. I don't want to be bad at this like everything else, and disappoint my mom. (*Therapist notes that this might be part of client's "self-as-content" to keep in mind for later sessions.*)

T: So you would like to be able to do a good job of this? And other things too?

E: Yeah, I guess.

T: How come? (*Trying to elicit values.*)

E: (*Long pause.*) I'd like to be able to do something right for once. So I can contribute something to the world. To make it a better place.

T: (*Pause to take in what Erol said.*) That's a value. That's a really important value. And it took courage for you to share it with me. No wonder it was hard for you to answer the question. That's the thing about values. They're really important, so it's pretty hard to look at them. Our fears kind of come up with them. Saying them out loud can be hard. Thank you for being brave enough to do that.

If and when necessary, you can revisit these values conversations. Sometimes our clients get traction on values work, and then new, important values arise and clients get pulled back into fusion and avoidance. As always, we start by asking what stuck and then proceed to a mindfulness exercise at the beginning of each session.

Identifying Values with Individual Clients

Adolescents vary a great deal with regard to their awareness of what matters to them and their actual values. Some will come to therapy with values that parallel those of the clinician, others will not. It helps to know your own values as a therapist and keep those in mind as you navigate this work with your client. Genuine curiosity is another essential ingredient to fully understanding where your client is coming from. Note that we use the word "values" with some clients, and with others we may use "qualities that matter," or "describing words." As long as you are helping your client to think about who he is inside that matters to him, don't get too fused with the wording.

What Stuck?

We like to start with this question so that we can reinforce ideas that were introduced last time, or in earlier sessions. It can open up discussion about concepts or things that were confusing, and it then segues nicely into a discussion of any home practice they were willing to try—usually experiments based on what is now being reviewed.

Concepts introduced in the previous session include: the mind's job in keeping us safe and how it does this; the illusion we share that we can control our thoughts and feelings and that trying to get rid of this stuff will actually make it go away; and, of course, mindfulness. A review of DOTS and the quadrants of the matrix is also helpful.

Review of Home Practice

Two practices were assigned after the first session: engaging in daily activities mindfully and noticing DOTS. If your client was able to engage in mindful activities, ask for her five senses experience of what she noticed. This inquiry is meant to enhance noticing skills further, not to challenge the veracity of whether she did her home practice. Many adolescents arrive at the second session having "forgotten" about their home practice; it may or may not be helpful to tease out if this was genuine forgetting or if something got in their way. Regardless, there is no time like the present: you can engage your client in mindful noticing of something she is doing in the moment, with you, and role-model how to describe the experience. You can use any of the five senses to find out how the chair under her body feels, what she sees, smells, or hears in your office, what she is tasting if she has a snack with her.

You also want to know if your client was able to notice her use of DOTS over the last week, stressing the fact that she may not notice her DOTS until after the fact, and that noticing in "real time" will become more likely as her mindfulness skills progress. If she can identify DOTS from the past week, ask about short-term benefits and long-term costs to DOTS use.

Mindfulness

Through the practice of mindfulness, one develops a sense of standing back from inner experiences and observing what is happening from a distance. Before proceeding with a formal "Mindfulness of Thoughts" meditation, we describe "The Tiger," which seems to help clients experience a sense of distance from their inner events that can be a useful stance during the meditation.

The Tiger

This is a metacognitive exercise that we borrowed from Wells (2009). It can be done as an eyes-closed visualization that would go something like this:

Picture a tiger in front of you. Just notice whatever comes up. You just see a tiger, wherever you are. See if you can get a really clear and detailed image of a tiger, right there in front of you. You are not interacting with your tiger, just watching it from a distance. It doesn't even notice you. (Pause for a few moments to allow the visualization.) *Don't try to make it do anything in particular, just watch for a few moments and see what happens.* (Pause.) *See if you can feel what it's like to watch the tiger from a distance, without interacting with it. Notice what it feels like to do this.*

This can be debriefed when you are done. Ask if your client was able to visualize a tiger, and if so, what his tiger was doing. This is an opportunity to notice and to have fun with how busy our minds are and how easily they create something out of nothing, which is why our instructions are very sparse regarding what the tiger is doing. Allow for this noticing of whatever the mind creates. This instruction also helps to create a felt sense inside of being able to get distance from what is in one's mind, of being able to watch what is there in real time, as our minds are actually fabricating it, and experience being unable to control it. This is an opportunity to normalize our ability to watch our minds without controlling them.

Once you have done "The Tiger," you can refer to it later and it can become a shorthand for this neutral, detached, observing stance toward one's own mind; you can encourage your client to come back to it order to regain this stance whenever he needs it. Feel free to customize this. Some adolescents may prefer to "look at" something other than a tiger to gain that internal felt sense of observing at a distance. Use whatever your client can relate to, such as his own pet or another animal he prefers, as long as it develops the sense of distancing. An animal mimics the mind nicely, because a visualized animal is likely to do something independently, outside the control of the observer. This helps to emphasize the idea that our minds have minds of their own. Knowing this, it becomes more apparent how debating the truth of our thoughts is not always helpful.

Before engaging your client in the next formal mindfulness practice, remind her of the definition of mindfulness and ask whether she thinks it may be helpful. You can let her know that the practice is all about training her brain to pay attention to something, whether it be her breath, sounds, sights, or any other five senses experience, and noticing when her attention drifts off from the focus.

Mindfulness of Thoughts

A script for "Mindfulness of Thoughts" may be something like the following:

Bring your attention to your breath as it comes in and out. See if you can focus on noticing your breath as it comes all the way in and goes all the way out. (Pause.) You might notice as you do this that your mind can be pulled away by thoughts that come up, like thoughts about what we are doing now, thoughts like, "This is strange," or "I can't listen and focus at the same time." (Pause.) Or you might have thoughts about something you saw on the way here, about something you did earlier today or something you are planning to do later today. (Pause.) Just look at your thoughts like you looked at the tiger, with a sense of distance. Then, kindly and gently, detach your attention from those thoughts and return it to your breath. (Longer pause.) Now see if you can do the opposite.

97

See if you can just watch those thoughts as they come up. (Pause.) *See if you can just watch your thoughts as they arise, stay for however long they stay, and fade into the background as a new thought comes up.* (Long pause.) *See if you can watch as one thought leads to another and another, like a monkey swinging from one branch of a tree to the next.* (Pause.) *Just keep watching where your thoughts lead.* (Long pause.) *If you like, try to picture your thoughts as you did the tiger, at a bit of a distance, so you can watch them but you are not interacting with them.* (Long pause.) *Now you can open your eyes and bring your attention back into the room.*

At the end of the mindfulness meditation, a question as simple as "What was that like?" or "What did you notice?" will give you an idea of your client's ability to observe her internal events and the degree to which she avoids them. Your client may tell you she noticed some thoughts and may even be able to relate in considerable detail the sequence of thoughts she observed. There may have been so many thoughts it was overwhelming. Or she may say that when she looked for them, there just weren't any thoughts in her mind. Her mind was "blank." This inability to see what is inside can sometimes actually be a kind of involuntary avoidance, and can be processed as such, with compassion. It doesn't really matter what your client's experience was. You can normalize whatever happened, because both extremes as well as everything in between are normal. Then you can use your client's particular experience as a jumping-off point to explain that it is normal to have troubling thoughts popping into our minds, especially when we are doing something new or challenging, and that it is equally normal for us to tend to avoid these thoughts by using DOTS or sometimes by just going blank, being unable to get in contact with the thoughts that are present. If the client has not been able to notice any thoughts, you could consider repeating the "Mindfulness of Thoughts" exercise later in the session, perhaps building more slowly into it from "Mindfulness of Breath" and mindful awareness of the body.

Mindfulness and Paddles

We introduce at this time another form of "Paddles." This time we provide red circles made from construction paper, about eight inches in diameter, taped to popsicle sticks. If you have not already introduced the concept of judgments at an earlier time, you can introduce it now. When you notice your client engaging in judgments, you can ask her to restate the judgment as a fact, which tends to lessen the emotional intensity and serves as a way of defusing from unhelpful judgmental thoughts. For example, if she states, "I'm so stupid," you could ask her to notice the judgment and how she feels inside when it appears, and then ask her to restate what she said as "facts only," which may result in something like, "I did not do as well on a test as I wanted to," again noticing how she feels inside as she tells the facts of the situation.

Having clients try to identify facts and judgments about objects in your office or visible out the window can be a fun method to engage them in this activity in a way that is less threatening than starting with their thoughts. You can take turns doing this to illustrate the point. Once clients have the hang of it, you will need to monitor your own speech and the workings of your mind to catch judgments and rephrase them as facts for and with your client. Starting with your own speech will be good role-modeling for your client. At this point, we each take a red paddle and we ask our client if she would be willing to hold it up when she notices either her own judgments or the clinician's, and we do the same. Paddles can be used as often as you like, and we sometimes reintroduce them in later sessions if they have fallen by the wayside.

Another way to use the paddles is to have the red paddle stand for "getting caught up in our head," regardless of whether it is in judgments, rules, time traveling to the future with worries, or ruminating about the past. When your client's mind is focused on internal events, as opposed to external, five senses experience, and it's taking her away from the moment and what matters (such as being the person that matters to her while she is in the room with you), the paddle is a way to engage in and indicate "noticing." You can ask your client as she raises her paddle if in fact she is "caught up" in her mind, and if she was trying to "fix" her mind, then gently ask about her ability to control her mind, and help her come back to the room. This gives a nice opportunity to remind your client that what's on the inside can't be "fixed," while external, five senses experience often can be fixed.

Identifying Values: What Matters

The focus of this session is values, the qualities within our self that are important, descriptive terms of who we want to be in the world. Values are a way of being. Many adolescents are able to identify such qualities without much of a nudge; however, for those for whom the task is more challenging, we have found it handy to use Louise Hayes's "values cards" as a means of stimulating conversation and discovery. These cards are included in her book *The Thriving Adolescent* (Hayes & Ciarrochi, 2015).

Formally, we use Russ Harris's "Values Identification Form" (2008), which he adapted from the Valued Living Questionnaire, or VLQ (Wilson et al., 2010), and have clients complete the sheet in session, a throwback to earlier data-collection methods when we began the ACTion groups. When working less formally, we may just inquire about values very broadly, or weave the domains into a conversation or simple chart. For many adolescents, relationships in general are their priority, and you can limit your discussion of values to domains that include relationships (such as friendships, family, and romantic relationships), as opposed to inquiring about each domain separately.

Basic Inquiry into Values

Some clients make this easy. Let's start with that scenario! You can introduce the idea of values with something like this:

We have spent some time talking about what's on the left side of the paper (we don't always refer to it as a "matrix") and about the idea that as thoughts and feelings you don't like come up, you use DOTS to get rid of them. This works for a little while, and then when you stop "dotting," the stuff inside comes back, so it does not work permanently. So round and round you go, caught up between the upper and lower left, because when DOTS stop, the stuff below comes back. (Look for agreement.) Let's look at the right-hand side now, this is the side that includes what's inside, on the lower right, but this time, it's the stuff inside you that matters to you, it's the qualities in yourself that are important and the people in your life who matter. The stuff that will go in the upper right part is the behavior we will see when your values are directing your behavior, and when you are treating those who matter as if they are important.

There are many ways to get at what matters, and here we will outline a few. Following a discussion of values, we compare and contrast values to goals to help clients see the difference. We might start with something like this:

Values are the qualities inside you that matter to you, so no matter what you do in your day, whether you get an "A" on your test or not, whether your friends are mad or not, whether your part-time job is in a restaurant kitchen or your dream job, it does not matter, it's about who you are as you move through your day. To get us started, is there a part of your life that you really want to put some attention into, where things don't feel fulfilling, or are there people in your life who are important to you, who matter, but your relationship doesn't feel good in terms of who you are in that relationship? (Let them identify life "domains" such as school or work if they have trouble identifying people who matter, or if that just makes more sense in the moment.) *So, first, if I had the people who matter to you in my office, instead of you, and I asked them what they liked or loved about you, what would you hope they would tell me? What would be the qualities you hope they would point out because they are the qualities that matter to you?* (Or you can change the language to reflect a domain that matters.) *You mentioned that school is an area of your life you want to change. If I had your teachers in my office, what qualities in you would you hope they have noticed, if I ask them to describe you as a learner?*

100

Once your client has some ideas, we ask the second question:

Now, I have a second question. Of all the qualities you just identified, which ones would still matter if no one actually noticed them? Which qualities would still be important to you?

We only include qualities in the lower right quadrant that were answers to both questions, not just the first one. What we have learned is that sometimes "rules" mimic "values." Rules can take the form of "I have to be _____ or else _____ will happen." Going back to our thinking about evolution and our brain's job of keeping us safe and part of a tribe, the biggest fear that emerges for our clients, in one form or another, is that if they don't behave in a certain way, they will ultimately be rejected. If living according to an inner quality is mostly about that quality being noticed by others, so that they stay connected to us and don't leave, it may not be a value. It could be a value, however, in certain contexts, which we will talk about a bit later. Let's assume for now that our client is identifying values. (We'll discuss rules shortly.) If the previous discussion of values has not brought much up, there are more ways to elicit what matters.

The Party. Another way of getting at what matters that is often cited is to ask, "If we had people who matter at your eightieth birthday party and they were giving speeches about you, what would you hope they would say about you?" However, adolescents don't often think that far ahead, so we changed the timeline and use things like your high school graduation party (for those who can envision this event as realistic), next year's birthday, or a day in your honor, or anything else that seems relevant to your client. Again, we would also ask what your client might hope his loved ones say *because it's important to him.* Then (the trick question), we would ask, "What if no one noticed any of these qualities? Would these qualities still matter to you?"

Why Did You Do Something Difficult? Another way we help clients identify values is to ask them if they have done anything, however big or small, that filled them with anxiety, hesitation, or any other emotions that they judged unpleasant, and why did they do it? Hopefully they will be able to identify something that is either recent or memorable, or both, so that a "felt sense" of the experience remains.

Sometimes coming to their session with you is the answer to this question, and this can open up a conversation about what matters in showing up week after week and who they want to be in the room with you. Many will respond with, "My parents are forcing me." This may be true, but we often suggest that they might be able to get out of coming if they really wanted to, so perhaps there is more to it? This conversation may help to pick up on values in the therapeutic relationship, and generalize to those outside the session. We often ask the "What did you do that was scary?" question again in future sessions to maintain traction by helping our clients remind themselves that they have already done things that matter, things that were difficult, taking unwanted thoughts and feelings with them in the process

For Any Domain. We have found it helpful, regardless of domain, to ask a question like the following: "If I had your favorite teacher in the room, someone who meant a lot to you, what qualities would you hope this teacher would have noticed about you as a student?" This example rests on the assumption that your client has, in his history, a teacher that he liked or admired. You can use this question for any domain, really, changing it to be more specific. For example, if your client is trying to identify values in the domain of physical health, and works out at a gym, or wants to, the question can be rephrased as: "If your trainer was in my office with me, what would you hope he noticed about you when you are working out with him?" And then, "Suppose that other person never noticed the qualities you just identified. Would those qualities still matter to you?" Asking this of your client can be very helpful in teasing apart honest, gut-level values from ways of being that your client believes he has to enact merely in order to keep people close and to prevent rejection.

Values Traps

There are several points during values identification where you and your client might get a bit trapped in ways that will make it difficult, ultimately, for her to move ahead with values-based goals or behavior change. Several common traps, described below, highlight the ways in which values can be confused with goals, rules, what we want other people to think or feel, or values that belong to other people. The good news is that if this happens and you and your client fall into a trap, you will see it eventually. You can both climb out of the trap later, when you realize things are not progressing as your client would like.

Values Versus Goals

Many times, our clients identify qualities, outcomes, or goals, such as being smart, happy, content, or successful, as values. At these times we refer back to exercises done to illustrate the illusion of control, and ask the client how realistic this is. Is being happy, or having any particular feeling, really theirs to control? The answer here will be no, and so this quality may not be a value. This can lead, however, to the more useful question, "If you were content or happy, what would you be doing?" which will likely lead to values. If being "successful" or "rich" is offered as a value, we make a similar inquiry, given that these are arbitrary states and not necessarily under your client's control to achieve. We might ask, "Once you are successful or rich, then what would you do with your life, what would matter to you?" For the sake of simplicity, we don't consider the achievement of an emotional state as a value or as a goal, although you might possibly come across exceptions.

We have discovered several fun ways to help clients differentiate values from goals. We took from other ACT books the strategy of using "going west" as an example of a *value*, and specific destinations that one might reach along the way (cities that are further west) as examples of *goals* (Dahl et al., 2009). This conveys the distinction well. We also explain that values can't be checked off on our "to do" list as complete, but goals can. For example, you could never say you have finished going west; there is always somewhere else to go by heading west. But you can say you reached Tokyo, or Istanbul, or any other city that is west of you. We try to be aware during this discussion that some clients who struggle with geographical or directional concepts could end up caught in thoughts about being stupid and not having an answer. You could modify this idea and make it more concrete for clients who don't seem to be staying with you by asking, "Where would you end up if you moved to your left?" By repeating the question a few times, you can demonstrate the difference between "going left" as a value that guides behavior and arriving at a particular place in the room as a goal that can be considered "done." You can also give a list of items that could be values or goals, in a mixed-up order, and have clients identify which is which. You can also change roles part way through so your client takes a turn at providing a list of items (value or goal) and you identify which is which. Here is a sample list:

Goal	Value
Do homework	Kindness
Attend a party	Being attentive
Text a friend	Giving to others
Say one thing to peer at next table	Empathy
Get married	Honesty
Get a job	Commitment
Spend more time with someone	Humor
Do laundry	Caring
Do volunteer work	Adventurousness

Values Versus Rules

As mentioned earlier, sometimes an inner quality can be a value in some contexts but function as a rule in other contexts. For example, "If I do (or do not) behave this way, then this will (or will not) happen." This can be an example of the rule-governed behavior described in the "ACT Basics" section of this book, and as such it will be very resistant to disputation and evidence to the contrary. Often our adolescent clients tell us about how they engage in behaviors related to "being perfect," "caring for others," and "listening to others," not as a valued action, but to avoid rejection. In this sense, the behavior may not be an upper right behavior on the matrix, but may be an upper left DOT, functioning to avoid rejection (lower left). This may lead the adolescents into relationships that are unfulfilling because they don't provide the opportunity for the adolescent to be the person who really matters to himself. Erol explained it like this when talking about his recent interactions with his mother:

T: Sounds like you are really upset with your mother?

E: I do so much for her, I haven't even done my own schoolwork yet, but she keeps piling stuff on me to do.

T: What do you say when she asks you to do more?

E: I say yes, what else can I say?

T: Can you say no, or let her know that you are overwhelmed?

E: No, I can't disappoint her, I have to keep her happy so she knows I care about her and doesn't leave me again. (*Erol is describing rule-governed behavior, an augmental.*)

T: What makes you think she'd leave?

E: Well, when I was a kid, I didn't always do what she told me to do. I wasn't always such a good kid. And she left me behind when she emigrated. Afterwards I just kept thinking she thought I didn't care about her. I thought that's why she left.

T: Sounds like there is a rule in here: you have to make sure she knows you care or she might leave you?

E: Exactly!

T: How do you feel when you keep saying yes to things even though you don't really have time to do them? (*Saying yes is a DOT, to opt out of or avoid rejection. The therapist is now eliciting consequences of using DOTS.)*

E: My stomach feels bad and I can't breathe well, then I get stressed, so by the time I have a chance to do my own stuff, I am too stressed and I can't do it. Then I get a bit angry.

T: Do you ever just do something for your mom to show her you care, but not because you are afraid she will leave, just to be caring when you have time? *(Trying to sort out if caring is ever a value, in the lower right quadrant.)*

E: Yeah, sometimes I make dinner and that feels really good for both of us. *(Values-based behavior.)*

T: Can you tell me what "good" feels like? *(Adding to client's ability to notice how he feels.)*

E: Yeah, kinda warm inside, just happy.

T: So when you do something to show you care, just because you want to, you feel warm inside, and when you do something that looks caring, but you are really doing it to avoid the thought that your mother might leave you, your stomach feels bad and you can't breathe, then you get overwhelmed, stressed, and angry, is that right?

The conversation could be expanded here to inquire whether Erol feels this more broadly, across other domains. This may bring to his awareness that he has been feeling a need to be there and show support in some other areas as well, and that this is connected to the rule: *People who are important to me will leave me if I don't show that I care and do things for them*—an old "story" left over from the time his mother emigrated and left him alone. How Erol behaves when feeling overwhelmed, stressed, and angry can be explored in terms of the impact of that behavior on his relationship with his mother. You could also explore here how this rule plays out in other domains. Or you may decide to leave things at this level; you can always expand the work later.

Once Erol can differentiate the feelings associated with behavior that is rule-governed versus values-based, he may be in a better position to make conscious, freely chosen decisions about his behavior in the future. And once the distinction between values and rules is clear, we can talk to our clients about what caring, for example, feels like inside when it is coming from the lower right as opposed to the lower left. The majority of our clients can tell us how it *feels* different inside and can use this as a guide for later behavior. Erol may move move toward being the type of family member he wants to be, taking feelings of uncertainty and anxiety with him if he says no to someone, and learning to adapt to their response. Some mindfulness in the moment will help your client notice others' responses so he can find out with his five senses if they are leaving or rejecting him, as opposed to listening to what his mind tells him.

Using the matrix or just through conversation, you can help your client differentiate between values and rules, and the consequences of acting according to each. For example, striving to be "perfect" can reduce time available for other activities or relationships, can turn people off (depending on how they interpret our need to be perfect), and can set us up to try and reach a bar that is always moving out of reach, leaving us living in a way that is undoubtedly not values consistent. As one client put it, "I am hanging on tight to a bar that is really high (holding arms stretched high above his head), but it's so high I get tired from hanging on, too tired to do anything else, and eventually I slip off." He added, "Once I slip off, my arms are sore and tired, so I still can't do anything else, and I feel like crap about myself."

Sometimes the very same quality can function as both a rule and as a value, in different contexts. For example, the value (lower right) of caring may lead your client to do the dishes after dinner so that a tired parent can have a break (upper right). Or caring may be one of many DOTS (upper left) used to avoid rejection or thoughts of impending rejection (lower left) by doing things for others that your client really doesn't want to do, doesn't feel fulfilled by, and often does at his own expense, as was the case with Erol. Some adolescent clients talk about remaining passive with peers or in romantic relationships, in order to reduce the risk of rejection and quiet down thoughts from the lower left quadrant of the matrix, such as *They won't like me anymore*. Some may identify feelings of shame, embarrassment, anger, and resentment as a result of following their rules, which reinforces the use of DOTS to quiet down these additional and aversive emotions.

What Clients Want for Others

Another place where we initially got tripped up was keeping the focus on the adolescents' values. Many adolescents tend to veer toward what they want other people to think or feel and tell us things like, "I want my parents to be proud of me," or "I want others to think I am fun." We follow up statements like these with questions designed to get back to the illusion of control, such as "How easy is it to control how you feel, or how someone else feels?" Then we swing back to the idea of what is really theirs to control, and what matters in terms of how they live their day and the qualities they bring to the day.

Other People's Values

Some adolescents say they value things like "being organized" or "being less distracted." Often these are adolescents who struggle to be organized and focused, and who have been told throughout their lives, by parents and teachers (look at report cards), that they "should" be this way. Keeping an ear out for "shoulds" will alert you to the possibility that what your client is identifying are values or rules belonging to other people.

What You Value Makes You Vulnerable

"Values and vulnerabilities are two sides of the same coin." This idea has stuck in our minds throughout the years. We first heard it during supervision with Kelly Wilson, when we were working with a client whose values were hidden behind deep, long-held fusion. When clients talk about what frustrates them or makes them angry—a "bad teacher" who gives them "stupid work to do," for example—there is often a value (or several values) just around the next corner.

Let's return to Erol, whose avoidance often impacts his ability to go to school. He knows he is behind in his work because of absences and he has become increasingly anxious and avoidant. During one particular session, he became angry about being "centered out" because of his truancy.

E: It's just unfair that everyone is making such a big deal because I've missed some school. Everyone misses classes. I'm not the only one. Everyone talks like I'm the only one that doesn't have perfect attendance.

T: You are having feelings of anger about school right now and thoughts of how unfair it seems. I have to wonder if the possibility of not doing well, maybe even failing, matters to you?

E: No, I don't really care. Nobody really wants me there. They just say they do. The teachers don't like me. The other students don't like me. They blame me when I don't go. It's not my fault.

T: I find myself curious, do you often get this angry about things that don't matter? (*Therapist wonders if underneath Erol's anger is something he values.*)

E: Huh?

T: Let's say you weren't really concerned about whether your socks match, and you took off your boots and realized they didn't, how would you react with me right now?

107

| E: | I wouldn't care, no big deal, I'd just keep talking. |

| T: | But school is different, just talking about it is connected to a lot of anger and frustration. Does school maybe mean more to you than your socks? |

| E: | Yeah, I guess it does, I don't want to fail, but I'm really behind. There is no way I'm going to get an "A" now, and my teachers hate me, so there is no point in trying. |

Erol doesn't want to fail, but is worried he might and he is feeling vulnerable: he could lose something that matters. Because he agrees with the idea that school matters, the door opens for a conversation about the type of student he wants to be, regardless of outcome. The idea that the outcome is not always under our control, whereas who we are on the journey is, can be a novel idea for clients and will probably bring with it a combination of relief in finding some control, and hesitation in letting go of a familiar control agenda. Your client may need repeated noticing of how his desire to control what he can't control plays out, and an acceptance of what can and can't be controlled. This is particularly true for clients who fear rejection, because they are often fused with the idea that to be a worthwhile person, and in order not to be abandoned, they have to achieve at a particular level. The stress this places on them often prevents them from doing well and further strengthens their belief in themselves as "not good enough" and as someone destined for rejection.

Erol avoided the work altogether rather than risk a bad mark, which is what he was ultimately earning by not doing his work. Something like the following could help him, and may need to be revisited many times, perhaps using the matrix for added visual impact as you point to the different quadrants:

| T: | You have told me about how much you would like to do well at school. Finishing high school matters to you. (*Upper right.*) |

| E: | It does, I just feel so terrified to go to school. (*Lower left.*) |

| T: | And when you get pulled into thinking about how scary this is, how do you cope, what do you do? (*Upper left.*) |

| E: | I feel panicky and I distract myself for hours on the computer. (*Upper left.*) |

| T: | Yet you have told me that school matters, and that as a learner, being committed and caring is important. So you get anxious, and head up to the upper left quadrant, to your DOTS. How do DOTS |

relate to you being a committed and caring student? (*Trying to put upper left and lower right quadrants of matrix in a frame of opposition.*)

E: They don't, it makes me the opposite student: the one who isn't committed to anything and I feel like crap. (*Upper and lower left are now in frame of opposition as are upper left and lower right.*)

T: And if you were being a committed and caring student, what behavior would come from that? (*Hierarchical framing.*)

E: I would go in early so I wouldn't meet anyone in the hall and pretend to be studying when others come into the classroom. Or maybe ask the guidance teacher if I can go to class right after the bell rings, when the halls are quiet and there's no time to talk to anyone. Or even to work in a separate room.

T: The strategies you describe, are they something you can control?

E: Yeah, I can. I just wish I could control my grades too.

T: You can control your behavior, what you decide to do, but not the outcome?

E: That sounds right, I can make myself go to school, but I have no clue what grade I'll get.

T: If you go every day, from your sense of being committed and caring, how do you imagine it would feel inside?

E: I think I would feel proud of myself instead of how I usually feel disappointed.

T: Does school and being a caring and committed student matter enough to you that for the sake of being that student, you would be willing to take your thoughts and feelings with you and really turn up at school every day?

E: I would, as long as it isn't too overwhelming.

Erol brings up an important point, that goals will need to be set such that the intensity of ensuing thoughts and emotions is not so high that he isn't willing to have the thoughts and feelings. In this way, setting goals is not dissimilar to the traditional CBT hierarchy for exposure with response prevention. With ACT, however, the steps aren't about exposing oneself to increasingly anxiety-provoking situations in order to extinguish anxiety, they are about approaching what matters in a gradual manner and taking thoughts and feelings along for the journey. Except in unusual circumstances, most of our clients have been willing to take what is inside if it does not overwhelm them.

The Cue Card

As an experiential exercise, we find our clients can really get a felt sense of what this all means if they are given a cue card, to write their values on one side and the thoughts, emotions, physical feelings, and urges they are likely to notice as they proceed toward their goal on the other. We start by having them read aloud the side with their thoughts and feelings (lower left quadrant of matrix) and then ask them how they feel as they take it in, and where they would prefer to hold the cue card, assuming it is now super-glued to their fingers. Most clients will position the cue card out of view above their heads, off to the side, or under their legs, depending on their flexibility! Keeping their hands where they are, we ask them to turn over the cue card and to read the other side, the side with values on it. Depending on where the cue card is, they may have lost sight of values completely, and literally. If this is the case, we allow them to bring the card back in front of them. Then we have them read the values aloud, and ask where they would like to hold the card now that the values are visible. Many clients pull the card in toward them at this point. We then ask them to flip it over again, and inquire what else has now just moved closer. The answer will be the lower left quadrant stuff. Playing around with the cue card in this way makes the point that to be close to what matters (the lower right stuff), the thoughts and feelings you don't like (the lower left stuff) come along for the ride.

Now that your client has a basic sense of values, we will end the session with a mindfulness meditation and home practice.

Mindfulness

Your client is given the usual instructions for how to sit for a mindfulness exercise. You may want to engage your client in "Leaves on a Stream," since it evokes defusion, acceptance, self-as-context, and mindfulness. A script for "Leaves on a Stream" would be something like:

> Imagine that you are sitting alone in a beautiful landscape under some lovely trees on the bank of a river or stream. See if you can picture this in as much detail as possible. Keeping your eyes closed, look around in your imagination and see where you are. (Pause.) Look at how the water in the stream flows or swirls past you. (Pause.) As you look to one side, you notice a leaf coming

toward you. Sitting back, you watch the leaf as it makes its way past you and then off to the other side, until it disappears into the horizon. You turn your head again and notice another leaf, and on this leaf is a ladybug. (Insert whatever item you like.) *Still sitting back from the stream, just watching the leaf and the ladybug from a distance, as it floats past and down the stream, into the horizon. You turn your head once again and notice there are lots of leaves making their way slowly toward you. The next leaf has a stick on it. Just let the leaf and the stick float past you and continue down the stream until you can't see it anymore. You may notice, as you are doing this, that thoughts may come up, like "This is weird," or "Am I doing this right?" Or maybe you are having thoughts about what is on the leaf. Now just notice these thoughts as each comes up, one after the other. As each thought arises, see if you can imagine you are taking it in your hands and placing it on a leaf in the stream. Don't try to push the thought away and don't try to hang on to it either. Just let the water take it. Watch as each thought floats away down the stream, disappearing into the horizon in its own time and in its own way. Then as your next thought comes up and the next, just place each one gently on another leaf and let it float away as the stream carries it.* (Long pause.)

Debrief the above. This can be a good exercise to practice distancing a bit from thoughts without trying to stay in control of them. The discussion can highlight client observations that distancing was possible. Depending on your client, you can expand the above script by suggesting that she place specific thoughts or images on the next leaf. These can include thoughts and images she does not want, the things she tries to get rid of, as well as "pleasant" thoughts or images, to really enhance the sense of watching what is inside from a distance.

Some clients may have trouble with doing any visualization exercise at this stage in therapy. They may be generally unable to visualize images, in which case you may need to rely more on other experiments or other ways to practice distancing from thoughts. Or they may still be too busy in their heads to make space for visualization. Don't worry if your client isn't fully able to follow through the experience. There will be more opportunities to practice. This one will be recommended again in the next session.

Assignment of Home Practice

At the end of this session, you can ask your client to do several things throughout the week: first, to continue his efforts at noticing DOTS as well as the short-term and long-term costs and benefits; second, to practice mindfulness throughout the week, either informally by doing mindful activities as he did the previous week, or by listening to one of the audio tracks for this book. (We suggest one of the first few tracks, focusing on "Mindfulness of Breath" or "Mindful Walking.") Finally, you can suggest to your client that he try to do something in the next week that is consistent with his values. Some adolescents will benefit from some preplanning with you; others are happy to leave the session with some curiosity and a sense of discovery about what they might do, preferring to find their moment more spontaneously. Here you can remind your client of a simple way to change his language, just a bit, to help unstick from thoughts, by using the phrasing "I'm having the thought that…" This "unsticking" can help him move ahead with values-based goals.

Modifications for Group Work

As mentioned earlier in this book, only modifications are described below. What is not mentioned in this section is largely the same as outlined for individual therapy. It is worth keeping in mind that talking about "values as a group member" can be very helpful for bringing the work into the moment with a group of adolescents. Doing so is likely to result in meaningful conversations about who they want to be in relationships, both in general and, more specifically, with one another.

Mindfulness with Paddles

After engaging the group in a mindfulness meditation, you can give out the paddles, one to each group member, as described in the section on individual therapy. You can then ask each group member to raise a paddle if they notice either themselves or another group member or a facilitator engaging in judgment, and then have a "group think" about how to change the thought to a fact.

Identifying Values: What Matters

This is a great opportunity to have participants work in small groups, allowing an opportunity for vulnerability, compassion, and a deepening awareness of each other. Group members often hold on to the perception of others as "normal," seeing only themselves as flawed in some way. Getting to know each other and discovering the part they share, the part that is hurting, vulnerable, and scared, within the context of this "normal" other is incredibly powerful. Each adolescent starts to build a sense of his peers as both normal and suffering at the same time, and this starts to change his experience of himself to someone who is not just suffering but perhaps "normal" too, and deserving of compassion. The compassion that emerges in this session and those that follow seems to supercharge defusion and acceptance.

To get the group members started, you can ask about who they are as group members, and then move to asking about the other domains. We typically divide the group into smaller groups of two or three participants, with a facilitator joining each small group or moving among groups, facilitating discussions about whether qualities the adolescents identify are values, goals, or rules, and helping them sort this out with each other.

Values Versus Rules

This is a great opportunity to ask your group members about "rules" they have for engaging with others, and to put these rules "on the table." As group members talk about what they do or what they avoid in order to keep others close and engaged or held at a distance, it allows a sense of understanding and compassion to build in the room. Something may trigger one adolescent to feel left out, and how he reacts in this situation can be brought to the forefront of the conversation. Clients from our ACTion group have talked about behaviors they engage in when it looks like they might be rejected or when emotions start to feel too intense. Common examples include: using humor, changing the topic, pulling back and dissociating, disengaging eye contact, becoming angry and dismissive of others, or contributing less or contributing in a more superficial way. Having clients identify their behavior allows us as clinicians to identify it when it happens in sessions and process it "in the moment."

Conclusion

The focus of this session is to help clients identify their values, and it ends with choosing a step they might take toward those values. For this first step, we ask for just a small one, since there is still lots to experience together: defusion, acceptance, mindfulness, and self-as-context, all of which will help your client on her journey as the slope gets steeper.

Session 4

Setting Goals: Putting Values into Action

Committed action embodies the right side of the hexaflex and the matrix and is based on values identification. Once your client knows what matters to him, it is time to head in that direction. Keep in mind that goals are set in order to move in a direction consistent with values, not for the purpose of habituating to thoughts and extinguishing feelings.

Focus of This Session

This session builds directly on the previous session: taking the values our client identified and helping him connect what matters with values-consistent goals. We begin the process by teaching LLAMA, an acronym adapted from Chad LeJeune's LLAMP (2007) that provides a linear way to incorporate ACT in the moment. Although ACT is far from linear and mechanistic, clients have told us that beginning their journey with LLAMA helps them to be less overwhelmed by the variety of options. They are able to use ACT more flexibly over time. After LLAMA, we walk clients through a formal goal setting that incorporates the ACT processes. This session will not, of course, give them everything they need. We keep building their sense of mindfulness, willingness, acceptance, defusion, self-as-context, and self-compassion as they continue to head toward what matters throughout the remaining sessions.

Fictional Client: Erol

We return again to Erol, who was introduced in session 3.

Setting Goals with Individual Clients

Now that your client has identified what matters to him, it will be important to listen with awareness as he works toward goal setting. Allow time for him to describe his goals in some detail, so you can get a sense of them as goals, and not as rule following or attempts to please you or others in his life.

What Stuck?

As you and your client review concepts from the previous week and his experience of home practice, he may return to the next session having taken a step consistent with his values, or not. In either case, you will usually hear that he eventually hit a brick wall and could go no further. For example, Erol told us that he was able to think about asking the guidance teacher to help, but that he was unable to follow through with the idea in the moment because "thoughts about being seen as weird or different flooded into my head." Clients often report that at some point their efforts were stifled by thoughts they are fused with or emotions they are avoiding. In order to take steps toward what matters, they may need a more intense dose of defusion and acceptance, as well as a structured process to get them started.

Review of Home Practice

At the end of the last session, clients were asked to try several things: to notice when they used DOTS and the corresponding short-term and long-term costs and benefits; to practice mindfulness, either formally or informally; and to move toward a values-based goal or take a values-based step. You can review your client's progress with each of the tasks sequentially and expect to spend a good amount of time with the last item, values-based goals. It is not uncommon for adolescents to report that they "forgot" to engage in their home practice; further discussion will usually bring up the thoughts and emotions that they were trying not to experience by avoiding their home practice. Conversely, for those who remembered, this gives you a chance to reinforce why they did it, referring to the values that were driving their behavior.

Mindfulness

To augment the more formal mindfulness practices from earlier sessions, we introduce an informal mindfulness exercise in this session and follow it with a repeat of "Leaves on a Stream" from session 3. Many adolescents struggle with formal mindfulness practice for a variety of reasons, so we like to introduce less formal ways of enhancing the ability to "notice." In addition to having your client engage mindfully in daily activities, you might want to incorporate activities that are specific to one or more of the five senses. Whatever the sensory focus, you and your client can use this as the anchor on which attention rests, while practicing watching what's inside from a distance when attention veers to inner events. There is no tightly held "rule" about which sense to start with, and your choice may depend on what you have handy in your office.

Informal Mindfulness of Taste

This is an adaptation of the frequently cited "raisin" practice, which you may know from Jon Kabat-Zinn's *Full Catastrophe Living* (1990). Using taste as the sensory anchor for this session, ask your client to pay attention, on purpose, in the present moment, without judgment, to something she is eating or drinking in your office. It may be something she has brought with her, or you can provide any number of things and ask her to "notice what it tastes like" and describe it to you. You can ask your client to slow down, let the food or drink sit in her mouth, swish it around or bite into it slowly, swallow it slowly, and just "notice" the experience. You can remind your client, if necessary, of the "Tiger" experience and "Leaves on a Stream," for example, if she gets caught up in her mind and needs some distancing from what is inside. You can ask her to notice what she is experiencing, and to notice when her mind wanders, to label where it went, and to gently shift back to the object or anchor of her focus—in this case, what she is eating or drinking. If you have your own snack, engage in this practice with her, sharing what you notice. Some suggestions of food to have in your office include: gum, small candies or mints, chocolate of various flavors, or a variety of drinks, with a little bit poured into small cups for her to sample and describe.

Leaves on a Stream

Often engaging in a particular mindfulness exercise once is not enough for most clients, so now may be a good time to repeat "Leaves on a Stream" from session 3, after you give your client the usual instructions for a meditation exercise.

Debrief the meditation by asking what your client experienced. Again, reinforce any observation that it was possible to get a little distance from thoughts. The usual observation reported is that there was a sense of relaxation or relief from letting go of thoughts. This is another exercise for learning to detach lightly from thoughts without trying to control them. Hopefully clients who had trouble visualizing previously will be more able to this time.

Getting Ready to Set Values-Based Goals

Behavior change, in the form of goals that are consistent with values, is what you are supporting throughout ACT work (that's why it's called ACT) and you can provide your client with structured ways to gain traction. While working on goal setting, it is important for clinicians to remain curious about whether identified values, and their corresponding goals, are values, not rules, and whether they are values that belong to your client, not to her parents, her peers, or you, her therapist, as mentioned in the previous session. Remember that as your clients think or talk about moving in the direction of their values, they will experience some intensity of internal events, of thoughts and emotions. Depending on the intensity of the internal events, clients may have trouble engaging in goal setting, and may instead spiral down into experiential avoidance. In order to make a move in the direction that matters, LLAMA is taught first so that clients can use LLAMA, both to help them think about and organize goals and then to engage in behavior change.

LLAMA

Even if clients have a sense of their values or what matters, the next step may not come easily. They are used to getting pulled into their thoughts and feelings and then moving to avoidance. They may need some help with ACT ways of moving toward who or what matters, and this is where LLAMA can be helpful. The steps in LLAMA overlap with each other, so it may not be a single linear process, but can be used as such to start with. It helps to let our clients know that while moving through LLAMA, they might get stumped, for example, at the first "A" and need to go back to the beginning. Or later in the process, clients may move through LLAMA and start heading toward their values-based goal, but then get pulled into or stuck with stuff inside and have to go back and use LLAMA repeatedly. All of this is perfectly normal. Although you can define what each letter stands for in this session, you may want to explain the first "L" in LLAMA in more depth now to give clients something to work with as they move toward goals. For this purpose, the entire acronym is defined below, along with a more detailed description of the first "L." Deeper explanations of the remaining letters are provided in later sessions.

To demonstrate how clients can use LLAMA to move toward values, we can follow Erol as he worked through LLAMA with a problem he was experiencing. Erol had a lot of difficulty with doing schoolwork of any kind at home. He knew he had to do assignments or he was not going to complete his courses. However, every time Erol tried to do his work, uncomfortable feelings would surface and he would avoid homework to avoid his feelings—his behavior was under aversive control and not "workable." You will see below how he was coached to use LLAMA to deal with this.

Labeling

The first "L" stands for *labeling* and refers to the labeling of inner events such as thoughts, feelings, physical sensations, and urges in a descriptive way. We involve clients in actually *feeling* how using this method could change their internal experience and their relationship with thoughts and feelings. For example, if the thought "I am a loser" is one that a client gets pulled into, we have them repeat the thought out loud, slowly, trying to *feel* the experience of saying it. We then ask them to "label" it by repeating, "I am having the thought that I am a loser," and again ask them to notice what it *feels* like inside as they say it this way. We then add one more step to labeling by asking them to repeat with us, "I am noticing that I am having the thought that I am a loser," again noticing what it *feels* like inside to label the thought. For some adolescents, this is a simple yet powerful way to experience a sense of distance from thoughts, and it supports a sense of looking "at" their thoughts as something their mind conjures up and not as a description of who they are.

The process of labeling can be applied to emotions, physical sensations, and urges. You can ask your client to label an emotion she is noticing inside, such as, "I am noticing that I am having emotions of sadness." You can leave it at this, or ask your client to further describe what the emotion feels like, to which she may reply, "I am noticing I have feelings of tiredness everywhere in my body." An example of labeling sensations would be something like this, "I am having a sensation of tightness in my chest," or "I am noticing I am having sensations of tightness in my chest." When a client reports an urge, you can ask her to *describe* the urge, such as, "I am noticing that I am having an urge to leave the room and I am feeling this in my legs, which feel tingly and energized."

Labeling supports defusion by using language to place some distance between your client and her internal events. Incorporating descriptions so that "I notice I am feeling anxious" becomes "I notice I am having feelings of butterflies in my stomach and tightness in my abdomen," may help your client to loosen her grip on verbal networks related to stimuli such as "anxiety" or "sadness."

If we have a sweater, jacket, or scarf handy, we wrap ourselves up in it and liken being surrounded by the garment to being surrounded by our thoughts when we say "I am a loser." Then we remove the garment and hold it at a distance, repeating the statement with arms outstretched, looking "at" the garment—and, in parallel, looking "at" the thoughts. When you do this, it is ideal if your client will then take a turn with you and "try on" the garment to experience the difference in this way. Many adolescents can see, hear, and feel the difference labeling evokes. This little exercise incorporates the processes of defusion, acceptance, mindfulness, and self-as-context, all at once.

Erol found that if he tried to do his math homework, or study for a history test at home, really uncomfortable feelings would come up. He would have a flood of anxious thoughts suddenly going through his mind, a stab of anxious feelings in his stomach, and tightness in his chest, making it hard to breathe. He learned first to label these, "I'm having thoughts that I can't do this work, that it's too hard," "I'm having a feeling of cramps in my stomach," "I'm having a feeling of tightness in my chest," and then, "I'm having the thought that I can't breathe." This is the point where he would previously have gone to the computer and started playing video games.

Letting Go

The second "L" refers to *letting go* of the struggle to control thoughts, feelings, physical sensations, and urges that come from inside. This is essentially about willingness, and as such is very closely connected to the "A" that follows. We explain that this "L" is like hitting a pause button, which is what we can do when we notice we are getting stuck to our thoughts and feelings and are about to engage in DOTS, moving away from being who matters. We label what is happening inside, and then we stop, we don't move, and we agree to stop trying to get rid of what is inside. Letting go of the struggle to control what's inside involves developing a sense of willingness to have our thoughts and feelings, consenting to whatever comes up.

Erol learned to remind himself that he didn't have to push back the uncomfortable thoughts and feelings he was having. He could let go of the struggle and stop fighting.

Allow

The first "A" refers to *allowing* what is inside to be present. This is a shift that seems to be made as an internal, felt sense, and your client will know when it happens. You can define this step to clients as simply "finding space inside for whatever comes up, letting it settle." Allowing what is inside to simply be there is supported by a sense of willingness (see session 5) and enhanced through the process of defusion (see sessions 6 and 7).

Erol found that when he consciously turned his awareness to the thoughts about not being able to do the work and the physical feelings of anxiety in his body, they did not get worse. He found he was able to make room for them instead of fighting them, which gave him some stillness and space.

Mindfulness

The "M" refers to *mindfulness*. At this point you can remind clients what mindfulness means. This may spark some discussion of how being in the present moment is a lot less emotionally intense, which may allow for clarity and better decision making. When we bring our focus back to the present moment, we remove the "extra" layer of thoughts and emotions that are likely linked to rules and judgments, to past and future—to things that are not presently happening. When your client can return to the moment, as it is, he can make choices based on what is actually going on. Perhaps feelings were triggered by relational frames to past or future, and what is left once they settle is the sense that they were just "triggered" and that it's time to move on with the moment. Alternatively, there may be some sense of emotion that needs to be felt, understood, and perhaps acted on in some way. It's an opportunity to remind your client of mindfulness practices he has already done, and perhaps give him a hint of what is to come. It's also an opportunity to convey to him that regular practice of even small moments of mindfulness can strengthen the "muscles" in our minds that help us notice when our attention has wandered off and bring it back to the present moment.

For Erol, having this moment of stillness and increased clarity freed him up enough to be able to weigh his choices, such as whether to avoid the schoolwork and experience temporary relief from discomfort or whether to move toward values. He focused on his room, in his present moment, noticing what he saw: his desk, and his schoolwork, taking in the present-moment experience with a sense of intentionality. Erol engaged in writing mindfully, noticing how he felt when doing so, and read his book aloud to better take in the words and stay present.

Approach What Matters, or ACT

The final "A" refers to *approaching* what matters, or ACTing. Once your client has labeled what is happening inside, let go of the struggle to control the uncontrollable, allowed some space for what is inside, and brought himself back to the present moment and what is actually happening, he is in a better position to approach what matters and to take a step in the direction of his values. This is an opportunity, if it hasn't come up already, to discuss long-term goals that matter to your client, so that you both know where you are going for the rest of this session, and in the ones to come.

Erol recognized that avoiding the uncomfortable feelings worked for him only in the short term, but caused more anxiety in the end, because his work was still not done and he knew he wanted to complete it. He realized that, uncomfortable or not, choosing to do the work was taking him in the direction of the values he held to be important for himself as a student—being committed and caring. When he thought about it, he realized that making the choice to take steps in the direction of these values, every day, meant that he would eventually reach his long-term goal of completing high school.

Values-Based Goals

Once values are identified, setting behavioral goals that are consistent with values is the next step. It is helpful to keep in mind that goals are chosen behaviors that can be "checked off" on a "to-do list." Although we have said it already, it bears repeating that you may not want to have clients set goals that sound anything like an emotional state. You have, after all, invested time and energy generating creative hopelessness, the idea that one cannot control thoughts and emotions. Clients often want to commit to goals of "being happy," "feeling calm," or "feeling content." To get out of this trap, you can ask them, "Okay, so once you feel this way, what would you want to do?" Another popular adolescent "goal" is "I want to be rich," which in and of itself often leads nowhere in terms of connecting with values. On the other hand, asking, "What would you do with your life if you didn't need to worry about money?" often leads to goals and values. Such a question can elicit meaningful goals that are values consistent, such as "I would go to school," or "I would spend time with my family or friends."

For some clients, keeping their values in mind as they head into the week and trying to engage in behavior consistent with values is sufficient in terms of planning behavior change. For others, however, a more systematic approach may be helpful. The acronym "SMART," outlined below, can be used with clients to help them identify and structure their goals.

Specific

It is helpful to have clients set specific goals by specifying the actions they will take, when and where they will do so, and who or what is involved. An example of a specific goal in the domain of peer relationships might be: "I will talk to one girl in my class each morning and try to keep the conversation going for at least two turns, and I will ask two questions." By setting specific goals, there is less likelihood of getting caught up with clients who return and tell you, "Well, I did talk to someone, *but* it was only twice." While this allows your client to maintain consistency in his relational network, or "story," it also results in a dismissing and devaluing of his achievement.

Meaningful

Goals should be personally meaningful to your client. This can be challenging if parents are involved in the sessions and have a different priority than the adolescent. If a goal is genuinely guided by a client's values, as opposed to following a rigid rule, or trying to please others (pliance), or trying to avoid some pain, then it will be meaningful. If it lacks a sense of meaning or purpose, check in and get curious.

Adaptive

Goals are considered to be adaptive when they take your client in the direction of what matters, and don't reinforce further experiential avoidance. It can be difficult at times to differentiate an adaptive from a nonadaptive goal. For example, a client who avoids feeling sad by watching endless amounts of television may decide that instead, she is going to work on her domain of health, guided by her values of being involved and conscientious, and go to the gym six times per week. There is a "driven" quality to her new goal that suggests it may be yet another DOT, which ultimately will not take her in a valued direction, and this is at least worth being curious about. Asking your client how she feels when she goes to the gym may help her to notice if her behavior is coming from a place of values or avoidance.

Realistic

Client's goals should be realistically achievable. Clients need to consider variables such as their physical and mental health, competing demands on their time and their parents' time, financial resources, the needs of others who may be involved, and whether they have the skills to achieve their goal.

Time-Bound

To increase the specificity of a goal, make it time-bound by setting a date and time for each step. If this is not possible, make as accurate a plan as is possible.

We often provide handouts to clients so they can record what area of their life they are working on, what their values are, what the next step is, and what internal events (thoughts, feelings, emotions, urges) they are willing to take with them so they can live in a way that matters. An example is provided at the end of this chapter, and available for download at http://www.newharbinger.com/33575. We start out by asking clients to commit to a new step, a new behavior that is in line with their values and that they can complete before the next session. As we build momentum over several sessions, longer-term goals can be identified and then broken down into smaller steps.

Mindfulness

An eyes-closed meditation, "Demons on the Boat" (Harris, 2009), is helpful at this point, since it includes pretty much all of the ACT processes and the elements of LLAMA. We have occasionally changed the word "demons" to "monsters" or "creatures," to suit our client's sensibilities. You will notice in the transcript that we don't explicitly tell our clients that the demons are a metaphor for their internal events, for their thoughts and feelings. Most figure it out for themselves by the end, but some may need a subtle prompt. It goes something like this:

Imagine you are on a boat, whatever type of boat you like, and you are on the water. It is calm. Let your imagination create whatever type of background you like. It could be a lake or an ocean, a tropical or a cooler climate. You are not going anywhere in particular, you are just drifting about as your boat rises and falls gently with the motion of the water. You decide at some point that you are tired of drifting about and that you want to go somewhere. You take a look around and up ahead you see an island, and on that island is something that matters to you, perhaps an image of yourself talking to your teachers or starting your schoolwork. You grab the boat's wheel (or tiller) and you aim your boat toward that island, toward what matters to you. As you do this, you notice that the water quickly becomes dark and murky. Waves start to rock your boat around uncontrollably, and then, out of the water, come the demons. They are stinky, snarly, vicious-looking creatures, with big teeth. They drool and make horrible noises. Just let them be however your imagination creates them. (You can ask your client to describe the demons at this point, or check in to determine if she can visualize the scene.) *As they fill you with fear, you take your hands off the wheel and start to push them away from you and off of your boat. As you do this, the water starts to brighten and calm and you find yourself alone again on your boat, drifting aimlessly, but without the demons and the waves. But this doesn't last long, drifting aimlessly doesn't feel satisfying after a while, and you find yourself wanting to go to the island, wanting to head to what matters, so you grab hold of the wheel again, and aim toward the island.* (Repeat the description of demons coming into the boat, and leaving once you fight them off and aim nowhere, as many times as you like, then move to the next section when you are ready). *Once again, the water settles and you drift about in your boat, aiming nowhere. Again, this only lasts for a while, and you aren't satisfied, so you aim your boat toward the island once again. As before, the water becomes rough, the demons come up over the side of the boat and they are gnashing their teeth and snarling all around you. This time, though, you don't let go of your wheel, you notice the demons, acknowledge to yourself that they have arrived, you label your demons and your urge to fight them off, but you don't let this control your behavior. Instead, you hit the pause button and you stop fighting. This time, you allow the demons to be there, you make some wiggle room for them and you hang on to the wheel, mustering your qualities of caring and commitment, and you head toward your island, where you see yourself as a student, talking to your teachers and getting your work done. The demons are still on your boat with you, snarling and stinking. This time, however, as you really take in the present moment with your senses, you notice something new: you notice that they aren't actually touching you. Yes, they stink, yes, they are scary, yes, they are "sticky" in that they try to get your attention, and you want to get rid of them because the very thought of them makes you feel anxious and nauseated* (or whatever symptoms your client can relate to), *but as you hold on to the wheel you notice that the demons just stand beside you. So you allow the demons their space, you let them stay on the boat, and you keep your mind in the present moment and your eyes on the island ahead. The waves may rock a bit harder for awhile, the demons may do more to get your attention, but you continue to allow the waves, allow the demons, and continue to use your sense of commitment and caring to go to the island ahead. You notice soon that you have reached the island, and your boat pulls up on the sandy shore. As you hop out, the demons hop out with you. Imagine yourself on that island of what matters, in as much detail as you can. Imagine heading toward what matters, and imagine the demons tagging along with you. Can you look at that scene and tell me what you see, what the demons look like and what is happening?*

At first, we didn't always ask for a description of what they imagined at the end, but we learned that for many clients, their demons were smaller, or changed in some way that made them less aversive, and they were able to imagine taking the demons along as they did what mattered. If we don't ask, clients can miss this subtle change in what they are seeing, so we make a point of inquiring and giving them an opportunity to "track" what happened in the moment.

We allow time for clients to share their feelings about the "demons" experience and many will combine elements of that with LLAMA quite readily, taking with them whatever appeals and whatever may be useful. As we mentioned earlier, we don't tell clients that the "demons" are their thoughts and feelings. By the end of the meditation, we hope they have gained a felt sense that the demons are whatever gets in the way of values-based behavior. The demons are not simply "bad" or "negative" thoughts; we don't dichotomize that way in ACT. If a "positive" such as *I am smart* is held too tightly, for example, this can create an inflexible life that steers our clients into a narrow world of doing things, or not doing things, so as to avoid risks of being "not smart." But this does not steer them toward valued living.

Assignment of Home Practice

Now that your client understands values and goals, her practice for the week is to take one or more steps that are in line with her values, to do something that matters, and take her thoughts and feelings with her. We also ask that clients continue to notice when they use DOTS, and the consequences of doing so. Mindfulness practice can also be given if your client is willing, either formally or informally (through "noticing" in daily activities). There are brief versions of "Leaves on a Stream" and "Demons on the Boat" available at the website for this book; you can remind your client to listen to those as a "booster" outside of session. You want to remind your client about LLAMA at this point as well, depending on how much of it you went through with her, and perhaps "The Acetate" if you think that might help her to proceed with goals.

Modifications for Group Work

The sequence for group work is the same as for a session with an individual client, with some suggestions to modify the content. Values work is very interesting when done as a group. In particular, when "rules" are explained, many adolescents will opt to share their interpersonal "rules," and it is not unusual for peers to comment on how they felt on the receiving end of someone else's rules. It requires some degree of established safety and intimacy among group members to share such vulnerabilities, and for peers to share their responses. Once in place, however, awareness of a client's moves toward what is important or away from uncomfortable internal events allows clinicians to notice the moves in the moment and use to opportunity to process what is happening.

Once you are more comfortable moving within the ACT processes in the moment, you may find that sharing of interpersonal rules can become the focus of this session, or of many sessions, which is why our group curriculum was designed to allow several sessions for values work. Often the interpersonal values and rules emerge as sessions progress and intimacy and compassion are established. Whereas values may lead to prosocial behavior between group members, rule following may be detrimental to group engagement. When clients perceive a threat to their position within the group, they may resort to longstanding behaviors, driven by rules, about what they must do in order to maintain their position. Behaviors that may emerge include things like being inappropriately agreeable, contrary, cheerful, or disengaged, or oversharing of personal information. It is worth remembering that any of these behaviors may represent either a flexible, values-based response to what is happening in a given moment, or an inflexible reaction to an internally held rule (fusion). As is always the case, context is important.

For example, a client may overshare as a way to show caring or empathy with a peer (values-based behavior), or she may overshare as a means of feeling "seen" or valued in a moment when she is reacting to perceived rejection or invisibility (experiential avoidance). Occasionally a client will disclose that sharing "personal trage-dies" is the only way she knows to feel secure that others are connected and invested in her and that she will not be abandoned. In response, other group members might say that they tended to remain distant because they did not know her well enough to feel comfortable in learning such personal information, and were overwhelmed by the content, but that they felt closer to her now, when she shared genuine emotions and seemed to connect to their emotions. Others have revealed that they are afraid to connect, to feel vulnerable and intimate in relationships, and approach peers with caution, showing nonverbal behaviors that are interpreted as angry, off-putting, or distancing in some way. Pausing the group so that members can notice their own thoughts, feelings, and behavior can be an important "felt" experience that, in combination with group processing, may lead to increased awareness and change.

We have generally found interpersonal dynamics to be a worthwhile detour from any given topic and we recommend engaging in this with clients to the degree you are comfortable. Therapists new to ACT may be tempted to resort to previous ways of engaging in such moments that are not ACT consistent, such as cognitive disputation, reassuring, lecturing, "fixing" things, or trying to "cheer up" the group and move away from aversive feelings and thoughts. As you continue through this book, you may find that LLAMA helps you work through difficult interpersonal moments with clients. Debriefing among group cofacilitators is essential after such sessions so that facilitators can track their own engagement in experiential avoidance when intense affect arrives in the group, as well as their own reactions to the various "rules of engagement" that clients enact in sessions.

We also recommend caution if you are not experienced using ACT with clients who present with very difficult ways of relating, such as those who are typically described as having personality disorders. The dynamics of pushing people away or trying to move closer can collide for them in ways that are painful and emotionally evocative. When that has happened, we use each and every ACT process as best we can, infused with compassion, to help clients experience whatever comes up for them in these moments.

Basic Inquiry

In our group sessions we often begin values work by drawing a matrix on flip chart paper, asking members who, as a member of the group, they want to be during this session, and writing this down in the bottom right quadrant beside each group member's name. This leads into the top right quadrant, as we ask each person what their behavior will look like when they are acting according to their values as a group member. Usually qualities such as being a good listener, being caring, and being compassionate emerge and are connected to behaviors such as looking up and making eye contact with each other. It does not take long for group members to identify internal behaviors that arise when trying to connect (lower left), that take them away from values and lead to DOTS (upper left), the use of which often gives the opposite impression of who they really want to be. Members identify behavior such as doodling, eating or drinking, zoning out (vacant stare), repeated trips to the bathroom, use of humor, sarcasm, or angry comments as DOTS, designed to help them avoid the thoughts and feelings that surface during a discussion of what matters. Group members fill in the rest of the matrix quadrants as they talk about their DOTS within the group and how that plays out interpersonally. This discussion also allows clinicians the opportunity to ask permission to inquire with group members if clinicians think a client is using DOTS in real time, in the group process. Then you can ask group members once again what their values are and if they can go in that direction instead.

Values-Based Goals

We have group members commit to behaviors within the sessions that are values based and connected to changes they are working toward. For example, clients who want to participate more in class, in line with their values of being an active and responsible learner, may choose to do so in group as well, whereas those who are moving toward being more connected with others may identify active-listening behaviors like making eye contact, looking at their peers instead of down at the table, and nodding while others speak as values-based goals within group sessions. This allows facilitators to reinforce values-consistent behavior within the sessions and is a very powerful means of motivating clients. As clinicians, we often decide ahead of time how to divide the group members so that each of us is responsible for noticing values-based behavior in specific clients and no one goes unnoticed. But we remain flexible about this: we may also reinforce values-based behavior in clients assigned to other facilitators if we happen to be the one who notices.

Because our group design includes a three-month follow-up session, we have each group member identify a change he or she would like to make that is reasonable to achieve by the time of the follow-up session, so that he or she can commit to something explicit and work toward it weekly and during the gap between the last group session and the three-month follow-up session.

Conclusion

By the end of this session you want clients to have a good idea of their values and of several "next steps" that they can try to take between now and the next session. Reminding them to change their language to "I'm having the thought that…" or "I am having feelings of…" can be helpful, and ending with a reminder of the first "L" in LLAMA will give them something to work with.

Goals Worksheet

I want to make changes in this part of my life: _____

_____

I want to head in the direction of the following values: _____

_____

I am willing to feel emotions of: _____

And I am willing to have thoughts or physical feelings or urges of: _____

_____

So that I can (ultimate goal): _____

The steps I will take are (daily or weekly goals, leading to long-term goal):

_____

_____

_____

_____

The ACT strategies I will practice include:

_____

_____

_____

_____

LLAMA:

L = Label thoughts, feelings, urges, story. "I am having the thought/feeling that…"

L = Let go of the struggle, stop trying to control what's inside, hit "pause."

A = Allow thoughts and feelings, unstick from story, allow it to be there since it isn't leaving anyway!

M = Mindfulness, return to the present, without judgment, using your five senses.

A = Approach what's important, follow values, or simply "ACT."

Example:

The area of my life I want to make changes in is: *school.*

My values are: *to be caring, hard working, courageous.*

I am willing to have emotions of: *anxiety and fear.*

And I am willing to have thoughts or physical feelings or urges of: *thoughts of being a failure, worries that no one will like me, butterflies in my stomach, an urge to be alone.*

So that I can: *pass my math class.*

The steps I will take are:

1.   *Role-play, with my father as the teacher, so I can practice asking for help with math.*

2.   *Text my friend Tania just to say hi, because I haven't seen her for a while.*

3.   *Text Tania to help me with math after school.*

4.   *Ask teachers for help (still deciding which one to start with).*

The ACT strategies I will use include:

1.   *Use LLAMA to label and notice thoughts and feelings.*

2.   *Practice and use "Leaves on a Stream" and "Demons in the Boat" to allow and unstick from thoughts.*

3.   *Remind myself of my values and why this matters to me.*

4.   *Try to be mindful when I ask for help, so I can really know how others are responding.*

Make sure your steps are SMART:

- Specific: *Specify the actions you will take, when and where you will do so, and who or what is involved. Example of a specific goal in the domain of school: "I will ask Tania for help with math once this week, after school, when no one else is around."*

- Meaningful: *The goal should be personally meaningful to you. If it is genuinely guided by your values, as opposed to following a rigid rule or trying to please others or trying to avoid some pain, then it will be meaningful. If it lacks a sense of meaning or purpose, check in and see if it is really guided by your values.*

- Adaptive: *Does the goal help you to take your life forward in a direction that, as far as you can predict, is likely to improve the quality of that life?*

- Realistic: *The goal should be realistically achievable. Take into account your health, competing demands on your time, your financial status, and whether you have the skills to achieve it.*

- Time-bound: *To increase the specificity of your goal, set a date and time for it. If this is not possible, set as accurate a time limit as you can.*

Session 5

Willingness and Allowing of Feelings

In this session we move to the left side of the hexaflex as we continue with the second "L" and first "A" of LLAMA. These letters stand for "Let go of the struggle to control what's inside" and "Allow what is inside," respectively. When we let go of the struggle, we are essentially tapping into a felt sense of "willingness" to have thoughts and feelings. Once willingness has been engaged, your client may be able to "allow" some breathing room for her thoughts and feelings. The second "L" and the first "A" in LLAMA are closely connected and not really separate, but they are presented here and in our discussions with clients as two separate steps for ease of understanding.

Focus of Session

Having spent the last few sessions helping your client to identify her values and to try to take steps in the direction of her chosen values, you may find she either has hit a bit of a "brick wall" or anticipates a collision in the near future. At some point in her journey, as she takes steps toward what matters, vulnerability lies around the corner, ready to pounce. If she was comfortable with vulnerability, she wouldn't be in your office, so it's safe to assume that DOTS are going to emerge sooner or later as you encourage her to move in the direction of what matters. Nurturing a sense of willingness and allowing can help your client move toward values-based goals. This is the focus of this session. We are essentially working with processes on the left side of the hexaflex in order to help our client make changes on the right side. In this session we focus on nurturing a sense of willingness to experience whatever is inside, and on acceptance of feelings. Acceptance of thoughts, also called "defusion," will be the focus of sessions 6 and 7.

Fictional Client: Destiny

Destiny is a fifteen-year-old girl who experienced racial discrimination throughout middle school. She had a hard time trusting peers and making friends. She has always loved drawing, and spends most of her time by herself, sketching. Her father left the family when Destiny was two years old, after which her mother was in an abusive relationship with a new partner until just last year. She and her mother have been living in a subsidized apartment on their own. Destiny would like her mother to pay more attention to her and help her, especially when peers at school are treating her badly. She knows her mother cares about her, but she sometimes seems so far away, even when she's right there in the room with Destiny. Sometimes Destiny finds herself far away, too. She can be sitting in her room watching something on her computer after school and then suddenly she notices that hours have passed and she has no idea what she's been doing in the elapsed time. She wants to go to art college when she finishes high school, but it is hard for her to stay focused, both in class and when she is doing homework. She sometimes experiences intrusive images of her mother's former partner and feels intense fear or anger. During the last six months, when the feelings have been really bad, she has started to cut her arms with a razor blade.

Willingness and Allowing with Individual Clients

To engage a sense of willingness and allowing with clients requires that we, as clinicians, engage our own sense of willingness to share in whatever thoughts and emotions they bring to the session, as well as our own thoughts and feelings that may arise in response. This is also a good time to check in with your own fusion in terms of expectations for your client as well as any tendency toward avoidance when particular feelings enter the session. She may be watching you for very subtle signs of pride or recognition, as well as disappointment or avoidance, the latter of which may be interpreted as "My emotions are too much," or "My feelings are dangerous." Depending on your own comfort level, and with boundaries in mind, you may want to share your own moments of avoidance and engage in willingness exercises in the moment, especially if she has noticed a lack of willingness on your part.

After the usual review of past material and home practice, we focus on letting go of the struggle with internal events, or willingness (the second "L" in LLAMA), followed by allowing (the first "A" in LLAMA), and then circle back to values-based goals, which are really what the steps in LLAMA are meant to facilitate.

What Stuck?

You may want to spend some time reviewing your client's understanding of values, as compared to rules and goals, and the idea of SMART goals. It is helpful at this point to remain mindful as to whether your client is truly embodying an ACT stance or whether she is using LLAMA and other strategies as a means of avoidance.

Review of Home Practice

At the end of session 4, clients were asked to think of a values-based goal and to commit to it. Whether or not they attained their goal, much can be learned from how they approached what matters. Sometimes clients go beyond the goal they set for themselves, other times they have tremendous difficulty gaining any traction. Either way, it's worth checking in with your client to get more information about her experience.

For the client who meets or exceeds her goals, it is important to understand how she did this. Knowing what ACT processes were helpful, and how she used LLAMA (if she did), will be important in order to maintain motivation and direction.

Equally important will be identifying any pitfalls or obstacles to her progress, or any potential obstacles to future goals. Sometimes clients make it confusing and engage in what seems like values-based behavior, but they do it in the service of avoidance. Such can be the case with clients who report that they spent "hours working on a project," except that we discover that their efforts were in the service of avoiding something else, such as peer contact or other work that was actually more pressing. This is why a functional understanding of client behavior is essential, taken in context.

At other times, clients may avoid their goal if the intensity of emotions that accompany the behavior is more than they are willing to have. If this is the case, it may be helpful to have your client pick a different step toward what matters, one that will titrate the "dosage" of thoughts and feelings that are likely to arise inside.

Sometimes clients commit to "empty" goals that do not really hold any meaning or relevance for them, and they complete them either easily, without any sense of anxiety, stress, pride, or accomplishment, or they don't complete them at all, reporting an accompanying sense of boredom with the task. This may signal a need to circle back and revisit creative hopelessness, DOTS, costs and benefits of DOTS, values, and defusion.

Figuring out where clients are stuck will guide clinicians in where to go next. If your client reverted back to DOTS, or got stuck in *wishing* or *worrying*, more defusion practice may be helpful. Some defusion strategies have been presented in previous sessions and more are to come in sessions 6 and 7. Meanwhile, she will benefit from time and effort spent on willingness and allowing.

Perhaps previously identified values were not really meaningful to your client and need to be unraveled a bit more to gain some traction on goals. The bottom line is this: if values-based goals are not happening, it is worth the time and effort to figure out what that is about before proceeding. Spend time where it's needed, perhaps revisiting creative hopelessness, or values versus goals, or "The Acetate," for example. It's also a good idea to be curious about the goals that were set. Did your client freely choose them, based on her own values, or was someone or something influencing her decision?

As we reach the halfway point, this is a good time to inquire about formal and informal mindfulness practice, to ensure that that practice does not get lost in the other ACT processes. Once you have sorted this out with your client, at least for now, a mindful visualization as well as discussion and experiential moments can enable "willingness" and "allowing" to take center stage.

Mindfulness

We start this session with an informal mindfulness experience, anchored in the sense of hearing. At the end of this session we engage our client in a meditation to help her develop a sense of willingness and the allowing of her emotions.

Informal Mindfulness

Continuing with informal practice anchored in "noticing" with one of the five senses, ask your client to close her eyes and use her sense of hearing to notice sounds within and beyond your office. Guide her to notice sounds near and far, loud and soft, constant and intermittent. Bring in LLAMA by periodically reminding her to notice if her mind wanders, to label this, and to let go of the struggle to control her mind, and gently bring her focus back to listening. Allow a few moments to debrief.

Willingness

In this session, we explore willingness: an inclination toward the thoughts, feelings, and urges that come up inside, rather than a move away from internal events. When we are willing to have our internal experiences, we let go of the struggle to control them. As clients stop struggling they will be left with their "clean" emotions to adapt to, as opposed to the additional or "dirty" emotions that come with struggling. Experiential exercises will help your client get a felt sense that willingness to experience discomfort is going to be essential in order for her to reach a goal that lies in the direction of her values.

It may help to start the session off by asking your client what comes up for her when she thinks of "willingness," and then exploring the concept together briefly before you both head off into experiential exercises. Keep the matrix handy and if you sense resistance, go back to her matrix and creative hopelessness.

In your conversation about willingness, the idea that willingness means "succumbing" or "playing dead" might come up. You and your client need to be clear that willingness does not mean that we *want* unpleasant stuff inside or that we have *given up* in any way on making things better. Willingness just means we know we can't change what's inside us or what's behind us in the past, or other people for that matter. We need to change our inclination to one of consent, and allow inner events to be present. This runs contrary to our normal human inclination, because we have minds that are problem solvers, always trying to move away from discomfort and to "fix" things.

You can ask your client for examples of when "fixing things" works for the outside world, or alternate with your client in giving examples. You can start with the idea that if it is cold, we can put a jacket on, or adjust the thermostat for the building. If we have a broken shoelace, we can replace it. Unfortunately, we tend to apply the same problem-solving strategies to things that are inside, where we are powerless to effect any lasting change (LeJeune, 2007). We tend to be frustrated with ourselves for not being able to "fix" anxiety, anger, or sadness in the same way we can deal with a splintered finger. This frustration, the felt sense that we "should" be able to solve the problem of unwanted inner experience, only amplifies feelings that were difficult to begin with. Although it is counterintuitive, these inner experiences can really only become less problematic when we make space and allow them to be there, effectively "letting go" of the impossible struggle to "get rid" of them.

Experiential Exercises and Metaphors

The point of this session is to demonstrate that willingness to experience discomfort is something that is essential in order to reach a goal that lies in the direction of one's values. Tying willingness to values gives clients a way to transcend the stuck place they may be in. Willingness is described as a kind of "on or off" phenomenon. You can't be half willing. You either are willing or you aren't. We use several metaphors to get at the idea of willingness that are described in the section below. We often start with the "Jumping Off a Chair" metaphor, which gets at this all-or-nothing quality of willingness, and it works well to use it as an actual experiential exercise. We typically follow this with the "Wrinkled Sock," which we prefer to do early in a session so clients can sit with their wrinkled sock for the remainder of the session. Some clients resist the "Wrinkled Sock." We find that warming them up with the "Chair" experience helps them ease into the "Sock" one. Several other experiences and metaphors follow, ending with an adaptation of R. D. Zettle's "Rocks" exercise (2007) that seems to fit beautifully for our adolescent clients with depression.

Jumping Off a Chair

The "Jumping Off a Chair" metaphor can be done in several different ways. Ask your client to climb onto her chair. You can do the same if you like. Then ask her if there is a way to jump halfway off the chair. Although there may be solutions offered like stepping down with only one foot, or hanging onto the arms of the chair and swinging halfway to the floor, these are stepping and swinging, not jumping. The answer is ultimately no, it can't be done. Your client will recognize that she has to either be willing to jump off it or not. You and your client, or one or the other of you, can actually execute the jump, if you want, for a really visceral demonstration. (Caution: It's best to do this exercise using simple, stable chairs, like institutional stacking chairs. It is dangerous to use chairs that are on wheels.) This is one of those moments that demonstrate the importance of our advice about obtaining "buy-in" from parents before beginning ACT: their adolescent may tell them some strange things about what they did in today's session. Although your client may be able to understand the principle of willing-or-not from just talking through the "Jumping Off a Chair" exercise, ACT is an embodied experience. The more experiential and visceral the learning is, the more likely your client is to internalize it in some way, and use it.

Wrinkled Sock

We adapted the "Wrinkled Sock" from Chad LeJeune (2007) and engage our clients in an eyes-closed visualization followed by an experiential version of the metaphor that goes like this:

Would you be willing to close your eyes with me, and imagine the scenario I describe? Imagine you are getting ready for school, perhaps running a bit late, and you have an important test in the first period. You are in such a rush that you skip breakfast and get dressed as fast as you can. The socks you put on, unfortunately, are the ones that you don't like because they keep wrinkling up and falling down. In fact, this is what happens. As you rush to the kitchen to grab your lunch, your sock has slipped down and is now wrinkled under your foot and it's driving you nuts. You stop and pull it back up, then grab your lunch and head to the door. You throw on your boots and coat and then pick up your backpack. Before you get to the front door, the sock has wrinkled itself up again and you just can't stand it. You put down your backpack, take off your boot, and yank that sock back up again. You put your boot back on, grab your backpack, and race out the door. You are now feeling frustrated, perhaps angry, and disgruntled to say the least. You know you have a test soon and you try very hard not to think about the sock, but it just keeps coming to mind. As you race for the bus, your sock does it again; it is now down to your ankle and totally wrinkled under your foot. You stop to pull it up and notice the bus passing you by. Since you don't want to be late for your test, you run to school, stopping every few feet to pull up that sock. Finally you arrive at school, sweaty and exhausted, and get to class just in time for the test. But before you can start, however, you have to pull that sock up again. You are so frustrated and angry at this point that you can hardly focus on the questions and you spend half the test time trying to calm down.

While this is a somewhat extreme version of events, it does resonate with our clients and makes the point that effort to avoid what we can't change usually gets in our way. When you have finished the visualization, ask your client what "comes up" for her and allow a few moments for her to process the experience. It is helpful to ask, "What was it that ruined your day?" Most clients will initially respond that it was the sock that was responsible for all of the stress of the morning and the poor test result. With just a bit of discussion, your client will likely compare the sock to other things in her day or her life that she can't control, that can't be changed, and where efforts to try and change these things usually proves futile and often makes matters worse. Now that you are done with the visualization, it's time to turn the wrinkled sock into an experiential exercise that goes like this:

Could I ask you to do an experiment with me? Could I ask you to actually have a wrinkled sock and see what happens? Take your sock on one foot and roll it down so it's wrinkled up under your arch in the middle of your foot. (Do this at the same time with your client. If the client is not wearing a sock, hand her a wad of tissues to stuff under her foot in her shoe.) *Next, we are going to do some walking with our socks all wrinkled up. For the sake of this experience, can I ask you to agree that your wrinkled sock is something you cannot change? Like other things in your life that you may not like, it is here to stay, and it won't change.*

Most clients laugh at this point and are easily engaged in the experience; some will find they are fused with thoughts about how utterly annoying this will be. Once your socks are set, it's time for both of you to move around the room with your wrinkled socks. This can be done as mindful walking, slowly, trying to notice when thoughts go to the sock, using LLAMA to return to mindful walking. It might sound something like this:

> *Let's try to walk mindfully, being aware of what our body feels like as we walk, noticing the physical sensations in our feet* (pause), *our calf* (pause), *our thighs and hips* (pause), *just noticing what it's like to walk.* (You may notice we have skipped over the gluteus maximus. This is purposeful because it can result in fits of giggles that interfere with the experience.) *As you walk, you may notice that your mind gets stuck on the sensations of the wrinkled sock in your shoe. When this happens, label the thoughts or feelings you are having, try to hit the pause button, let go of the urge to control what's inside, just allow whatever rises up inside to simply be there. Notice that you have gotten caught up in wishing you could change something that you can't change, and just allow it to be, as it is. As best you can, allow space for thoughts and feelings, and loosen up around whatever else you notice. When you are ready, mindfully return to the present moment, and proceed with what matters, in this case, walking mindfully.*

You can walk as long as you like with your client, leaving time for silences and reminding her of how to use LLAMA to allow the sock to remain wrinkled, while gently turning her attention to the present moment. Once you are finished, process the experience with your client. Lots of clients say they totally forgot about the sock after a while. You can also ask your client if she is willing to keep her sock wrinkled for the remainder of your session. As you go on with the session, notice times when your client is focused on her sock, maybe trying to pull it up, or lost in thoughts, and use that as an "in the moment" opportunity for more LLAMA and more willingness. You can go back to creative hopelessness at this point, too, weaving in the costs and benefits of focusing on the sock during the session. Lots of clients totally forget about the sock as they focus on the session and are pleased to notice this later on. In fact, those who do forget about it sometimes leave with it still wrinkled and you might hear about that when they return the next week! When we have clients who have a difficult time with this experience, we try to repeat it in future sessions as a gauge of their ability to accept what can't be changed, and the feelings and thoughts that come with it.

Struggle Switch

A less active way to demonstrate willingness is the "Struggle Switch" (Harris, 2009). This can be done as a metaphor or as a visualization and is quite simple. It goes something like this:

Imagine there is a switch on the wall, like a light switch. When it is on, you are struggling. When it is off, you're not. The struggle switch is the decision to stop trying to avoid unpleasant things inside, such as thoughts and feelings that are uncomfortable. When the switch is on and you are fighting against experiencing these, you are in a constant struggle. When the switch is off and you choose to let yourself experience these, the struggle stops. But you have to be willing to flip the switch.

This exercise does not usually need much debriefing. It's fairly self-explanatory. It is a good "shorthand" metaphor for willingness that you can refer to later to remind your client that willingness is required in order to accept whatever will flood in when she is moving toward her values.

To enhance the experiential part of this metaphor, you can ask your client to enact the struggle switch idea by allowing some of the thoughts she gets hooked into. When she finds herself fighting them, ask her to visualize herself turning the switch on. As she lets go of the fight, ask her to visualize turning the switch off. You can then ask her what else she is able to do while caught up in the struggle, when the switch is on as opposed to off. Asking questions like "Can you do your math homework?" or "Can you really focus on a conversation with your best friend?" while the switch (that is, the struggle) is on usually gets a no from clients and helps them experience the conflict between struggling and values-based behavior. For some clients, it can be more impactful to have them get out of their chair and flip a switch on your wall, like a light switch, every time they go between willingness and not willing.

Wade Through the Swamp

"Wade Through the Swamp" (Hayes, Strosahl, & Wilson, 2012) is a metaphor that applies to acceptance in general. It can be done as a metaphor, just relating it in conversation with your client and drawing it on a whiteboard if you like, but it is probably more effective when done as an eyes-closed mindful visualization. A script for it in the visualization form would be something like this:

Imagine that you are on a trek in the mountains, and your goal is to climb a particular peak. You have wanted all your life to climb this peak and you have prepared for months to do this trek; for whatever reason, it matters to you. You have all your equipment with you and you are prepared and determined to reach the peak. There is a long road approaching the mountain and from a distance it looks like the way is clear all the way to the foot of it. But as you get closer, you realize that there is a huge swamp surrounding the foot of the mountain. You can't even begin your climb without getting across that swamp. You try to think of every possible way to avoid the swamp because it's cold, wet, stinky, and muddy; there are slithery creatures in it. You know you can't set foot in it without getting wet up to your knees. You would like to turn back, but then you remember that your goal was to reach the peak. There is no other way to do that than to just plough through the swamp. So, focusing on that peak, you hold your nose and wade in. You take a few steps and realize that, although it is slow going, you can move forward. The mud is cold and wet, but you find that you can get through it. Before you know it, you are through the swamp and starting up the mountain. Your feet are drying and you are doing what you always dreamed of.

This can be processed easily enough by just asking your client what this was like for her, what came up as she listened to your description.

Gnats

We created a mindfulness exercise that we ask clients to engage in with eyes closed. It involves those pesky little bugs called gnats. You may or may not have these where you live, but if you don't, you can substitute another bug that is pesky, annoying, and out of your control, but harmless, such as fruit flies or midges. Ask your client if she is familiar with gnats or another irritating type of bug before you begin the exercise, to make sure that it will resonate. Questions to ask your client have been inserted in the exercise as it is described below. You can insert them into the body of the exercise as shown or save them for afterwards. "Gnats" can incorporate LLAMA nicely. The exercise goes like this:

Try to imagine now what it feels like to be outside in the summer, with the warmth of the sun, maybe birds chirping, and imagine yourself doing something you like to do, like riding a bike, or walking and talking with friends. (Pause and ask client what he is envisioning.) *Now, imagine that you come into a huge cloud of gnats. Do you remember what that feels like, and how it felt when the gnats swarmed around? Maybe they got in your eyes and up your nose?* (Pause, allowing time for client to share his felt sense of the visualization.) *What did you do?* (Client usually replies that he swatted at the gnats and walked or rode faster to get through the cloud.) *Did they go away?* (Client will often say that the gnats kept coming back.) *So no matter how hard you tried, they just stayed with you? They returned to swarm around your head?* (This part gets at creative hopelessness. Swatting at the gnats is like a DOT, meant to get rid of them, which doesn't work.) *I wonder what happened to your experience of riding your bike or talking with friends while*

you were busy trying to get rid of the gnats, which you couldn't do anyway?
(Many clients reply that they lost touch with the experience.) *Imagine*
yourself now, doing what matters, with the gnats around your head, and this
time, imagine just letting them be there. Don't try to get rid of them. Instead,
notice them, and label what you are noticing inside, including your urge to swat
them away. Hit a pause button and stop struggling; let go of the urge to control
them, and see if you can imagine letting them be. Try to stay in this moment as
best you can, letting the gnats be present while you gently shift your attention to
doing what matters.

As part of debriefing this exercise, ask your client if he might be able to think
about gnats the next time he tries to do something challenging and experiences
moments that are unpleasant. ("This is kind of like going through that cloud of
gnats.") If it's actually gnat season, you can ask your client if he would be willing to
try this the next time he encounters gnats. The "Gnats" metaphor is good for addressing both willingness and a sense of allowing.

Driving on Ice

This metaphor and the next will resonate with clients in cold climates. The first
one, "Driving on Ice" (LeJeune, 2007), like other metaphors, can be done with eyes
open or closed. It goes like this:

Do you know what you're supposed to do if you are driving and you start to
skid on ice? (Clients who are already driving or studying for their licenses
will know and can answer. If not, you can explain.) *It seems like you*
should turn the wheel to steer the car away from the direction that it's skidding
in, and that's what we're inclined to do. But you will actually pull out of the
skid more successfully if you steer in the direction of the skid, until you get
some traction again.

To engage your client in this as an eyes-closed experience, ask her to imagine
driving, set the stage for winter, for an icy drive, with her hands on the steering wheel,
and ask her to imagine hitting ice and veering off course in a particular direction.
You and your client can both hold your hands as though you are driving, and move
your hands and body accordingly as you enter the skid. Ask her to imagine trying to
steer out of the skid and back in the right direction. Then ask her to repeat the experience, but this time, guide her to gently touch on the brakes and aim her car into the
direction of the skid. Process her experience of the two different versions. See if she
can notice how she felt in each as part of the debrief.

Downhill Skiing

If your client has done any downhill skiing, you can try this one, as an eyes-open or eyes-closed exercise (LeJeune, 2007). Before you proceed, set up the "scene" in as much detail as you can, from a five senses perspective, what she would see, feel, and hear (taste and smell may not be relevant); and if eyes are open, perhaps stand in a ski position, if either of you is familiar with it:

When you come to a steep slope and you are afraid you are going to fall, what do you tend to do with your body that your instructor probably told you twenty times not to do? (The client will say she leans back, trying to pull away from the hill below.) *And what happens if you do this?* (Client will say she falls.) *So what are you supposed to do?* (Client will likely repeat an instructor's advice to bend the knees and lean the upper body forward, toward the bottom the hill. This feels scary because it makes you go faster, but gives you much more control because your weight is balanced over your feet and you will be less likely to fall.) *So let's see if I have this right: doing the scary thing, leaning toward the bottom of a steep hill, will make you go faster but actually gives you control, whereas trying to stay more comfortable by leaning away from the bottom of the hill ends up in a fall, and then you aren't going anywhere.*

Harry Potter

This one is easily recognized and understood by many adolescents.

Do you remember in Harry Potter and the Philosopher's Stone, *when Harry, Ron, and Hermione were trapped in the "Snare" as they fell through the trap door under the three-headed dog? What did Hermione do?* (Your client may remember that she stopped struggling, pulled her arms in, and stayed very still until the snare loosened and she was released.) *That's right—when she stayed still, the Snare let her go. But when you struggle against and try to resist thoughts and feelings, the way Ron and Harry did with the Snare, they hold on even more tightly.*

The Rocks

You will need a small sand pail and enough small rocks to fill it. Decorative river rocks purchased from a garden or florist shop work really well. Here is how it went with Destiny:

T (Therapist): Can I ask you to try an experiment? Could I ask you to hold this pail and imagine that the rocks inside are all of the thoughts and feelings you don't like to have? (*Hands her the pail.*) So if the pail is full of things you don't like, the thoughts, feelings, sensations, and urges, what do you want to do with them? The trick here is, though, that you can't let go of the bucket. The same way you have not been able to use DOTS to permanently get rid of what's inside, you also can't get rid of the pail or the rocks.

D (Destiny): Well, I'd want it to go away, so I guess I'd hold it out here like this. (*It may take some experimentation, but sooner or later your client will try holding the pail as far as possible, often with fully extended straight arms.*)

T: So, how are you feeling?

D: Okay, but it's kind of heavy.

T: Okay. Now I'm going to ask you if you would try to do something while you hold the pail, something that is like what you do during the day, something that matters to you. I brought a sketchbook. Would you be willing to try and draw something while you hold the pail?

D: (*Laughs.*) Okay. (*Starts drawing.*) My arm is getting sore, it's hard to focus on the sketch. (*Puts down pencil and reaches out to hold pail with both hands.*)

T: Hmm, what do you think is going on?

D: Well, the more I hold my arm out like this, the heavier these rocks get, I can't think of anything else.

T: But you don't want those thoughts and feelings anywhere near you, do you?

D: Nope.

T: What do you think you would have to do so you could have at least one hand free to do the drawing, or to do anything else that's important to you? Remember, the pail isn't going anywhere. You're still going to have those thoughts and feelings. You can't get rid of them, you can't leave them anywhere. So if you can't let go of the pail, is there anything you can do with the pail so that you can focus on the drawing?

D: Yeah, I could try moving it somewhere else. (*Plays around with different positions.*)

T: Let me know when you find a position you prefer.

D: I could bring the pail in and hold it against my side like this. (*She brings in the pail and presses it against her side and then tries pressing it against her stomach with one hand. She lets go with the other hand. It took some more experimentation here, but she eventually thought of this. The therapist would have prompted Destiny if she hadn't.*)

T: How is that for you, with all those thoughts and feelings so close to you like that?

D: Yuck.

T: Not so nice, huh? But can you do your drawing now?

D: I guess. I can do it with one hand.

T: And how do your arms feel?

D: Better.

T: So do you think maybe it works better for you if you don't spend so much energy trying to push away those thoughts and feelings and maybe just let them be there?

D: Maybe.

In this example, Destiny would need a hand free to work on her drawing. You can substitute any task that would be a step in the direction of your client's values, based on the situation your client is facing and the steps she would have to take during the home practice. This exercise can be debriefed to be sure that your client has had the experience of working hard to keep feelings and thoughts away (and getting tired from it) and has made the connection between this and being unavailable to do things that are meaningful and important.

Now that you have worked on letting go or willingness, you can move next to the first "A" in LLAMA, *allowing*, and work on allowing feelings. Allowing thoughts, or defusing, will follow in the next two sessions, although you have already given her some ways to defuse from thoughts with "The Acetate" and with language such as "I'm noticing I'm having thoughts of…"

Allowing Feelings

Allowing is closely related to the previous steps of labeling thoughts and feelings and letting go of the struggle to control them, but it entails a slightly different and braver process. Letting go involves disengaging from the struggle to push unwanted thoughts and feelings away. Allowing means consciously making space for unwanted thoughts and feelings to be present and accepting that they will be there as long as they want, since we have no control over them. Once your client has let go of the struggle, she has, in essence, consented to her thoughts and feelings being present. Allowing can be thought of as making room for thoughts and feelings. We engage clients in a quick experiential exercise called "Making Room," and then proceed with the full "Observe, Breathe, Expand" mindfulness meditation, allowing time for debriefing.

A word of caution: it is not uncommon for clients to tell us they have "allowed" or "accepted" their internal events, when really they have given up or are coaxing us to move on so they can avoid their inner experience. This is not acceptance in the ACT sense.

Many clients don't want to have their feelings, let alone allow them, so this can be a tricky idea to pitch. And you don't want to get into a debate with your client. To support your client with the risk he is taking, find out what he thinks about moments when DOTS are and are not helpful, when stopping the struggle may or may not be helpful.

Sometimes DOTS are helpful. For example, a bit of distraction at the dentist's office might not interfere with valued living. It might make it more manageable, in fact, if it gets you through the appointment. It may even work in concert with a value in the domain of health and looking after oneself. At other times, though, DOTS are not so helpful. If your client is having trouble with the concept of allowing, you may want to go back to his matrix and the idea of creative hopelessness, and work with willingness a bit more. A brief exercise involving you and your client is described below.

Making Room

We describe two experiential exercises that were created during sessions, both of which help clients to feel what it's like to make room for what's inside and make the idea of "allowing" a bit more concrete. For the first exercise, adapted from Russ Harris's "Clipboard" metaphor (2009), stand up facing your client, a foot or so apart. Put up one hand each and press against your client's hand while she presses back. Let your client know that you are her unwanted thoughts and feelings. As you push against her hand to get her attention, ask her what she would like to do. With little prompting, most clients will tell you they want to push you away, and you can ask her to do so by gently pushing your hand away from her. Allow your hand and arm to move, and then push back on her hand to mimic how her unwanted thoughts and feelings would return. Engage in this back-and-forth briefly, and ask her to try to do, or to imagine doing, something that matters while she is engaging in this with you. She will probably tell you it would be difficult. Next, ask her to assume her fingers are glued to your fingers so that she can't get rid of you. What can she do so that she is no longer doing battle with you—her thoughts and feelings? If she can't quite figure it out, ask her to back up, slowly, until her fingertips are barely touching yours, and then ask her to notice what this feels like when you gently push against her fingertips. She will likely tell you that you (her thoughts and feelings) are far less noticeable and she may be more willing for you to be there. The discovery we hope for here is that by backing up and making space for you (her unwanted experience), she may be better able to engage in values-based goals.

Another way to capture the essence of making room is to ask your client to imagine being in a crowded bus. This can be done eyes open or closed: we often used eyes closed so clients can imagine the scene in as much detail as they can. Once your client has an image of this scenario, you can suggest that the bus is so crowded that others are poking her in the ribs with their elbow and she is bumping into other people as she is jostled around with the crowd. Most clients can relate to such an experience and feel a sense of discomfort in just imagining it. We then ask, "If none of the people are leaving, how do we make more room for those on the bus?" Clients often arrive at the idea of making the bus bigger, which is similar to what we are asking of them in expanding around feelings.

Now that your client has an idea of willingness and allowing, it's time to move to a mindfulness meditation, "Observe, Breathe, Expand," which we adapted from Russ Harris (2009). In our experience, many adolescents struggle to even locate their emotions (which makes it next to impossible to "observe" them), while others have a hard time staying with the idea of observing feelings or breathing into them. They might say things like, "There is so much stuff in my head I just can't do it," or report a sense of impending panic at the very idea of getting close to their feelings. It helps to keep in mind that your client is likely proficient at DOTS as a means of avoiding feelings, so asking her to stay with them, to cozy up to them, is not going to be an appealing idea.

To help ease your client into the "Observe, Breathe, Expand" meditation, you can ask her first to engage in an exercise that we call "Hedgie."

Hedgie

For this experiential exercise your client will need a hard, spiked plastic dryer ball. We called ours "Hedgie" because we found some dryer balls that were actually formed in the shape of a cute small hedgehog, but any shape of spiky plastic dryer ball will do. "Hedgie" is based on an adaptation of an example Kelly Wilson gave in a workshop, using the idea of a spikey, prickly pear cactus. In that workshop, Wilson described asking a client to imagine squeezing down with one hand on something spikey, like a prickly pear, and then, alternatively, to imagine loosening the hand around it, giving it space. This metaphor imparts a sense of how making space for something that is painful, although counterintuitive, is actually less painful than trying to crush it. To make this even more concrete for adolescents, we give them an opportunity to physically try it out with the spiky dryer ball.

Holding one Hedgie yourself, give one to your client and say:

Hold Hedgie with both hands wrapped around him, squeeze him tightly, and notice what that feels like. Notice what feelings come up in the rest of your body, such as your shoulders, neck, back, and forehead. (Chances are, as she is squeezing Hedgie, tension is developing in many areas of her body.) *Now, slowly release your hands, so they are just lightly floating around Hedgie's spiky surface, but still touching and holding him, and notice what that feels like.* (You can ask your client to repeat this a few times, so she starts to notice the difference between "tightening around Hedgie" and "loosening up around Hedgie," which usually does not take long.) *Now, as you are holding Hedgie tightly, notice what thoughts may be coming up, label them, and try to gently detach from them and come back to focusing on Hedgie.* (Pause.) *And now, imagine what it would be like to try and focus on homework right now* (incorporate whatever your client is struggling with). *Could you be the student you want to be, if you kept your tight grip on Hedgie? Now, loosen your grip on Hedgie, give him some space to be there.* (Pause.) *And then imagine doing your homework. What would it be like to do your work with a looser grip on Hedgie?*

Not only does "Hedgie" provide a physical sensation of tightening up versus loosening up around something for her to notice, it complements the ideas of willingness and allowing that are the focus of this session. Once she notices the "felt" difference between tightening up and loosening up around Hedgie, it is time for the next experience.

Observe, Breathe, Expand

Ask your client to think of a values-based goal that she would like to achieve, and let her identify this goal prior to starting the meditation. Having her bring the goal to mind during the meditation will likely bring up some level of feelings that she tries to avoid, giving you both something to work with in the moment. The "Hedgie" experience can be woven into this mindfulness meditation. Once you have introduced the meditation, and are seated in preparation, it could go something like this:

Try to bring to mind the goal you just identified, in as much detail as you can. Notice where you are, who is with you, and what your surroundings look like. Just notice as much as you are able to in this moment. As you bring your goal to mind, notice any feelings that come up in your body. (After a pause, you can ask your client if she notices any feelings. If she doesn't, give her more time to visualize and then check in again.) *Can you tell me where the feelings are? Try to look "at" your feelings from a distance, noticing their color, size, shape, texture, notice if they are moving or still. There is no right answer to this, nothing you are "supposed" to see, just try to notice whatever comes to mind as you look at your feelings. Can you tell me what you see?* (Allow time for description.) *As best you can, maintain that stance of observing your feelings, from a distance, and as you take your next in-breath, imagine the air going all the way to the place where the feelings are and then going right into the feelings, washing over them, filling them up. Then start to breathe out from that same spot. If thoughts take your attention away, simply notice, label the thoughts, let your thoughts settle—don't get into a conversation with them—and gently shift your attention back to your feelings, where you're breathing in and out from them. As you do this, take a look at your feelings and notice if they have changed in any slight way while you've been standing back looking at them.* (Pause and allow client time to share with you.) *Now, as you observe your feelings and breathe in and out from them, try and see if you can give them more room. Expand around your feelings in whatever way works for you. Imagine that there is a way to somehow open up more around them and make space for them. If Hedgie was helpful, imagine squeezing him and then unclenching around him, and as you do, see if you can let your body ease up this way around the physical sensations inside that you have been observing.* (Pause.) *Just like you loosened up around Hedgie, making more room for what is there. Make some room for whatever your body is feeling, and try not to push down on the feelings, try not to clench up around them, or tighten up around them. If thoughts take your attention away, simply notice, label the thoughts, let go of your struggle with thoughts, and gently shift your attention back to your feelings, to breathing in and out from your feelings and giving them some room. You may not want or enjoy your feelings, but since they are here and we have discovered that they are hard to control, try to approach them with a sense of willingness to let them be there, and allow them to have some more room. You may notice that, at times, your body has clenched up around the feelings again. If that happens, just notice this has happened, label your feelings, and try to bring back a sense of willingness and allowing, give your feelings some space, some breath, and loosen up around them. If it helps, think of the feelings as flowers whose petals are opening and try to give them some space and room to gently unfold. Just like with Hedgie, try to loosen your grip on the feelings and notice what happens. Notice as you observe your feelings standing back from a distance. Continue to breathe into them. Look at their size, shape, texture. Notice what stays the same and what, if anything, changes as you breathe in and out from your feelings, as you try to loosen your grip on them, making more room for them. (Allow time for this.) Do your feelings seem settled enough that we can end the meditation now, or do you need more time with this?* (Allow client to reply, and if she needs more time, continue, repeating instructions as you see fit.) *To end the meditation, I'll ask you to let the image of your feelings gently dissolve. Shift your attention back to the room you are in, noticing sounds, noticing the feeling of the chair under your body. Just come back to the present moment and we'll open our eyes.*

If your client was able to engage a sense of willingness and allowing, you can add in a step near the end that weaves in some self-compassion. Here is the piece we add to the end:

As you continue to breathe in and out from your feelings, and make some room for them, imagine yourself somehow being inside your own body, with your feelings. Maybe you are sitting next to them, or standing near them, whatever comes to mind, just see if you can imagine yourself inside, with your feelings, still looking at them. As you do this, imagine telling your feelings, in some way, that you are willing to have them be there, that you aren't going to try and push them away. You might tell them this by your body language, your facial expression, a gesture, or words, whatever comes to mind; just see if you can let your feelings know that you are trying to give them some air, and some room to just be, that you will allow them the space to come to rest.

For clients who struggle with the "expand" portion of "Observe, Breathe, Expand," it can be helpful to isolate the "expand" sequence of the mediation through the "Hands" exercise outlined below.

Hands

Using one's hands as an external "marker" of sorts and visualizing a flower is something that Sheri learned from her Pilates instructor, Alison Crouch. It expands nicely on Russ Harris's (2009) brief mention of "healing hands" as a way to add an element of self-compassion to the processes of willingness and allowing. In this exercise, your client's hand functions as an external marker to guide her experience. It will give her a sense, from the outside, of what "expanding" might feel like on the inside. This experiential exercise is most effective if you can introduce it at a moment when your client appears to be feeling her emotions physically, but not too intensely, because we present it here as a sort of "primer" for the full mindfulness experience.

> *Are you willing to place your hand, gently, where the feelings are and let it rest there just barely touching you?* (Pause.) *Imagine that as you breathe in, the air gently lifts your hand, where you placed it over the feelings, from the inside, and as you breathe out it lowers it again.* (Pause.) *Now notice the pressure from your hand. Try to keep it light, loosening your grip on your body.* (Pause.) *As you breathe in and out, to and from your hand and your feelings, see if you can gently loosen up around the feelings, just like you loosened up your hand on your body.* (Pause.) *Try and lighten your touch, or unclench, inside, around your feelings.*

You can also suggest to your client: "Try to imagine a flower, closed up, and make enough room inside to allow it to open, for the petals to unfold slowly and gently, with enough room so they don't get stuck." If this is helpful, you can add "Hands" to the full version of the "Observe, Breathe, Expand" meditation described earlier in this session.

Spend some time debriefing this experience, taking note of your client's willingness to have her feelings and to give them some space. A sense of willingness and allowing takes time to develop, so be mindful of titrating her values-based goals in terms of the intensity of feelings they evoke. If the intensity is too high, she may not be willing to have her feelings or complete her goal.

Three-Month Goal

Before you bring your session to an end, this halfway point is a good time to talk with your client about longer-term goals, such as three months from now, or whenever you might see her again after the weekly therapy sessions end. Using the SMART acronym is essential to make sure that you both know what she is working toward as a long-term goal. Together, you can ensure that she takes weekly steps in the direction of this broader goal.

Assignment of Home Practice

For the remaining sessions, home practice is much the same: taking steps toward what matters, toward values, while using LLAMA to label, to let go of the struggle (willingness), to allow thoughts and feelings, to mindfully return to the present moment, and to approach what matters. Help your client create a SMART goal that she can commit to until your next session. A given step may be something she does once or repeatedly, but it is in the service of moving toward values, not habituation of feelings.

Continue to stress mindfulness practice, whether formal or informal. The more she moves toward values, toward something that matters, the greater will be her sense of risk and vulnerability. Mindfulness practice will help her to notice and make conscious choices about her behavior. If she struggles with physical sensations of emotions, practicing the "Observe, Breathe, Expand" meditation will be important; you can give her the guided audio version available at the website for this book to practice with.

Modifications for Group Work

Much of what we described for individual work can easily be accommodated to group dynamics, and in many cases makes for a rich discussion of each person's experiences. When engaging a group of adolescents in mindfulness experiences such as "Observe, Breathe, Expand," however, it helps to know if group members have been able to reach a certain point, such as "observing," before you move them on to the next step.

Let your group know ahead of time that during this mindfulness meditation you will be asking them, with their eyes still closed, to raise and lower their hands at certain points in the experience, and that when you do this, you will be opening your eyes to see where each person is at. This helps group members to stay engaged, as they are asked to raise their hands from time to time, and it reduces the usual "comparing" that they would get looped into if they were asked to indicate their progress aloud.

Jumping Off a Chair

When doing this exercise with a group, we highly recommend having your clients *actually* jump off their chairs. (Again, using only good sturdy ones!) It's a good way to wake the group up and it's a terrific way for them to experience the "yes-or-no" polarity of willingness. You can remind them of the "Chair" exercise in later sessions when they struggle with willingness to attempt a goal, and the memory, if they have actually jumped, will be vivid. As clients get ready to do this exercise, their normal human minds start racing with comparisons and worries about their performance of jumping, as compared to that of their peers, and whether they will look silly. It can be a great "in the moment" opportunity to Label, Let Go of the struggle to control, and Allow, returning mindfully to the experience and trying anyway. It can also be an "in the moment" opportunity to remind group members of their mind's natural tendency to compare—to make sure they are doing the jump just right and won't be voted out of the tribe.

Gnats

You may want to have group members "act" this one out if they are willing. You can do this by having two group members walk together, perhaps sharing a story about their day. Have each of them identify their interpersonal values, who they want to be while listening and talking to each other. Then have another group member, or two, walk behind them and move their fingertips annoyingly between and around the two who are talking, or make annoying little noises behind them. This gives the group members who are talking an actual "in the moment" experience of trying to stay focused on each other.

Three-Month Goal

Divide your group into partners and ask them to help each other devise SMART goals that they can move toward over the next few sessions, and ultimately a goal they want to achieve by the time they return for the three-month follow-up group. Group leaders can float between dyads to assist and coach.

Conclusion

By the end of this session your client understands LLAMA and has some experience in using the steps and in allowing feelings and thoughts, although the latter is expanded upon in the next session. As she moves ahead with values-based goals, willingness and allowing of feelings is crucial. Practicing this stance will be important throughout the remainder of your work with her.

Session 6

Defusing from Thoughts

Defusion is the process on the left side of the hexaflex that refers to getting some distance from inner events, such as thoughts. It involves looking *at* them instead of engaging *with* them. The ACT stance suggests that when we look at our thoughts simply as something the brain does, we can then ask whether following those thoughts takes us in a values-consistent direction. This process is important in giving clients the skills to make conscious choices about their behavior so that they are more often in control of the direction they take.

Defusion refers to ways of changing one's relationship to thoughts, but to some degree clients may find these strategies are appropriate for unsticking from feelings as well. Similarly, as you saw in session 5, acceptance strategies relate mainly to feelings, but to some degree they are also helpful with thoughts. Ultimately, the distinction we make between the process of defusing from thoughts and the process of accepting or allowing feelings is a bit artificial. Because thoughts and feelings are often closely linked, so are the strategies for addressing them. More confusingly, both of the processes on the left side of the hexaflex, acceptance and defusion, are referred to jointly as *acceptance processes*—meaning the acceptance part of acceptance and commitment. However, it is worthwhile to separate the two out and to deal here with defusion separately, because defusion of thoughts and acceptance of affects are targeted somewhat differently.

Focus of This Session

Now that your client has explored values and begun setting goals that would be small steps in the direction of his values, it is time to introduce *defusion*. Because "what you value makes you vulnerable," it is a given that uncomfortable thoughts, feelings, and other private events will temporarily intensify as your client risks moving toward values. If he becomes "fused" with these inner experiences he will be unable to act. Taking thoughts like "I will never be able to do this" to be facts, instead of just thoughts, and assuming that feelings, like the big knot in his stomach, must mean his new steps are wrong will be immobilizing for your client. Fusion with thoughts and feelings, something that can happen because of our use of language, is seen through the ACT lens as contributing to suffering. Defusion ("unsticking" from thoughts and feelings) is seen as crucial in order for a person to be ready to stop depending on avoidance (DOTS) to manage unwanted inner experience, and to start making choices and taking steps toward values.

With defusion, we are going to work on the left side of the hexaflex, encouraging clients to take a different approach to managing the difficult thoughts that have been coming up for them. We want to help them unstick from thoughts rather than resorting to the DOTS we discussed earlier, because DOTS provide only short-term relief. You will likely hear lots of "yes but" arguments here, when you ask your client to consider relinquishing DOTS. You will also hear lots of reason giving about why it's not possible to allow the uncomfortable private experience to happen—as if anyone could stop it. The "yes buts" and reason giving will create a repeating "whack-a-mole," propelled by the unrealistic expectation that we should somehow be able to just get rid of difficult personal experiences. The DOTS are likely to keep happening and your client may need to revisit creative hopelessness and the illusion of control with you.

Fictional Client: Cody

In this discussion of defusion, you will meet our client Cody. He is a sixteen-year-old boy who was always a physically active child, engaged in many sports activities, but has become much less so since becoming a teenager. Cody has had difficulty in school from the very beginning. Teachers complained that he was not paying attention in class. They have all been frustrated because they can see that he is intelligent and able to learn, but his grades have never reflected this. In addition, Cody has always been a very social boy and fairly popular. Teachers told his parents they saw leadership qualities in him. In fifth grade he was diagnosed by his doctor with attention-deficit hyperactivity disorder (ADHD) and given a prescription for medication. His parents and his teachers thought this helped, but he hated the idea of being on medication and refused to take it from seventh grade onwards. He told his mother that he thinks only "losers" take medication. His grades progressively declined along with his attitude. He was often in trouble at his high school for talking back to teachers and refusing to follow school rules. The only class he liked was band, in which he had started playing the trumpet. Cody really enjoyed the trumpet and received a lot of positive feedback for how well and how quickly he was advancing; the music teacher had even asked him to play in the school band. But Cody stayed away from all his other classes if he thought he would have a hard time holding his temper when teachers made demands. His vice principal told his parents that he was a good kid, but that if he didn't change his behavior he would be suspended from school. He was given an ultimatum to attend every class and show completed homework. When his parents tried to talk with him about this, he became enraged and put his fist through his bedroom wall. He was smart enough to know that his anger was a problem, but he couldn't control it. He wanted things to be better. Learning to defuse from his angry thoughts and feelings was important for him.

Defusing from Thoughts with Individual Clients

The focus of this session is defusion—"unsticking" or "unhooking" from thoughts. As clinicians, it is important for us to keep clients' values and goals as the broader context in which the work is being done. After going through some defusion experiences, we bring the client back to our trusty LLAMA to help him move toward what matters.

A word of caution here. It is not uncommon for clinicians to want to help their clients defuse, or unstick, from absolutely everything and to obliterate the use of DOTS entirely in favor of moving toward values. This tendency is something that we, as clinicians, need to hold with a loose, flexible grip. DOTS are not inherently evil; they may at times be helpful. For example, if being in a bus or subway car that is crowded with people is enough to make an anxious person avoid them, then distracting from the environment with music in headphones may be helpful. In fact, if it supports someone in getting to school or treatment, it may actually be in line with values related to education or health. It is when engagement in DOTS becomes an inflexible, mindless way of reacting that takes someone away from values that DOTS become counterproductive.

In this chapter we provide some categories regarding the types of thinking that may be helpful to defuse from. These categories have helped us, as clinicians, to be alert and sensitive to particular ways of thinking. It also helps to have a sense of what to defuse from so we don't insult or invalidate our clients by asking them to defuse from painful, present-moment circumstances, at least not too quickly. For example, if a client has just broken up with her boyfriend and is feeling sad and noticing thoughts of *I miss him and I can't believe we aren't together anymore*, this is a moment to stay with her feelings and share in them, creating a compassionate space for her to work through her grief. This is not a moment to ask her to deliteralize the thought by singing it to the tune of happy birthday. So we want to be careful about encouraging our clients to accept and defuse from everything inside, all the time, as a rigid rule. Context is important here; we as clinicians need to be mindful of "the big picture."

In the "ACT Basics" section you learned about elements of the therapeutic stance that work well with ACT. We are reiterating a few of them here because we believe they can be instrumental in helping our clients take this important step, changing their relationship to their thoughts. Phrasing thoughts as *I'm noticing I'm having the thought that I'm weird* can help clients loosen up around the literal meaning and get some distance from their thoughts; they can look *at* their thoughts instead of *through* them. You can do a lot to encourage defusion by the language you use. Responding to a client's expression of thoughts by saying, "So you are noticing that you are having the thought that..." implicitly demonstrates to your client how to create a bit of distance from thoughts and shows him a way to have his thoughts without fighting them.

In this session you will do lots of experiments with your client, and it is best to *ask* him if he is willing to try things out with you. "In the moment" opportunities will likely arise for you and your client to engage in an ACT way throughout the session. If your client is struggling to take small steps, watch out for your own urges to reassure and dispute thoughts and feelings. Getting pulled into a dispute with him will just make you look like his parents on a bad day.

What Stuck?

In the last session, the idea of willingness and allowing what was inside was introduced, and several experiential exercises were conducted to help clients feel what willingness and allowing are all about. Before continuing with defusion, it is helpful to review the contents of that previous session, correcting any misperceptions or confusion. Clients often revert back to thinking that "allowing" means they have to passively succumb to whatever is happening in life. This may need some clarification and discussion.

Review of Home Practice

There were several suggestions for home practice at the end of the last session, including noticing DOTS, with their short-term and long-term impact, practicing mindfulness, and taking a step toward what matters and toward a long-term goal.

Ask your client what he did in the service of values, what did he do that mattered, debriefing how the process went. What unwanted inner experience came up while he was heading toward what or who matters? Did it prevent him from trying? This may bring into the room a real-world discussion about how your client navigates his own DOTS in a real situation. It's likely to make the content from the previous session more relevant and personal. As we mentioned earlier in this book, it is important to ask clients how they feel when behavior is for the purpose of avoiding, when it's a DOT (upper left), versus when behavior comes from values (upper right). It likely feels quite different, and this "noticing" can be helpful for continued behavior change. For example, doing something that represents genuine caring for a friend feels a certain way, but the same behavior will likely evoke different feelings if it was done in a frantic effort to avoid rejection.

If your client was able to attain his goal, ask if unwanted thoughts, feelings, physical sensations, or urges came up, and what he did in order to persevere. Was he able to recall and use LLAMA, "The Acetate," or mindfulness, for example, to help him move in his valued direction? If your client reports an absence of unwanted thoughts or feelings, the goal itself may have been quite meaningless and probably needs rethinking.

As we review home practice, we can weave back and forth between revisiting DOTS, creative hopelessness, and willingness, and introducing defusion. Having the matrix available can be helpful, so you can point to quadrants as your client describes his experience or ask him where things fit after he has told you about his efforts. As you can see in the session with Cody, below, fusion and avoidance got in his way:

T (Therapist): How did it go, attending every class at school this week?

C (Cody): Not so good, I was right on the verge of blowing up every day. My science teacher is a jerk. He tries to make me look bad in front of the class.

T: So you noticed you were having the thought *My science teacher is a jerk*, and it sounds like that one's pretty sticky. You must have been tempted to follow it and stay away from his class. (*Defusion and LLAMA.*)

C: Yeah, I could hardly make myself go in that classroom on Thursday. I could see the teacher glaring at me the second I got to the door. I got so angry that I started to shake, and when I'm feeling like that I just really don't want to go in. I know avoiding class is a DOT, but I really hate being in school if I think a teacher has it in for me.

T: Sounds like it was a pretty hard situation for you. And it really took courage for you to go to that class.

C: It was bad all right.

T: You were really feeling that anger. (*Pause.*) Remember we talked about trying to fix something that's on the inside using the same ways we try to fix things on the outside, by trying to get rid of it?

159

We all do that some of the time. It's wired into the way our minds work. We're trying to problem-solve all the time. So your mind is telling you if you don't go to class, you won't feel the anger. Hmm. How is that working for you? Do you feel better if you don't go to class? (*Bringing in values and workability of DOTS.*)

C: No. Even before the vice principal put me on this attending every class thing, I didn't feel better if I missed classes. I knew I was just getting further and further behind and getting lower grades for not participating. But I really don't want to be in that room.

T: So what would happen if you kept choosing not to go? (*Eliciting consequences of DOTS.*)

C: I'd get kicked out of school. That's what the vice principal said.

T: Is that what you want? (*Eliciting values.*)

C;   No. I want to finish school. And I want to be able to play in the band.

T: So school really does matter to you. At least, some things about school.

C: Yeah. I'd like to be able to get through school. I could do it if I could just be in the classroom. And it would be really cool to play in the band.

T: What's important to you about being the kind of student who goes to class and plays in the band?

C: (*Pause.*) I'd be with everybody else. I'd have friends around me. I like the guys in the band. It's kinda lonely if I stay away from school.

T: Being with people you like is important to you?

C: Yeah. It's really important to me. I like to have friends around me. It feels like we're all going through the same thing together. Like maybe we can help each other.

T: So (*pointing at matrix and quadrants while talking*), just to make sure I've got it, you get stuck in thoughts like the one about your science teacher being a jerk and trying to make you look bad (*lower left*), which leads to staying away from class (*upper left*), and then you are facing suspension from school (*upper left*), which gets in your way of being the student who wants to be together with everyone else and help each other out (*lower right*), the student who would go to school every day (*upper right*).

C: Yup, that's it exactly. I'm being the opposite of who I want to be and that just makes me feel worse. But I keep thinking over and over about how my science teacher just wants to take me down.

T: Do you think you can get rid of those thoughts whenever you want to or feel you need to? (*Back to creative hopelessness.*)

C: No, I wish I could, but I know I can't, it always comes back, sometimes worse.

T: Would you be willing to treat these thoughts the way we treated them with the "Acetate" exercise?

C: (*Smiles.*) Oh yeah. Like last week. (*Sighs.*) I guess.

T: Let's try it now, we can even write them down if you like. And today, we'll learn more ways to get some distance from thoughts and unstick from them. (*Spend a few moments either making a new acetate and working with it, or imagining one.*) (*Willingness and defusion from thoughts.*)

T: How are those thoughts in your head?

C: A bit better, but still there; it's hard not to think about them and the shaking feeling I'm getting.

T: Would you be willing to try the mindfulness exercise we did last session, where we did "Observe, Breathe, Expand" around feelings? (*Willingness and allowing of feelings.*)

C: Yeah, okay. That one sorta helped—to just let stuff be there.

T: I guess the ultimate question is this: are you willing to make room for the thoughts about your teacher, and that shaking feeling that you get, to allow some space for those just to be there, for the sake of going to school and being the you who matters? (*The ultimate workability question, emphasizing values and values-based behavior.*)

C: Well, it doesn't seem there is any other way, and I want to go.

Once you have reviewed your client's learning from the previous week, and his experiences with the home practice, check in on his long-term goal if you began that work last session. If you didn't get to it, this is a good time to flush out a longer-term goal and set SMART steps in that direction. Once you are done, you can begin mindfulness. Some of the content to be addressed in this session can be embedded within the mindfulness exercises that follow.

Mindfulness

In this session we engage our client in several steps of a "Mindfulness of Thoughts" meditation. It serves as a nice introduction to defusion of thoughts. In this mindfulness practice, we like to incorporate bubbles to give it a more informal flavor. Yes, the bubbles you blow through the little wand. Bubbles can make this experience fun and memorable, which may increase your client's ability to recall and use the experience outside of session.

Mindfulness of Bubbles

This is an excellent eyes-open exercise that is great for beginner mindfulness practice. It's helpful to keep a few dollar-store bottles of kids' bubble soap (with enclosed wand) in your office. They are good for learning mindfulness skills at this point in therapy, but can also be useful to pull out at any point later when you want to highlight mindfulness and defusion skills. Hand your client a bubble-soap bottle and let him know you are going to ask him to blow bubbles and that you would like him to choose a bubble and watch it as it floats away. Ask him to follow the bubble with full attention as it moves away and pops, or slowly shrinks to nothing in the air, or crashes and splats on the floor or another surface in your office. (If your office holds any treasured furniture or art, you might want to take this exercise outside.) Playing with bubbles seems to be as popular with fifteen-year-olds as it is with five-year-olds, so you are unlikely to get any opposition to this request. Before you end this step, ask your client what he noticed about the bubbles. It might be things he never noticed before, or things he had forgotten about, like the reflective rainbow of color on the surface of a bubble or the way it wobbles as it leaves the wand. You can ask your client to notice with different senses each time, such as sight (what the bubbles look like), sound (the sound they make when they pop), and sensation (what they feel like as they settle or pop on his hand). Needless to say, you should have your own bubble wand and participate with your client. Once you have debriefed this experience, you are ready for the more traditional experience that follows.

Mindfulness of Thoughts

After engaging your client in some fun bubble play, a simple "Mindfulness of Thoughts" that includes elements of defusion from thoughts can follow. It might go something like this:

Bring your attention to your breath as it comes in and out. See if you can focus on noticing your breath as it comes all the way in and goes all the way out. (Pause.) You might notice as you do this that your mind can be pulled away by thoughts that come up, like thoughts about the bubbles we just did or about what we are doing now, thoughts like "This is strange" or "I can't listen and focus at the same time." (Pause.) Or you might have thoughts about something you saw on the way here, about something you did earlier today, or something you are planning to do later today. (Pause.) When you notice these thoughts, just kindly and gently detach your attention from them and return it to your breath. (Longer pause.) Now see if you can do the opposite. See if you can just watch those thoughts as they come up. (Pause.) See if you can watch your thoughts as they arise, as they stay for however long they stay, and as they fade into the background when a new thought comes up. (Long pause.) See if you can watch as one thought leads to another and another, like a monkey swinging from one branch of a tree to the next. (Pause.) Just keep watching where your thoughts lead. (Long pause.) Notice where your thoughts are located, try to notice a location within your mind if that's where they are, notice if they are words or images. If they seem to be words, are you hearing them or are you seeing them in writing? Are they like writing on paper or on a computer screen? Do you notice the words in colors or a type of font? Are the words or images moving or sitting still? If they are moving, how are they moving? Try to notice the direction they take, whether they move quickly or slowly, smoothly or in a different way. Just watch your thoughts, watch what your mind does, without judging, without getting tangled, just watching from a distance. (Long pause.) Now you can open your eyes and bring your attention back into the room.

At the end of the mindfulness meditation, a question as simple as "What was that like?" or "What did you notice?" will give you an idea of your client's ability to observe her internal events. Try to elicit details about the form of your client's thoughts, the color, location, font, and mobility; this discussion will help her to gain a perspective of distance from her thoughts.

Your client may tell you she noticed thoughts and may even be able to relate in considerable detail the sequence of thoughts she observed. This is fine, to some degree; but be a bit careful here. Letting her share all of her thoughts may lead to both your client and you getting stuck in her thoughts—the lower left quadrant. Her regaling you with minute details of her thoughts may be a way to avoid the emotional experience you have just shared, for example. Conversely, she may say that when she looked for them, there just weren't any thoughts in her mind, her "mind was blank." This inability to see what is inside can sometimes actually be a kind of involuntary DOT, and can be processed in the manner similar to processing any DOT. You can begin by asking, "What might happen if you noticed your thoughts; what do you think that would be like?" If your client has some ability to self-reflect, she may help both of you understand what inner experiences she is avoiding (lower left of matrix). Clients have shared such fears as "I'll be overwhelmed by my feelings." A fear like this could be what maintains the avoidance of inner experience. Knowing this tells us to proceed patiently, that our client needs a more titrated "dose" of emotional experience.

It doesn't really matter what your client's experience was like of paying attention to thoughts during the mindfulness exercise. You can normalize whatever happened, because both extremes (noticing thoughts in elaborate detail or "going blank") as well as everything in between are all normal. You can use your client's particular experience as a jumping-off point to discuss that it is normal to have troubling thoughts popping into our minds, especially when we are doing something new or challenging, and that it is equally normal for us to tend to avoid these thoughts by using DOTS or by sometimes just going blank, being unable to get in contact with the thoughts that are present. If she was not able to notice any thoughts, you could consider repeating this mindfulness exercise later in the session, perhaps building more slowly into it from "Mindfulness of Breath."

If she was able to notice some thoughts, you can proceed to the next exercise. Otherwise, wait on this next one until your client is better able to be aware of thoughts.

Back to Bubbles

If your client has been able to observe thoughts, and you can hear in the debrief that he was able to stay aware of them at least for brief moments, you could do a reprise of the "Bubbles" exercise to reinforce the learning of "Mindfulness of Thoughts." Ask your client to pick up the bubble soap again and, with eyes open, pay attention to thoughts arising in his mind in the same way that he did in the "Mindfulness of Thoughts" exercise. Ask him, when he notices a thought coming up, to blow a bubble and imagine placing that thought into the bubble. Ask him to watch what happens to the thought (bubble) in the same way he watched the bubble before, as it floated away on its own, without being pushed, and eventually popped. Ask him to keep blowing a bubble each time he notices a new thought coming up and to keep placing each thought in a bubble and watching as the thoughts in the bubbles make their way around the room. The diminishment of the bubbles as they float off nicely mimics the natural decay of our thoughts as they give way to new ones.

Besides just "going blank," some adolescents report either heavy sleepiness or irritating restlessness when doing mindfulness exercises. These effects are not uncommon even for adults in mindfulness practice, because our minds resist staying present. But they are especially likely to happen for adolescents. For them it could simply be coming from too little sleep or too long sitting still in class all day, or it could be avoidance. Depending on circumstances, we don't challenge this unless it becomes a repeated pattern that we can bring to their attention. We just remain curious as to what it may be about. Adolescents are told what to do all day long, so it's important to notice your own urge to "teach" them what they should have gotten out of a mindfulness experience. Clinician acceptance of whatever they experience here is key, because it provides good modeling for their acceptance of their own internal events.

After working through "Mindfulness of Thoughts" and "Bubbles," your client is ready to continue with a few quick metaphors to normalize what his mind is doing, outlined below, before proceeding with defusion.

Metaphors to Normalize the Mind's Job

We have already likened what the normal human brain does, and why it does this, to a "fix-it machine" and a "comparison machine." You can remind your client of these ideas, and also introduce two new metaphors, "The Bear and the Blueberry Bush" and "Survivor," each of which is described below.

The Bear and the Blueberry Bush

"The Bear and the Blueberry Bush" is not a new metaphor. It is one that you may have read in other ACT texts or heard in workshops (Wilson & DuFrene, 2008). It can be done with eyes closed to enhance the visual imagery, and goes like this:

Imagine that, many millennia ago, one of your early ancestors is looking out of the cave one morning, along with a friend who is with him. He sees a dark shadow on a hill across the way and begins to wonder what it is. It's too far away to be sure. His friend is convinced it is a blueberry bush, and suggests going out to pick berries. Your ancestor, on the other hand, tended to be a bit more cautious and is worried it might be a bear. The friend decides to go out and get some berries, but your ancestor chooses to stay inside the cave, just not sure enough what that dark shape could be. The friend never returns.

You can process this metaphor by asking what your client thinks might have happened to us as a species if this kind of scenario repeated itself over and over, and only the more cautious of our early ancestors tended to survive. What you want to pull out here is that those of us who are around today probably have an evolutionary bias toward caution. Early humans who made more reckless choices in the face of ambiguity were less likely to be around to produce offspring. Once your client gets this, having an anxious mind becomes normalized and easier to accept.

The Survivor Metaphor

A second metaphor you can share here is one we call "Survivor." We have already described the quality of our minds, as they evolved in our early human development, as being like "comparison machines," constantly vigilant about how we compare to our peers. The function of this tendency, according to evolutionary science, is that we needed to be vigilant to ensure we were contributing enough to our tribe and not lagging behind, which could have resulted in abandonment and (most likely) being eaten by something. As a shorthand for this concept, we like to refer to the reality television series *Survivor*. Even adolescents who haven't watched the show seem to have some familiarity with the *Survivor* premise, but it can be easily explained if they are not familiar with the "rules" of the series. As tribe members get to know each other and work together, it is generally those who are perceived as comparatively less hard working, less physically fit, less strong, and less socially skilled that are at risk of getting "voted off the island." If you use this metaphor, you can point out that ensuring we are as likeable, as fit, and as useful as other tribe members is very adaptive if we were living as part of a tribe several millennia ago, just as if we were on *Survivor* today. To make sure we "measure up," our archaic minds are always making us self-monitor, comparing our own ability with that of others. Our mind, however, doesn't know that we aren't living in archaic times and that we are not on a reality show, so our mind encourages constant comparing when it fears we might get voted out of the tribe.

Thus, in our contemporary world, your client's constant vigilance and comparison regarding her own performance may or may not be necessary or even helpful. As was the case with DOTS, this requires a less than rigid "hold." There are moments when self-monitoring and comparisons may be helpful. For a client who struggles with peer relationships, for example, it may be helpful for her to check in and notice if she is talking too much and not allowing others to reciprocate in a conversation. There may be some advantage in dressing like others if blending in is preferred, but there might also be some advantage to asserting uniqueness by not adhering to the "uniform" among peers. This is where the ACT processes overlap. Your client's ability to stand back from herself (self-as-context) and notice (mindfulness) what is really going on in her current circumstances will give her an opportunity to decide what to do. Is she really in a game of "Survivor" at a particular moment, or does the actual five-senses-based information coming from her environment suggest that she is not really in danger of being voted out of the tribe?

When your client is stuck in thoughts about being rejected, and is not really taking part in the conversation going on around her, others will notice and may judge, over time, that she isn't interested in them. They may assume that she is bored by them, or come to any number of other conclusions. This will likely result in some degree of the peer rejection that she was trying to avoid by ruminating in the first place.

That said, although we have shown that it is normal for our minds to send out worry thoughts and to compare, it is often not helpful for us humans to get stuck in these thoughts when there is no actual risk. To help unstick, we remind our client of LLAMA and note that the first "A" is the focus of this session.

LLAMA and Defusion

We usually write the letters of LLAMA and the meaning of each on a whiteboard, flip chart page, or piece of paper, and explain that it is something important that we will be referring to over and over again in the work we are doing together. Remind your client what the first two "L's" and the first "A" stand for, if this was not covered in a review of home practice, and then proceed with more of a description of the first "A," which stands for *allowing*. In the previous session, we focused on allowing emotions. Now it's time to learn how to allow thoughts, to unstick from them. We tend to use words like "unsticking" or "unhooking" from thoughts, as opposed to "defusion," but you can use whatever term works for you and your client. We proceed with a brief description of *allowing thoughts*, followed by some experiential exercises.

Allowing

So as we said, the first "A" stands for *allowing*, with *willingness* understood to be necessary and related to allowing. What you want to do is provide your client with as many experiences of defusion, or unsticking, as possible. This will give him the tools he will need to allow his thoughts as you continue to support him to move in the direction of his values. Then you can pull LLAMA together and explain to your client that after noticing and *Labeling* what is happening inside and *Letting go* of the struggle (hitting a pause button) and consenting to what is inside, he can unstick from thoughts (and emotions) and *Allow* them to be there, return *Mindfully* to the present moment, and then *Approach* what matters. Before going ahead with ways to unstick from thoughts that take us away from valued living, it can be helpful to highlight to your client what he is unsticking from.

What to Unstick From?

We find that it is helpful to point out some categories of thoughts that typically get us, as humans, stuck, and throughout this discussion we stress *workability*—whether sticking to thoughts is taking us in a valued direction. We provide a list of the types of thoughts we ask clients to watch for and to be ready to unstick from, along with some specific suggestions for unsticking from each type. We follow this with a list of experiential exercises that can be applied more generally to any sticky thoughts that are getting in our client's way.

Rules

"Rules" are a very common type of thought, and can often cause problems. We suggest that rules are like flypaper or the sticky pads used to catch rodents. We start out with rules given to us by parents and other authority figures, and later, as we become adept at deriving relationships through relational framing and transformation of stimulus function, we make up our own. They are sometimes helpful, but often not. As explained in the "ACT Basics" section, rules can often lead to the very outcome clients seek to avoid. Unfortunately, even when our rules give us unwanted outcomes, we often "stick" to them and will find reasons to maintain consistency among our networks of rules. For these reasons, rules are identified and addressed using LLAMA in the same way as a thought or feeling, without disputation. For example, in a discussion with Cody about what was going on inside him as he thought about dealing with his science teacher, here is how it might have been handled as he described a rule:

C: I just keep thinking my science teacher has it in for me and it's really unfair. I get really stuck on this thought and I feel horrible, I am so scared I'll fail and I know this isn't working, but if I go to his class and do what he wants me to do, people will think I'm a wimp and I'll have no friends.

T: So is this a rule that your mind gives you, that if you do what the teacher wants, you will have no friends?

C: Yeah, I guess it is. It feels like I'm going to get stuck on my own because he'll make me look stupid and no one will respect me. No one will chill with me.

T: Sounds complicated, like if you aren't respected, no one will chill with you. What do you do when this rule pops up and you feel worried no one will chill with you?

C: At home I play video games, sometimes for hours, then I get more behind in stuff, like my homework, so my mom and I end up arguing a lot. I try to get out of the arguing because she can't stand it when I'm upset or angry, so I go to my room and feel worse. I just numb out a bit with games, I can do that for hours. My friends have stopped texting me, I guess because I don't answer them when I'm like this.

T: If you follow that rule—that if you do what the teacher wants, if you aren't respected, you will have no friends—is it taking you in the direction of your values as a student, or even as a friend or family member? (*Therapist is getting at "workability" of thoughts.*)

C: No, I'm going the opposite way, I feel like I'm losing everything, I feel like I'm going to puke just saying that.

T: Would you be willing to walk through LLAMA with me around this thing about doing what the teacher wants?

C: Sure, what I'm doing isn't working. I'll try.

T: Do you remember what the first "L" stands for?

C: Yeah, Labeling.

T: So when you notice you are caught in that rule, could you label what you are experiencing? (*Working on defusion.*)

C: I'm noticing I'm having the rule about being rejected.

T: That's it, now what's the second "L" for?

C: Letting go of something, not quite sure what though.

T: It's about letting go of trying to control your thoughts and rules, it's about being willing to have whatever thoughts your mind comes up with.

C: Oh yeah, like the gnats, they just keep flying around, so I can stop swatting them and stop trying to get rid of them. (*Cody closes his eyes in an effort to visualize.*)

T: Exactly. Do you remember what's next?

C: The "A." I want to try that breathe and expand thing with my eyes closed because I'm shaking again now just thinking about my science teacher. And my stomach is in knots. I feel like I'm going to throw up.

T: Okay, I'll close my eyes with you and walk you through it. (*Therapist repeats "Observe, Breathe, Expand" mindfulness from session 5.*)

C: My stomach feels a bit better. The anger isn't gone, but I don't think I'll throw up, and I'm trying to picture looking at my thoughts like I look at paintings on the wall.

T: How are you doing?

C: Better, we can stop now (*referring to the eyes-closed experience*), I think I can try this at school.

T: Great. One last step, though, can you bring your attention back to the present, gently letting go of the rules and feelings you were noticing, and just pay attention to the here and now?

C: Yeah, I notice I am here with you, and you are smiling at me. (*Mindfulness, aware of present moment with one of his senses.*)

T: You sound surprised.

C: I am. I guess I expected you to have that look on your face that teachers get, that I'm stupid.

T: Do you see that look on my face now?

C: No, I don't, you look happy for me.

T: I wonder if in class, once you work through L, L, and A, when you get to M and come back to paying attention to the moment, can you pay some attention to the look on your teacher's face, or the faces of the other students? Maybe take in how they are really looking at you, if they are looking at you, and not just go with what your mind tells you?

C: I can try that, maybe they will surprise me too! And if they look at me like I'm a wimp, I guess I can deal with that after class.

From here, once you have labeled the rule, you can encourage your client to go through the steps of LLAMA with it—letting go of it (struggle switch), "unsticking" from it (allowing it, using perhaps some of the deliteralization techniques you will see described later in this session to defuse from the rule), and moving on to mindful noticing of his present moment, without judgment, and approaching what matters. As he returns mindfully to the present, he will be able to *respond* according to what is there, based on his five senses, with flexibility, as opposed to *reacting* mindlessly, based on internal events such as thoughts and feelings.

Often, your clients will *feel* the difference between behavior that is coming from rule following or reason giving (see below), as opposed to behavior that is values based. For example, when your client follows his rule of *I have to listen to people or they won't like me*, and tells you he listened to a friend complain about her boyfriend for hours the night before, and was left without time to study for his own test and now resents the friend, he can likely also tell you how he felt in the moment, physically, and how he is feeling now. This can be compared to how he imagines he might have felt if he were able to loosen up on his rule and set some time limits on listening, so that he balanced his value of being a caring friend with his values as a student. It is quite likely that your client will notice that behavior based on rules feels different than behavior based on values, even when the behavior looks the same. Excuse our repetition of this idea, but it's important! This is something he can look out for in the future: hints that his behavior is being driven by rules and not by what matters.

Reasons

Generating reasons to explain behavior is common but often problematic. Reason giving comes in many forms, and some reasons that we hear often from clients include things like "I can't go to school until my anxiety is gone," or "I can't make any changes until I lose weight." For these, we offer the "Kidnap" metaphor (Harris, 2009). To use this metaphor, ask your client who is the most important person in the world to her. Then, ask her if she would be willing to do the thing that now seems impossible to do (go to school, join a sports team, or speak to someone at lunch) if that most important person were kidnapped and the kidnappers were demanding the impossible action as a ransom. Usually the answer is yes. This is how the "Kidnap" metaphor unfolded with Cody:

T: So, it seems that taking a step and walking into that classroom with your teacher is really tough, with a lot of thoughts and feelings coming up and getting in your way.

C: Yeah, it just seems impossible, I want help, I need help, but my head is full of crap about what other people will think of me; they'll think I'm a wimp. I can't go in there when I have these thoughts; they're just too strong.

T: Could you tell me the name of someone who really matters to you, someone you love very much?

C: That's easy, my dad. He drives me nuts, but he's my dad. I guess I care about him.

T: Would you be willing to imagine something with me with eyes closed?

C: Okay.

T: Imagine that your dad, whom you care about, has been kidnapped, and the only way you can get him back from the kidnappers is to go in that science classroom every day. Can you describe the scene you are picturing in your mind? How are you feeling as you think of this? What would you do? (*You want your client to have a felt sense of potentially losing someone he loves, and of doing something that makes him angry and taking his anger with him because his dad matters to him—the visualization and request for details will help him to experience this from an internal, "felt" sense.*)

C: That's a dumb question, of course I'd go.

T: Wouldn't you feel angry?

C: Of course, but who cares, it's my dad. I'd do anything to get him back.

This part may or may not need debriefing. Sometimes our clients just "get it" and are ready to move on, while at other times it can evoke intense affect (thanks to relational framing and equivalence of stimulus function, it can *feel* real) that needs some compassion and patience. Processing may include a discussion of how to use LLAMA in this circumstance, and the idea that your client doesn't have to wait for life-threatening abductions before making a move to live according to his values. This metaphor can contribute to a growing sense of willingness and allowing.

The Past

Thoughts about the past typically involve *wishing* that things from the past, circumstances that have already unfolded, and even who we were in a given moment, had been different. This can lead to endless rumination. Reminders can be helpful here that mindfulness returns us to the present, and, in combination with unsticking, allows us to let such thoughts come to rest. Wishing can be unpacked a bit by asking your client if what she is wishing for is something that she can change—something that could be achieved (if she were willing) with actions in the here and now. If it could, then the outcome wished for can be tied at some point in your work to values and potentially carried out through committed actions. However, if the outcome that is wished for is not in your client's control, if it is something that has already happened that she cannot change, then wishing could be considered an example of the "T" (Time Travel) in DOTS. In that case, discussing the short-term and long-term costs and benefits of this wishing may help to loosen her grip and defuse from wishing. In the mindfulness practice described at the end of this session, you will also see how wishing can be addressed with LLAMA.

The Future

Thoughts about the future typically take us into the territory of *worry* and are also captured by the "T" in DOTS. Here we remind clients of how our minds are preprogrammed to solve problems that have not yet appeared.

For both thoughts about the past and about the future, a little mindfulness and defusion exercise we call the "Arm Timeline" can help to improve awareness of thoughts as they move away from the present.

The Arm Timeline

Ask your client to create an "Arm Timeline" by placing the index finger of her right hand in the middle of her left forearm (or vice versa, depending on handedness). Tell her to imagine that the center point on her left forearm represents the present in a timeline that runs on her left arm from her elbow to her fingertips, with the elbow representing the furthest, most distant past she can remember and the fingertips, the furthest point she could imagine in the future. Then ask her just to watch her mind and to let her finger follow where her mind goes in time. Starting with her finger in the center, in the present, she can move it forward toward her fingertips or backward toward her elbow, depending on where she sees her mind going. This is a simple little exercise, but can help to demonstrate how easily our minds slip away from the present into the past or future, and how returning to the present can be a way of unsticking the mind from rumination and worry.

The "Self"

Thoughts about the "self" create the self-description clients are fused with—the core of their "story." Common examples clients have given us include "I'm a loser," "I'm not good enough," and "I am unlovable." These can be addressed with the "Word Web," which is the focus of the next session, as well as by helping clients change their language, as we outline in the following sections.

Judgments

Judgments are opinions, as opposed to facts. We encourage clients to change their wording so that they are expressing only facts, particularly when a judgment pulls them into fusion and a lack of acceptance, taking them away from the present moment. For example, if the thought is *I'm a wimp*, we could encourage the more factual *I didn't yell back at my teacher*. Use of the "Judgment Paddles" helps to increase awareness of judgmental thoughts and also normalizes them, so that they can be seen as something that minds just do.

What we have learned from running groups is that the effectiveness of defusion strategies is very personal. Something that resonates with one adolescent may not resonate at all for another. You can keep going through them until you find one or two that your client really responds to. Some of these strategies tend more to address the "getting a bit of distance" aspect of defusion. Others address the more general concept of acceptance—staying with difficult experience.

In the debrief for any of the following strategies, you can review the obstacles your client faced in accomplishing the home practice from the previous session. Ask her to imagine using some of the defusion ideas and see if she thinks any of them would have been useful. Later in this session, you can also encourage the use of whichever strategies seemed to resonate the most while she tries to move in a values-consistent direction until the next session. Don't forget to remind your client of defusion exercises from past sessions, including "The Acetate" and using language like "I'm noticing I'm having the thought that…"

In thinking about rules, reason giving, wishing, worrying, judgments, and our sense of our "self," a caveat is in order. Although we discussed this in session 3, it bears repeating. Many of the adolescents with whom we have worked have experienced bullying and ostracism from peers. This can result in "rules" such as "Agree with everyone so they don't reject me." Many have struggled with attentional difficulties or impulsive behavior that has resulted in them being given rules like "You need to stop interrupting or no one will like you." Knowing when the present moment necessitates some self-awareness or self-reflection can be a useful, adaptive skill. There may in fact be moments when agreeing with others is socially appropriate and moments when it is not. There are moments when interrupting is okay, and moments when it is not. Being aware of our present moment allows us to discern the difference between and among various conditions as they are unfolding, not as they exist in our minds. When there is a past experience of rejection or criticism, patience and compassion are in order, allowing our client time to work through the emotions that come up. In these situations we try not to move too quickly to defusion, since that can feel very invalidating. It may be that our clients do not so much need to unstick immediately, as to be aware—to share with us, to make us feel what they feel and to receive compassion from us—and *then* to unstick when the present moment is not the same as the past. We urge our readers to bear this in mind when practicing defusion strategies with clients. Engaging in some of the deliteralization exercises outlined in the next section (such as "Funny Voice," the "Milk" exercise, and "Singing") can be incredibly invalidating if not applied thoughtfully, especially within the context of cognitions connected to trauma, rejection, and shame.

Defusion Exercises: How to Unstick

There are many ways to engage clients in the process of defusion, including the "Bubbles" experience outlined earlier in this session. We provide several additional options in this session that we borrowed and adapted from Russ Harris (2009), beginning with some that involve deliteralization strategies, such as changing one's voice, then moving on to some others that can be done as eyes-closed experiences. Be mindful that you don't overload your client with a smorgasbord of defusion options; if a deliteralization experience is really not to her liking, you may want to skip the rest and go to the eyes-closed visualization experiences. If she really liked "Bubbles," you can stay with that. Debriefing after a defusion experience will reveal what is working for her.

It is important to be aware of the possibility that DOTS are in play during defusion exercises. If the thoughts that clients are trying to unstick from are too evocative, they may resort to habitual ways of trying to "get rid" of them. If this is the case, you may have to help your client choose a less evocative thought to get some practice with defusion first, one that brings with it an intensity of feelings that he is willing to have.

Singing

Suggest that your client sing his thoughts out loud to the tune of a familiar song. This is usually seen as ridiculous and helps to undermine the intensity of thoughts by changing the context in which they occur. Go ahead and try it with him. Be as ridiculous as possible! You can use any familiar melody that works—"Happy Birthday," "The Alphabet Song," or any other familiar and preferably trite melody would work well. The more you allow yourself to be silly and vulnerable in this exercise, the more permission your client will have to do the same, allowing him to experience defusion of a difficult thought.

Funny Voice

You can have fun encouraging your client to say his thoughts out loud and use a cartoon voice, or to imitate the voice of someone famous. As was the case with "singing," having your client change his voice will change the context in which his thoughts occur and allow for unsticking.

Milk, Milk, Milk

This is a fun way to experiment with defusing from words and then from thoughts. You can invite your client to join you in reciting "milk, milk, milk," for forty-five seconds (Titchener, 1916). The repetition is extended for that length of time because that is usually how long it takes for words to become detached from their meaning. Then you can ask your client to repeat the process, this time repeating over and over a "sticky" thought (usually a judgmental thought about the self) until it becomes separate from any meaning. You can invite your client to use this strategy whenever following a thought takes him away from his values. After asking if he is willing to try something new with you, the "Milk" exercise can be done something like this:

T: Can you close your eyes with me and say the word "milk"? As you do so, imagine milk. Tell me what comes to mind, whatever you can imagine with your five senses.

C: I am picturing a huge glass, it's cold, I actually don't like milk that much. It tastes chalky.

T: Okay. Sounds like you've got it. With eyes open (*pause*) can you repeat with me "milk, milk, milk"? We are going to say it together as fast as we can until I say "Stop." (*Repeats the word out loud for about forty-five seconds.*)

C: (*Stares at therapist, makes a funny face, and joins in repeating the word for forty-five seconds, laughing.*)

T: Now can you say "milk" again and tell me what comes to mind.

C: "Milk." It doesn't sound like it means anything anymore and I started to pronounce it in this weird way when we repeated it. The word sounds strange, not much is coming to mind when I say it.

T: Okay. Now could we try another one? Could you repeat with me, "He's trying to make me look bad," and as you say it, notice what comes up inside. (*Therapist is now bringing in one of Cody's thoughts that he is fused with to see if the repetition can have the same "deliteralizing" effect on him as it did with "milk."*)

C: (*Repeats: "He's trying to make me look bad."*) I feel that knot in my stomach that I get when I think about going to school and seeing my teacher, I want to get rid of this thought, but I can't.

T: Can you allow those thoughts and feelings and repeat it with me like we did with "milk," until I say "Stop"?

C: *(Smiles, then repeats the phrase with therapist for forty-five seconds.)*

T: Can you repeat, "He's trying to make me look bad" again now?

C: "He's trying to make me look bad."

T: What was that like?

C: The same as milk. The words started not to mean anything.

T: So, would you be willing to try that the next time you're about to walk into that science room? You can combine it with LLAMA, which we spoke about earlier. *Label* the thought, like "I'm noticing I'm having the thought that he's trying to make me look bad," then *let go* of trying to control it, just let it be. Use this experiment— repeat the thought, to just *allow* it to be there. And then ask yourself whether following the thought will take you in the direction of your values of being the kind of student who's there with everyone else and helping each other out.

C: Yeah. Okay.

By the end of the above experience, Cody has learned that he can begin to loosen his grip on thoughts, which allows him some room to move toward what matters. This may enable him to hold the thought *He's trying to make me look bad* a little more lightly and with less judgment. This was an experiential opportunity to discover that it might actually be possible to allow unpleasant internal experiences rather than make unproductive attempts to control them. It is important to work with adolescents to create a moment like this where they can actually experiment with accepting instead of controlling, but know that you will always need to be ready to revisit creative hopelessness if there is not enough willingness to try what matters.

Computer

You can suggest that your client imagine her thoughts scrolling as if across a computer screen. She can change the font to any different one, or even minimize the scrolling screen so that it is not visible in the center of the screen—but it will still be there. Have your client try it in the room with you so you can process the experience with her afterwards (Harris, 2009).

Thank Your Mind

Suggest that your client try noticing where his mind has gone, labeling it (for example, "I'm noticing I'm having the thought that…" or "I'm having a feeling of…") or simply labeling the mental process, such as "planning" or "worrying." Then ask him to *thank* his mind for being so helpful, working so hard to solve problems for him and giving him the thought (Harris, 2009). This suggestion usually brings a smile, but your client may actually remember to try it when dealing with difficult thoughts and it can be helpful. This is a great one to model, as well, by thanking your own mind for trying to solve problems for you, like what you're going to do next in your session, or how you're going to do all the things you planned to do before the session is over.

The Sky and the Weather Metaphor

You can describe your client's thoughts as a weather system that's passing through the area beneath a clear blue sky (Harris, 2009). This can be used as a metaphor and worked into the conversation in a session, or it can be done as a mindfulness visualization exercise, which is how we typically use it.

Bring your attention to your thoughts. You might notice how your thoughts come up and then seem to move out of the way, as new thoughts come in and replace them. See if you can notice as this happens. (Pause.) Now imagine that you are a clear blue sky, looking down at your thoughts as if they were clouds passing by below you. They might be clouds bringing rain or snow or sleet. There might be thunder or lightning with them. Just keep watching them, passing by below you as new clouds keep coming, bringing new weather. All these clouds, all this weather keeps passing beneath the clear blue sky that is you—the sky that's always there, still and constant, just watching the weather go by. (Pause.) Just watch as those thoughts pass under you like weather systems, arriving and leaving, knowing that you can always be there, watching those thoughts, quiet, clear, and blue like the sky above them.

This mindfulness piece also develops a sense of self-as-context, which is the focus of a later session, but here we can use it simply for defusion.

Chessboard

Another metaphor, done as a mindfulness visualization, is the "Chessboard" (Hayes, Strosahl, & Wilson, 2012), described below, which can help to develop a sense of willingness, allowing, self-as-context as well as defusion.

Imagine that your thoughts are like pieces on a chessboard. You might notice that you have some unwanted thoughts and then you might also notice thoughts that come up in opposition to the unwanted thoughts, countering them, in a fight with them. These two camps of thoughts are like opposing black and white chess pieces on the chessboard. Notice how your mind aligns first with one camp— with the black chess pieces—and then with the other, the white chess pieces, pulling you forward and backward across the board. Now imagine that you are the chessboard itself—just remaining still and watching the battle play out between the two sides, not joining with either. Just continue to watch, like the chessboard, as the thoughts play out their game.

This is an idea that appeals to many clients who are pulled from one side to the other in the battle between opposing thoughts in their minds. It gives them a welcome third option and sets up the experience of taking a neutral, defused stance. From that neutral place they can choose a direction based not on dueling thoughts but on *workability*, which is the focus of the next experience.

Workability (Pragmatic Insight)

Workability is a touchstone element in ACT (Hayes, Strosahl, & Wilson, 2012). It refers to the degree to which a proposed action is likely to move us in the direction of our values and to "work" for us, versus moving us away from values. The question you can ask to get at this is, "If you buy into this thought, how does your behavior change; what do you start or stop doing when this thought shows up? Does it work for you? Does following it take you closer to what is important to you?" Workability is the reliable truth criterion from functional contextualism upon which decisions can be made. Stress that thoughts are inevitable, but behavior is optional, and that your client can choose to follow only thoughts that take him in the direction of his values.

Turning Hands

This is a very simple little exercise (McKay, Lev, & Skeen, 2012). Ask your client to imagine allowing an unwanted thought to sit in the upturned palm of his hand. Then ask him to gently turn his hand palm down, allowing it to release and drift where it will. (This is not like a deliberate shaking off of an unwanted thought.) You can coach a gentle approach here that just *allows* the thought to be defused rather than pushed away, like the attitude taken in "Bubbles" or "Leaves on a Stream." You can ask him to predict where the thought would land—usually in his lap or on the floor nearby—bringing emphasis to the fact that, although unwanted internal events don't really leave, they may become less central. For a client who has trouble imagining or visualizing, you can use "Turning Hands" in conjunction with "Bubbles."

When "Bubbles" is introduced, you can ask your client to a let a bubble sit on his hand, then to turn over his hand to allow it to drop away. Then you can liken this to what we do with our thoughts, and refer to it afterward to evoke a sense of letting the thought go. Alternatively, you can have him write the thought on a small piece of paper, place it in the palm of his hand, and do the exercise by turning over his hand and allowing the piece of paper to fall to the floor. The thought and the experience are nicely concretized in this way.

The above are some of the many strategies that can be used for "unsticking" from thoughts. Coming back to Cody, we can try to pull it all together by using LLAMA when he identifies getting stuck in pursuing values-based goals with these "unsticking" tactics.

LLAMA Using Defusion

It's worth mentioning that the steps of LLAMA do not need to be followed in a strictly linear fashion. You may find as you work that you will need to loop back to earlier steps if emotions intensify, and sometimes jump back and forth between one step and another.

T: When you are at school and you're thinking about asking some of the others in your class to give you notes for the classes you've missed, what's going on inside? What are you experiencing?

C: I feel really embarrassed. I can't even picture looking them in the eye and saying that. The science teacher made me look like such an idiot that everyone thinks I can't do science. And it makes it worse to have to ask them to help me.

T: So you're noticing you are having the feeling of embarrassment, and the physical discomfort with making eye contact and the thought, *They think I can't do science?*

C: Yes. Exactly.

T: Okay. So when you say it the way I just did, you are Labeling. You are using the first "L" in LLAMA and labeling those things inside. Can you try that now, as if it's happening right here and now?

C: I'm noticing I'm having a feeling of embarrassment, and trouble making eye contact. And I'm having the thoughts *They think I can't do science* and *They think I'm a wimp.*

T: Great! That's Labeling. Now let's try Letting Go—that's the second "L"—to let go of the struggle to control what's inside, to get a sense of willingness to do that. Is there anything that helps you with having a sense of willingness?

C: I could use the "Struggle Switch."

T: Okay. What's that like?

C: I could just picture flipping the switch to turn off the trying. It turns off the trying to make the feelings and thoughts go away.

T: Did it help to make space for the feelings and thoughts?

C: Sort of. I feel like I can stop fighting.

T: Okay! And then the next letter in LLAMA is "A" for Allow. What could you try in order to get a sense of allowing your thoughts and feelings?

C: I can do the observing the shakiness and the trouble making eye contact, and just breathing, and allowing it to be there.

T: Okay, great. (*Pause.*) What about all that thinking going on in your head?

C: My stomach has settled, I'm not tightening up around it, but my head is still telling me stuff.

T: So what would you like to do now to unstick from those thoughts?

C: I could use a funny voice in my head. I could pretend the thoughts are like Homer Simpson said them. I could hear them like Homer's voice. Like the thought about how my teacher wants to make me look bad, I could hear that like Homer is saying it.

T: All right. What happens when you try that?

C: (*Cody tries and laughs.*) It sounds like a Simpsons thing. I don't have to take it seriously.

T: Good! You can feel free to hear Homer in your head any time you want! So, if we carry on with LLAMA, the next letter is "M" for Mindfulness. Remember this is about just being aware of what's here, right now, without judgment, and trying not to push it away. And then checking to see if you are about to follow what you are feeling and thinking, or what matters, which will it take you in the direction you really want to be going. (*Pause.*) What's happening?

C: It feels really bad, but I'm trying to allow it.

T: Instead of saying "It feels really bad," can you tell me what you are feeling, try to describe it without the judgment?

C: I can feel the shakiness coming back, and I feel a bit hot. I need to breathe and expand again. (*Give him time until he indicates he's ready to move to the next step—as mentioned, it's not unusual to go back and forth in the steps of LLAMA.*)

T: If you are feeling ready, can you picture yourself in that classroom now? Try to allow those sensations to be there, and at the same time, as you unstick from your thoughts and feelings, can you become aware of what you are doing, what's around you and what's going on in the present moment? Try to mindfully notice with your senses as much as you can about the room you are in and the people who are there. (*Pause.*)

C: Yes… I can see the teacher at the front of the room. The other students are all looking at me. I am walking in, and he actually said hi to me! Just "hi"—no mean jabs.

T: Okay, nice work! Now let's do the last "A" in LLAMA. Approach What Matters. Do you think you could imagine just being with those feelings and thoughts, remembering the value you have of wanting to be a good student who is together with other people at school, helping each other out, and see if you can picture yourself asking someone for notes?

C: I can still feel the knot and notice the thoughts, but they aren't taking all of my attention, so I can focus on everybody more. I want to ask for notes because that's being more like who I really am. Someone who cares about stuff and is together with everyone.

Bringing all of the steps together near the end of the session is helpful to give clients some clarity of how LLAMA may be used outside of session. Once the conversation is finished, it may be helpful to repeat with another scenario before ending.

Mindfulness

Before ending this session with a mindfulness meditation, you might want to expand on the meaning of mindfulness as the "M" in LLAMA. This can be confusing, since mindfulness really does overlap with each step of LLAMA—and in fact each step overlaps with each of the other steps to some degree. It helps clients to know this, and it bears repeating. In order to label internal experience (the first "L"), you have to *notice* it. That's mindfulness. And in order to stop struggling (the second "L"), it helps to be aware of the fight that's going on inside. Again, this is mindfulness. And in order to allow (the first "A"), you have to harness a sense of distance from thoughts and feelings, without judgment, which is also mindfulness. So how does the actual "M" for mindfulness differ?

We keep it simple with our clients and explain that yes, they all overlap, and yes, mindfulness is part of each step in some way, but here it is again just for clarity and simplicity. Once your client notices what is going on inside and her natural tendency to use DOTS to avoid thoughts and feelings, she can Label her inner experience, Let Go of the urge to control what's inside, Allow room for what's inside, and then, when she's ready, Mindfully shift her attention back to the present moment, to what is happening—noticing what is happening based on her five senses, and telling herself the facts of the current moment—and finally Approach What Matters. This may be a good time to revisit a definition of mindfulness, such as "paying attention, in the present moment, on purpose, and without judgment," before proceeding to a LLAMA-based meditation.

Mindfulness with LLAMA

After clarifying LLAMA and mindfulness, the mindfulness exercise that's called "Mindfulness with LLAMA" can be helpful in practicing the allowing of thoughts of any sort. We use it to demonstrate the use of LLAMA with a client who is stuck in "wishing." LLAMA helps when clients get caught up in the natural tendency to *wish for* things to be different from the unpleasant way they actually are, as discussed above under "What to Unstick From?" If you like, as a summary of the content covered in this session, you can do a review of LLAMA embedded right in the mindfulness exercise. Keeping in mind that you can substitute thoughts, feelings, and circumstances that apply to your client. The meditation might go something like this, with long pauses when necessary so that the client can work through each step:

Bring your attention to your breath and just follow your breath, in and out.
Notice if your mind is pulled away by any distractions. Just kindly and gently

detach from those and bring your focus back to your breath. (Pause.) Now, see if you can pay attention to something you sometimes find yourself wishing would be different in your life. Imagine circumstances that you wish were different, but can't be changed. Imagine the things that would seem possible for you to do if the past was different. (Pause.) Now bring your attention to the feelings and thoughts that come along with wishing. (Pause.) See if you can apply LLAMA to them, starting with the first "L." Notice what is coming up inside and Label it: "I notice I'm having thoughts of wanting to change the past" or "I'm noticing I'm having feelings of…" or "I'm noticing I'm having a sensation of a knot in my stomach." Now, for the second "L," see if you can just hit the "Pause Button" or pull the "Struggle Switch" and Let Go of trying to control those feelings and thoughts. (Pause.) They're not going anywhere. They're here for now. Like the "Gnats" or the "Wrinkled Sock," see if you can be willing to have your thoughts and feelings, let them be there. Next, for the first "A," try to Allow your thoughts and feelings to be present, looking at them, and making space for them. Knowing it's just your mind doing its job, looking at the thoughts like you looked at what was on your acetate, like looking at bubbles as they float around. As best you can, look at your thoughts from a distance, noticing their color, font, location. Are they moving, and if so, how? Just notice them from a distance. If you notice feelings, see if you can notice every detail about them. Where do you notice your feelings in your body? What do the feelings feel like? Do they have a color? A shape? Try to breathe in and out from your feelings, and expand around them, make some space for them. Place your hand gently on your feelings if that helps, and breathe into and out from where your hand is, resting it gently on your body as you unclench and allow some space for your feelings. (Pause.) If your feelings have found some space and come to rest, the next step is the "M"—to return Mindfully to the present moment. If you were in a classroom, for example, this would mean bringing your attention, with your five senses, back to the classroom, or the teacher, or your fellow students, wherever you need your focus to be, and telling yourself the facts of the moment. Because we are doing an eyes-closed mindfulness, we will return our focus to the present moment by noticing sounds in the room, and what it feels like to be in our chairs. In a few moments we can open our eyes and take in what we see in the room, including each other, and then we can do the last "A"—Approach What Matters by being who we want to be in this session, in this moment.

This mindfulness exercise leads naturally into a discussion of what your client is going to do in the upcoming week.

Assignment of Home Practice

At the end of this session, ask your client to identify a step she might take in the direction of her values. As in the mindfulness exercise, help her focus on a step small enough that she feels confident she could allow the unwanted thoughts and feelings that will come up when she attempts it. We also ask for continued practice of mindfulness, whether formally, using the audio supplied, or through informal mindful activities—doing a daily activity with mindful attention, such as walking, brushing teeth, loading the dishwasher, or putting away books in a backpack.

Modifications for Group Work

Much of this session can be done in groups just as it is outlined for individual clients. However, there are some changes, which are outlined below.

Mindfulness

It is not uncommon in a room of adolescents blowing bubbles for the comparing mind to flare up. You may notice some of your group members sitting back, not doing much, while others may be fixated, staring at their peers, and still others may make comments such as "I can't do this very well," suggesting that their mind is stuck in comparing. This is a good opportunity to ask if this is happening for anyone, and to normalize the experience of comparing. It connects back nicely to the "Bear and Blueberry Bush" and "Survivor" metaphors.

Review of Home Practice

If not already done, it may be useful at this point to help group members identify long-term goals either as a group or in pairs, ensuring that the goals, and each step that leads to the goals, are SMART and values based.

LLAMA and Defusion

There may be group members who just can't deal with the idea of allowing thoughts. This will require a return to creative hopelessness. Peers may be in the best position to challenge each other with the hopelessness of trying to get rid of unwanted thoughts and feelings. Clinician mindfulness is warranted here, so you can notice and allow this group process to happen. You don't need to be pulled into the debate.

What to Unstick From?

This piece can be very meaningful when working with groups, as interpersonal "rules" arise and "in the moment" reflections from facilitators can bring the rules to the surface if they are being enacted. Common rules and behaviors that have arisen in our groups include thoughts like, "I have to be empathetic all the time so people will like me," which can result in a group member who comments after everything others say, or who excessively shares her own experiences as a way to demonstrate empathy. Either behavior is likely to have the opposite result to that desired, with peers feeling invalidated and annoyed.

Defusion Exercises: How to Unstick

These can be done as a group, with thoughts that are common to the majority of group members being used as the basis for "Singing," "Funny Voices," and the "Milk" exercise. Depending on the progress of group members, be mindful to choose a thought that they are willing to have to some degree, otherwise they will simply DOT their way through the exercises when too much inner experience is evoked. For example, "She does not like me," may be less evocative than "I am not good enough" or "I am worthless," the latter two of which may result in dissociation, distraction, and other DOTS, as opposed to a felt, internal experience of defusion.

Conclusion

By the end of this session, our hope is that your client has a sense of how LLAMA works from beginning to end and can identify and practice ways to use each of the steps in the acronym as she moves in the direction of her values. The content of past sessions may need to be repeated, as her steps will likely evoke unwanted thoughts and feelings, just like in the past.

Staying on the left side of the hexaflex, the next session works with content similar to this one, but instead of defusing from thoughts, we engage our client in defusion from self-as-content, from the "story" she has of her "self."

Session 7

Defusing from "Story"

We use the word "story" to stand for the collection of thoughts that a client has about her "self." At times, emphasizing "story" can make us feel that we are caught up in this story along with her, perhaps even using it to avoid forward momentum. At other times, it will be important to give our adolescent client a safe, compassionate relationship in which to share her story and her sadness, anxiety, shame, self-doubt, and other feelings that are connected to the story. Once we have a genuine sense of our client's story, we can help her to defuse not only from individual thoughts, but from her story, from her self-as-content.

Focus of Session

In this session we extend the process of defusing or "unsticking" so that you can help your client identify and defuse from her whole "story." To be a little clearer, what we mean by "story" here is a client's fused version of who she is, what she can expect from others, and what the world has in store for her. In essence, it is the dense web of thoughts connected through relational frames that, outside of her awareness, have been influencing your client's behavior all her life. Your client's story is essentially about the ACT process known as self-as-content. This is likely a confusing mix of ideas about who she is and about her identity. Some of these ideas may be bestowed upon her by others, some she may have gleaned from her experiences, many will be rules, and some may represent her values. In this session, you want to help your client find the words for her story, as you lend a compassionate, understanding, and kind ear while being fully present with what is likely a shameful part of her self. Once she feels heard, you can help her to accept, defuse, and unstick from her story, allowing her an opportunity to choose her values to guide behavior instead of being guided by her story.

Fictional Client: Maya

Our fictional client for this session is Maya, a thirteen-year-old girl with a brief history of restricted eating. Maya lives with her parents and younger brother. She describes herself as a "people pleaser" and as such, tends to spend much of her time doing things for others. She struggles to say "no" and feels helpless to change or speak up for herself. Maya often begins sessions by stating, "I feel fat," and wants to talk about her sense of self-hatred, which she relates to her perception of her body shape and weight. She spends a great deal of time doing things for others in order to "make them happy." As a result, Maya feels exhausted and resentful and she is losing her sense of who she is and what she wants.

Defusing from Story with Individual Clients

From what you know of your client so far, you may have an idea of her story by now. It will be important that you let her put the pieces together and discover the bigger picture for herself. Try to let her do the mental and emotional work of recognizing her own story. Coming face to face with one's story can be very traumatic. Awareness of your own discomfort as the clinician will be essential, so that you can allow whatever emotions your client's story brings with it. Before proceeding with new content, engage your client in a review of past content and home practice.

What Stuck

A review of the last session will focus on LLAMA, to be sure that your client knows the LLAMA sequence, remembers what each step involves, and has a sense of willingness and defusion. Before moving into new territory with this session, it may be a good idea to check in with your client and make sure she understands concepts from earlier sessions, such as DOTS and defusion. As you move ahead, be on the lookout for a return to experiential avoidance, and a need to revisit creative hopelessness.

Review of Home Practice

At the end of session 6, clients were asked to practice mindfulness and to continue moving toward values-based goals, using LLAMA. Although this was not part of the home practice, feel free to check in with your client about her use of DOTS over the past week, just in case her creative hopelessness needs a boost. As for mindfulness, some adolescents are very hesitant to practice, and a patient and curious discussion will often reveal rules and judgments that are getting in their way. You may want to take this opportunity to have your client engage in a mindful activity in session while trying some of the defusion strategies from last session, to enhance her "in session" mindfulness practice. This may help her be more able to practice in the coming weeks.

Clients were also asked to take a step consistent with their values, using LLAMA to move forward. Debriefing how your client was unsuccessful and looking at what might have gotten in her way is as important as debriefing any success she may have had with a goal. Sometimes clients succeed with their values-based goal, but when reflecting on it they tell us that they did so by distracting or using some other DOT. Clients are often not initially successful, and what can emerge in reviewing this failure is that the step they were trying to take would have evoked an intensity of thoughts or emotions that they simply were not willing to have. If this happens for your client, it is reasonable to suggest that she back up and make the step smaller in some way, so that the level of distress is something she is willing to have. Help her identify a step that evokes only what she is willing to have inside.

Next, we move into an active mindfulness of walking.

Mindful Walking

We typically do "Mindful Walking" at the beginning and end of this session, adding in the "story" for the version at the end of the session. This can be tricky if you have a small office, and you may find you need to walk in small circles and very slowly. A sample of this meditation goes something like this:

For this meditation, we are going to pay attention, on purpose, to the sensations involved in walking. We will walk around my office, very slowly, and try to pay attention to what that feels like. (Begin.) If you notice thoughts coming across your awareness, label them, let go of the struggle to control them, and try to just allow them some space to be here, now, as you walk in this moment. You may want to try treating thoughts like you did with the acetate, or let them float around the room like the ones in the bubbles, or simply let them be there as you watch them, as if you are the sky and they are the weather. When you are ready, gently detach from your thoughts and put your attention back to the present moment, back to the experience of walking. Notice the sensations as your heel first touches down on the floor, and then as the rest of your foot rolls through and makes contact with the floor. (Pause.) Notice the sensations in your legs as you walk, any sensations in your hips or your back. Again, notice, label, and let go of trying to control the stuff inside that comes up, and gently bring your focus back to walking and what that experience is like for you in this moment. (Pause.) You might notice thoughts such as rules, reason giving, or judgments.

Try to notice them, and detach, bringing your attention gently back to the experience of walking. Try to put your attention on that moment when one foot is on the floor, waiting for the other foot to land. Notice what your balance is like; notice how this feels. Continue walking for a few more moments, noticing and letting go of thoughts and judgments, and feeling yourself walk.

Spend a few minutes debriefing her experience with mindful walking before you move into the next section, which begins with some user-friendly relational framing.

Everything Connects to Everything

Before getting into "story" too much, a simple, brief explanation of RFT (relational frame theory) and how "everything connects to everything" can be helpful. By the way, we never refer to RFT as RFT with clients. It scares most people. What we do say, however, is that we want to engage our client in some exercises designed to show her an idea about how the mind works, which may help her to understand why thoughts are so impossible to get rid of and why they seem to multiply. In order to make the point that everything connects to everything, and to help her identify her own personal story, we engage our client in a brief discussion of the mind and how it is both adaptive when faced with new problems, and not so helpful when we feel emotions about an event, especially when we feel emotions about an event that is not actually happening in the present moment. This latter bit is really "transformation of stimulus functions" from RFT. We follow this discussion with the "Word Link," then the "Toothbrush" problem, and finally the client's own "Word Web," or "story," as described below.

Our Helpful, Problem-Solving Mind

You can offer your clients a small glimpse of how their minds work, according to relational frame theory. Begin by asking your client if she has ever felt emotions or noticed physical sensations related to an experience that was not actually happening in the moment. Perhaps thinking about her favorite concert or vacation might elicit feelings of excitement as she tells you about the memory. You can switch gears and ask her about an exam in her least favorite subject. (She may look nauseated at the mere mention of this.) You can ask her to speculate about experiencing her feelings when the trigger for the feelings isn't there. How could that be adaptive? And how could it sometimes be problematic?

If your client doesn't think of it, you can suggest that words spoken or written can "equal" the actual object, or the image of the object in our mind, and that this would be very adaptive if someone yells "Fire!" when there is a fire. Your client will get that the fire would not need to be visible right in front of her before she reacts; reacting sooner may save her life. You can scaffold this idea by asking, "If there was a fire in this building and someone yelled 'Fire!' would you want to wait until the flames were in front of you before you did something, or would you act sooner?" So far, our clients have been unanimous in favor of acting sooner. If you want to have fun with this and really make the point, you can ask a second question: "If you were swimming and someone yelled 'Shark!' would you wait to find yourself swimming side by side with the shark and then figure out if it's hungry or not?" Again, the answer is usually the same: "I'd swim away without having to see the shark."

You can then ask your client how it is that she would know to take action before the danger was right in front of her. Many react with confusion to this initial question, so we prompt by asking, "What popped into your brain with the fire and shark examples?" Most tell us, "A picture of a shark or a fire." These examples make the point nicely that the human mind can create images or pictures of events, and we react to them with emotions that are the same as the actual event (though perhaps less intense), which in situations such as these can save our life.

Our Not-So-Helpful Mind

To examine how this tendency of our minds may be not so helpful, you can now ask, "How is it a problem that we may react to something we can't even see?" If your client doesn't have a quick reply, you can suggest something like the following: "I am going to say a word. When I do, try to notice what comes up for you, what thoughts, emotions, physical feelings arise." Then say something that is likely to be evocative for your client, something like "exams" or another word you know to be framed in coordination with something your client finds aversive. She is likely to notice internal events in relation to the word. Then you can ask how this is a problem. You want to move her toward awareness that unwanted inner experience could arise in response to a word, or to imagining an event, without the event actually happening in the present moment. You can then tie this awareness to the concept of avoidance, and to using DOTS (preferably ones your client habitually uses), and the short-term and long-term impact of using DOTS on her quality of life. Remind your client that her mind is just doing its job, keeping her safe, but in a way that is not so helpful when it has her reacting to events that are not there and she is in no real danger. You can normalize for her how, because of this very human process of the mind, we can all end up reacting to future-based worries with avoidance, and past woes with sadness, without really being in the present moment.

If you have gotten your client this far, you can move to a brief, simple, RFT-type of explanation. We do this on a flip chart. We don't use the term "RFT" but we do use RFT frames, demonstrated in triangle format, to show how complex connections are made. We use the written word "needle" paired with a picture of a hypodermic needle, paired with the written words "anxiety + pain" in a triangle format. You can use this to show how, when we just hear the word "needle," we may feel the way we feel in response to the actual object. You can also then demonstrate how things join up because they are the "same" or "opposite" or "better than," and so on, forming elements to our inevitable "story." Then, bring up the idea of how we try to manage anxiety about something, such as the needle. Perhaps your client has been told to "relax" when getting a vaccination shot with a needle. Whatever image conjures up relaxation for her, like perhaps a beautiful beach, can now be drawn, connecting to the needle "frame." This makes the point rather well that, in our minds, everything connects to everything, even though we may have no idea how some of our connections got made and this is often not a conscious or intentional process.

Word Link

This is an experiential exercise that gets at the processes operating in relational framing and allows clients an opportunity to see what their minds are doing (Törneke, 2010). Ask your client to give you a noun—any single word for a person, place, or thing. Write it on a whiteboard, flip chart, or page. Then ask for a second noun and write it below the first. Then ask the following three questions:

1. In what way is the first thing similar to the second?

2. In what way is the first thing better than the second?

3. In what way is the first thing the parent of the second?

Your client will almost certainly come up with an answer to all three questions, sometimes surprisingly quickly. You can congratulate him for his problem-solving skill, and then use this as a demonstration of how our minds work to link things in order to solve problems. For those who are interested, you can explain it in a bit more detail, such as, "Your mind has a box of everything it knows about each noun, what each is made out of, what it's used for, what it's similar to and different from. It automatically looks for places where the boxes connect, where things overlap. When you ask how the first noun is a parent of the second, your mind has to open its box about parenting, and what that means, and then find the overlap between parenting and the qualities of the nouns. Voilà! Problem solved."

Lighter, Toothbrush, and Screw

This exercise helps to make the point that our minds can connect everything to everything a bit more clearly. The more our clients see the inner workings of their mind as normal, the less intense is the desire to avoid those contents. For this exercise, we write each word, "lighter," "toothbrush," and "screw" on a piece of paper or a flip chart page, leaving some space between the words. Next, ask your client, "How can I use a lighter and a toothbrush to screw a screw into the wall?" (For kids who are not familiar with hardware, you may need to let them know that a screw has grooves in the head that make a shape.) To solve this problem, your client needs to think of the qualities and functions of each item, what it is made of, and what it can do. He will eventually realize that toothbrushes are made of plastic, and plastic melts. He will also come to realize that lighters give off heat, which melts things. This is the link—lighter melting and toothbrush being melted—that would allow someone to mold the toothbrush handle to the head of the screw and use it as a screwdriver. Most often, clients look perplexed after we present this problem to them and are not convinced they can solve it. To get things going, we ask our client for words that describe properties and functions of each of the three items. We put a circle around each of the three words, and as each word (describing a property or function) is offered by the client, we extend a single line from the circle of the relevant item, then write the new word, and circle it at the end of the line. We also write the "frame of coordination" along the line, such as "is made of" if "plastic" arises for toothbrush. This allows for a visual representation of the properties and functions of each item, and eventually of how a property or function of one item intersects with a property or function of another to offer a solution to the problem. This visual representation can be used later to demonstrate the fabulous human capacity for problem solving. ("So, you figured out that because the head of the screw has grooves, and because plastic melts, you can mold the melted plastic toothbrush into the head of the screw and use it to turn the screw! That's amazing that you have that ability!")

The Word Web

Like "The Acetate," the "Word Web" is central to our way of working with adolescent clients and the "story" of who they are. It begins as a simple pen-and-paper exercise, but it can yield lots of information and insights and can be brought out and revisited in subsequent sessions. Give your client a piece of paper and a pen or pencil. Ask her to write her most frequently experienced problematic thought in the center of the page and then draw a circle around it. Sometimes your client will know right away what this thought is; other times, it may take some inquiry to get there. More often than not, the core thought that clients are fused with is a version of "I am not good enough." Many times your inquiry will lead you down a path of judgments and rules and you will have to decide where to focus with your client. This transcript from a session with Maya illustrates this nicely:

M (*Maya*):   I feel fat.

T (*Therapist*): It seems like feeling "fat" has come up for you several times before, when you were overwhelmed and had too much to do.

M: Oh, has it?

T: Well, you did mention it over the past few sessions when you were talking about saying yes to things other people were asking you to do, like helping your brother with homework and your mom to paint the living room.

M: Oh, yeah, I guess so.

T: So, if this is a pattern, is it possible that you are overwhelmed today?

M: Yeah, my friend's boyfriend broke up with her, and I have exams starting, and she wants me to be with her all the time, and my parents got in a big fight last night so I feel like I have to be extra nice to them and do even more.

T: How do you feel about having to help your friend and be extra nice to your parents?

M: I'm kinda upset.

T: How does your body feel as we talk about this?

M: My stomach feels really bloated and I feel full.

T: Hmm. So it seems like when you feel fat, like today, your stomach is feeling bloated and full, it's also a time when you are feeling kinda upset and you have said yes to too many things.

M: Exactly.

T: So, I am wondering, since there seems to be some kind of connection between "I feel fat" and you being upset, what that means to you?

M: (*Pause.*) They both feel the same in my stomach. So maybe when I feel fat it's like I'm full of upset, kinda like when I eat too much. (*Notice the derived relations and transformation of stimulus functions through a frame of equivalence between physical sensations of satiety and sensations associated with keeping emotions inside.*)

T: So, when you have too much on your plate, you feel full!

M:	Yup, but I can't do anything about it.
T:	You can't say no?
M:	No way, I have to keep everyone happy.
T:	What will happen if you don't keep everyone happy?
M:	They won't want to be around me. (*Rule.*)
T:	That was a quick response.
M:	I know it doesn't make sense, but that's how I feel.
T:	So your mind gives you a rule, that if you don't keep people happy, they won't want to be around you.
M:	Yeah, it tells me that all the time.
T:	Other than keeping people happy, is there any other reason to hang out with you, another reason to like you?
M:	No, there isn't, there's nothing special about me.
T:	So keeping others happy is the only thing good about you?
M:	Yup, that's it.
T:	That can't leave you feeling very good about yourself?
M:	No, it doesn't. (*Hanging her head down.*)

For clients with anxiety or depression, for example, you may be able to guide them in defusing from what they give you, at face value, such as "I am stupid" or "Something bad is going to happen." For clients with an eating disorder who describe feeling "fat," for example, it may be the case that "nuances of affect, identity, and physicality had been collapsed into one attribute" (Halsted, 2015, p. 79). In such cases, you may want to unpack "I feel fat" a bit more, as you saw in the transcript above, so that you can help your client defuse from the thoughts and feelings that are at the root of the struggle.

It is not uncommon that a client will identify a deeply rooted belief, what we clinicians might know as a "core belief." We may be tempted to try to dispute it. This could be for a few different reasons. One may be that we have a very different perception of our client from the client's self-perception. Another may be that we have our own need to avoid pain and suffering, both our client's and our own. This moment can be a painful and deeply felt emotional one with your client. The therapeutic impact rests, at least in part, on the clinician's willingness to stay with the emotions: to not dispute, not change the topic, not reassure, but just be there with the client, in this painful moment.

For Maya, as outlined in her transcript, the thought *There's nothing special about me* may go in the center of the page, with domains of friendship, family, and school somewhere on the page, and feelings such as anxious, helpless, and resentment also on the page.

We learned over time that shame was felt by most of the adolescents with whom we were working, but none ever mentioned the word. Many had not consciously identified it or were afraid of being flooded with emotions (transformation of stimulus function) if they acknowledged it out loud. If shame does arise, it can be added to the "Word Web." If the transcript above with Maya were to continue, it might go like this:

T: How are you feeling now, as we talk about you not feeling good about yourself?

M: I just feel so embarrassed to be me, it's humiliating.

T: I noticed you are not looking at me anymore and are hanging your head down, and I wonder if you are feeling a sense of shame about who you are?

M: (*Squirming in her chair.*) Yeah, I do (*very small voice*). I just feel like I want to run right out of this room right now.

Once your client has identified a core problematic thought that is the one often leading her away from what matters, and has written that thought in a circle in the center of the page, ask what other thoughts or feelings are associated with that thought. Ask her to place those associated thoughts and feelings in circles adjacent to the original thought and to join the new circles by lines drawn to the original circle. Ask your client to keep noticing what other thoughts, feelings, and so on are evoked with each of the new, circled items, and to join those with lines to more new items as more content arises. Eventually your client will wind up with a page full of adjoining circles. Once this is done, you can ask your client to look at whether there may be connections between any items on the page that are not already joined by lines, and to go ahead and join these with more lines. This is likely to create a page that is dense and crisscrossed with lines joining circles all over it.

Your client may want to give a name to her "story." This will support defusion and give you both some shared way to refer to it. It might be called the "I have to keep them happy" story, or the "No one likes me" story, or whatever summarizes the content of your client's story. You can stress to her that it is called a "story" because there are so many thoughts they could likely fill a book, so she might want to name that book. It can be helpful to let your client know that you aren't referring to her thoughts as a story because you think they are fictional or false, because many adolescents have been told to "stop telling stories," so we suggest checking in on this. It is helpful here to normalize "stories" as something we all have.

When you begin the "Word Web," if you find that your client has difficulty getting started and can't identify the contents of her mind, you can write an affective word that has come up in a previous discussion, such as "shame," "sad," or "angry," as a "starter word" in the center of the page to lead off, or even write one affective word in each of the four corners of the page and let the client work inward from these. Another way to "prime" the story is to insert words that describe areas of life as "starter words." We have sometimes used the names of "domains" from the Valued Living Questionnaire (Wilson et al., 2010), taking into consideration which domains are relevant to our client. To evoke these, we write one term—"school," "friends," "family," and "job" or "health"—in each of the four corners of the page and let the client work inward from these. When we have clients for whom a part-time job is important (working at one or finding one), it has sometimes been useful to include this. If you think your client needs more prompting, you can put an affective word in the center and a domain name in each of the four corners of the page and let your client work inward and outward. When the "Word Web" is done, you can let your client look it over and ask what she notices and what she thinks about it. Using lots of compassion, stress that, although this is a very personal "Word Web," and everyone's is different, this is a very normal picture of the kinds of things that go on in our minds all the time.

Once the "story" is written, spend some time with your client helping her see the links or relational frames that connect the words on the page. This is where the idea of how everything connects to everything can be woven back in. You can remind your client that connections get made in our minds between things in several ways. These include the comparison (better or worse) of one thing with another, the timing of one thing relative to another, the cause and effect of one thing on another, and being the same as or opposite to something. Clients who suffer from depressed mood, for example, are often surprised to notice that they have both sadness and happiness in their "Word Web," joined perhaps by a frame of opposition, which explains why being happy brings with it a reminder that we may become sad, and takes away happiness in that moment as we become fused with the idea of becoming sad. Over time and with repetition, these connections form a "story of my life" that starts to seem real, but is only a web of connected thoughts. And the thoughts, just like when we yell, "Fire," evoke feelings even in the absence of an event. So thinking about our "story" will make us feel a certain way, and if we get stuck to those thoughts and feelings, we will behave a certain way, likely in a mindless way, without awareness. Once your client has come to see that thoughts are just thoughts, not necessarily anything more, you can extend that idea further to point out that, similarly, our "story" is just a story that we tell ourselves about our lives. This "story" may be true in some circumstances and not in others, so the issue of truth really is not helpful. What might be more helpful is for your client to notice when her story is active, step back from it, use LLAMA, and set her course based on values.

During this discussion, you can decide if you want to share a "story" of your own or an element of it, in order to reinforce the normalcy of "stories." But if you do so, do it in a way that maintains boundaries and does not overburden your client.

Mindfulness

At this point in the session your client has shared her most strongly felt, deeply rooted thoughts with you, and this likely evokes some sense of shame and failure. Compassion and patience is needed more than anything at this moment. When your client is ready to go ahead with mindfulness, we engage once again in mindful walking, but this time holding on to the "story," gently in our hands. If you have a Word Web "story" of your own, carry it with you. If not, we suggest that you create a brief version that you are comfortable with your client seeing, and use that to engage in the mindful walking along with your client. Introduce your client to the idea that you are going to experience more mindful walking, with a twist, perhaps like this:

> Before we start to walk, I wonder if you would be willing to take the "story" you just wrote and carry it lightly and gently with you, as we walk; and I will do the same with mine. (Once client agrees, continue.) As we did before, we will walk slowly, trying to pay attention to the sensations involved in walking. If you notice that you have hooked into your story, label that this has happened, let go of the struggle to control your story; allow thoughts and feelings to just be here with you, allow them to settle, and as you gently let go of your attention on "story," bring your focus back to walking and how that feels. (Pause.) Continuing to walk, notice sensations and physical feelings as you walk slowly around the room. If your story catches your attention again, try to treat it as you did the thoughts on your acetate, or the gnats in the summer; just let them be there, and gently shift your focus to the experience of walking.

Allow some time to debrief this experience, being curious to know what defusion strategies your client found helpful and what it was like for her, inside, to participate in this experience. This will allow you to find out if DOTS were at play, which they sometimes are. This mindfulness exercise can be repeated as often as you think helpful. Please consider repetition with this or any exercise in which DOTS leaked in during previous attempts.

Informal Mindfulness

Now that your client is familiar with the concept of the "Word Web" and how everything connects to everything, you can have a bit of fun in demonstrating this again before you end the session. To practice noticing what comes up, ask your client if she is willing to "free associate" and say what word comes to her mind immediately after you say a word. Begin by saying a word, any word, and then allow her to share whatever word comes up in response. Respond spontaneously to the word your client offers with another word of your own, and let your client respond in turn to that word. Continue for as many turns as you like. It can be fun to compare what word you started with and what word you end with, to illustrate how many ways everything connects to everything. To add to the experience, ask her if she noticed any judgments or feelings coming up for her during the exercise. You can engage your client in a second round if she wasn't sure, trying to notice this "extra" layer and pausing to use LLAMA when it happens.

Assignment of Home Practice

As the session draws to a close, ask your client to identify a values-based goal that can be accomplished in the following week, one for which she is willing to accept unwanted thoughts and feelings in the service of moving toward her values and what matters. Don't forget to make sure that it's a SMART goal. In addition, this is a good time to keep her thinking about broader, more long term goals, if that is appropriate for both of you. Perhaps her weekly goal is part of a longer-term goal.

In addition to values-based goals, remind your client of the importance of continuing mindfulness practice, or "noticing," in her daily life. You may also want to suggest that she practice taking her "story" with her in some way: perhaps she can think of a way to experience having her story with her while doing something else during the week, something that matters, using LLAMA to let go of her story.

Modifications for Group

While most of the content for this session with an individual client is easily adjusted for work with groups, there are elements of the "story" that are especially powerful in a group context. We describe below the group "story" and an additional element for groups, referred to as "Yarn."

Mindfulness

We typically do mindful walking with groups of adolescents by asking group members to push their chairs under the table in the center of the room and creating as large a circular space as we can around the tables. We ask the group members to spread out and to look down as they are walking, to make sure they don't tread on each other's heels—or ours. The meditation goes similarly to the one in the section on individual work, except that we add this instruction to group members:

> Be aware of any judgments coming up about you, or others in the group. Notice if your mind is caught in comparing, or rules about how you have to be with others, and after you notice, label these as "comparing" or "judgments." Let go of the urge to control your thoughts, and work with allowing whatever comes up for you.

Word Link

Let the entire group get involved in this. They usually have fun with it and don't easily forget the message contained within the experience.

The Thing About You

Now that group members are more comfortable with each other, we engage them in experiences that we hope will intensify group cohesion, safety, and a sense of willingness to be vulnerable with each other. In this exercise, "The Thing About You" (which we borrowed from Kelly Wilson), we ask each group member to write down on a piece of paper that "thing" about them they don't want others to know. We clarify that we do not want them to write down something they did (such as stealing or bullying another person) but rather a quality or judgment about themselves that they try to keep hidden. Once they have written down their "thing," we ask them to fold the paper up and hand it to a facilitator. Group facilitators also write down the thing they try to hide about themselves, and include their pieces of paper with those of the group members. We let group members know at the start that one or both of the facilitators will read each of their responses silently, and we assure them that the facilitators will not know who has written which particular response. Without knowing which client submitted which statement, a facilitator will let group members know of the themes that have emerged from all of the statements. In setting up the exercise this way, we make room for clients to be as honest and forthcoming as they can be.

Once everyone has handed in their pieces of paper, the facilitator scans them briefly and summarizes what was written on each of the pieces of paper in one statement, if possible, that characterizes all of them. So far, having run groups for many years, we can report that the "thing about me" statements written by clients have all boiled down to some form of "I'm not good enough." We share this with the group and ask if that seems to "fit" with what each person wrote down. Individual group members may have written a variation on the theme, such as "I'm unlovable," "I'm not smart enough," "I'm not talented enough," or "I'm not pretty enough."

The universality, now obvious, of this sense of being "not good enough" is often met with surprised looks around the room. Adolescents look at each other with a sense of: "But I like you and think you are pretty cool, how can you think that about yourself?" As facilitators, we are watchful for the tendency among ourselves to try to reassure group members that they are not inferior, or to dispute the felt sense of inferiority and shame that each member has acknowledged publicly. It does not take much discussion to help individual adolescents realize that reassuring and disputing won't help others, because it hasn't helped them. The idea of being so intrinsically flawed seems to be deeply rooted and not subject to logic or evidence to the contrary, and they "get" this.

After some time is spent processing the experience, you can move on to group "story." But don't rush. Many groups have spent quite a few moments engaged in what we can best describe as "speechless, silent compassion." We would encourage clinicians to just "be" with this. Afterward, you can try to help group members connect any unwanted belief, like the "thing about me" they have just written, to the matrix, identifying it as a lower left entity, and tracing how it leads to the use of DOTS in the upper left and takes away from values and values-based behavior. The fact that this sense of themselves based on "story" is so strong and so impervious to dispute strengthens the imperative that "not good enough" needs to be defused if clients are to move in a valued direction.

Group "Story"

Having created a safe and compassionate space for group members to share their innermost thoughts and feelings, you are ready to move to group "story." Creating the group "story" touches on each of the six ACT processes and really sends home the point that your group members likely already know: that disputing every thought that arises is futile and time consuming, and only seems to make their collection of thoughts "bigger." Because there is already some vulnerability and compassion in the room, this experience is timely and adds to the emotional tone that has been growing. You can frame this to clients as an experience to help them see what is connecting to what, and why unsticking is a valuable skill. Through the group "story," group members begin to have a better sense of what they are unsticking from, and this allows you to talk to them in future sessions about "getting stuck in story," as opposed to identifying individual thoughts. Let's face it, thoughts grow exponentially and they all have the potential to get in the way of valued living, so lumping them together in a volume, as a "story," can also make the work more effective.

So now that you have introduced the idea, here's how we do the group "story." We have the tables in the group room pushed together in the center of the room so they form a huge rectangle. We then rip off pieces of flip chart paper and arrange them over the tables so they are touching, taping together the points where they join, and taping each page to the table for stability. This creates an enormous writing surface in the middle of the room. Before your clients start to write on the paper, you as the facilitator can begin by placing some words on each of the pages. We suggest "Not good enough," in the center somewhere, and off in each corner, an emotion word such as "anxious," "happy," "angry," and "shame"; don't get too caught up about which emotions to write down, group members will add more. You may also want to write down some "domains," such as the words "friends" or "family," whatever is evocative for your clients. We provide felt markers and ask everyone to take one, offering lots of color choices, and take some ourselves. Then we ask group members to go around and write down whatever comes to mind as they look at the words we have put on the paper. You can suggest that they think of qualities, functions, or descriptions of the words already on the paper, physical feelings that come up as they see a word (transformation of stimulus function), things that are the same, or opposite (yes, they are relationally framing and deriving), better or worse, cause and effect, or now and then, just to name a few. As new words are added, ask group members to draw a line connecting the new word to the one that was already there. As clients start to write things down, encourage them to move around the table so they each have an opportunity to associate to the various words.

This process can sometimes have a slow beginning, but more often we find that group members dive into the project and cover the "page" quickly and thoroughly. When the pace of creative activity begins to slow down, and the page is filling up, we ask them to stand back, walk around the table reading all the contributions, and to draw lines between any inscriptions where they can see a connection that has not yet been linked with a line. You will know that the group "story" has been all done when the page is completely covered with crisscrossed lines. At this point we ask group members to stand back again and read what is there.

Encourage group members to comment on the process and any feelings and insights it may have generated. This can be an important moment for peer bonding, because group members are usually surprised at how closely the inscriptions written by others reflect their own thoughts and feelings. They will often say, "I could have written that," or "That sounds like me," or "That looks like how I feel."

Participating in the creation of the group "story" requires group members to take a pretty big risk. Writing the words and phrases to create the group story on paper can make them feel quite exposed and this can sometimes be intimidating. It can open them to feeling vulnerable if the group has not yet achieved, or at this moment is not quite maintaining, a level of emotional intimacy. When you have a group of adolescents who are still a little hesitant to open up and share, you can try the "Yarn" exercise outlined below.

Yarn

This exercise can be used at the beginning of the session, serving both as an excellent icebreaker and a warm-up to this session's content and process before you begin the "group story," as well as an alternative or additional way to engage group members in "story."

Icebreaker. To use the "Yarn" exercise as an icebreaker (a less evocative version), you can have one group member make a nonsense sound (a bleep, an animal sound, or virtually anything) and, while holding the end of the yarn, throw the remaining ball of yarn to another member. The next group member has to repeat the first sound and add a second one, which requires some mindful attention to the present moment. This continues with the list of sounds getting progressively longer. After each new sound is added, the group member making the sound holds on to the length of yarn, while throwing the ball of remaining yarn to the next participant, creating an eventual "spider web" of yarn joining all the group members together. If remembering all the previous sounds is too challenging for the group, you can ask participants just to repeat the previous two sounds. You could invent any number of alternative versions, such as group members each saying the name of an object, saying a color, saying a number, and so on, but we found that silly nonsense sounds encouraged a childlike playfulness and spontaneity that led to a nice sense of mutual acceptance and emotional safety in advance of doing the "group story."

Yarn After Group Story. We have also used the "Yarn" exercise later in a session following the creation of the group story, on paper, and prior to creating individual stories. When the "Yarn" exercise is done after the story, it can be used to provide another visual and experiential version of the story that has just been drawn out on paper, to heighten the idea that everything connects to everything. In this version, in an already pretty safe group, you can ask participants to volunteer a story element (like one of their previously written inscriptions) at each yarn toss and to repeat each

203

other's contributions. This underscores the universality of the elements of internal content they are noticing and the weblike nature of thinking. And a bonus: this playful context can have a defusing effect.

What Is My "Story"?

Once the group story has been processed, we ask each group member to sit separately and create a story on paper that is unique to him and that expresses his personal life history and experience of self. The process of doing first a group story and then a personal one "primes the pump" for the individual story and helps group members who have more difficulty identifying and accessing internal affective and cognitive events begin to notice their own. The normalizing of these events in the process of doing and reflecting on the group story can also somewhat detoxify previously unapproachable internal content.

Informal Mindfulness

For an informal mindfulness practice in this session, another adaptation of the "Yarn" exercise is good both for experiencing and for reinforcing defusion. This version adds another context where you can make the point that everything connects to everything and that we all get tangled in our thoughts. If you have a situation where you have group members who are already opening up and sharing easily with each other at the beginning of this session, before you get into the group "story," you can save this exercise to do at the end of the session, to reinforce what was learned.

For this group exercise, you will need a ball of yarn or string of some sort, and group members need to be standing up in a circle. Begin by holding one end of the yarn and saying a word. Any word will do, you can suggest one that links to what group members struggle with, such as school or friendships or a particular emotion, or leave it entirely up to the group to start. Next, after saying your word, throw the ball of yarn to another group member, but keep holding the end of it. The group member who catches the yarn says whatever comes to mind and then throws the yarn to someone else, while still holding on to the length of yarn. Allow this to continue for some time, with each group member having several turns, until the yarn has formed a big web, joining all the group members together.

Conclusion

By the end of this session your client may have a sense of her own "story" and ways in which to use LLAMA to defuse from it and move in the direction of her values. It can be helpful to use the written "Word Web" of her story in later sessions, so we suggest keeping a copy. If clients "forget" to engage in home practice of any sort, it may be prudent to have them set reminders on their cell phones so they can work toward independence as sessions draw to a close.

Session 8

Self-as-Context

Within the hexaflex model, "self-as-*content*," or the "conceptualized self," is located at the midpoint at the bottom of the hexaflex. This "conceptualized self" is simply the description of "me" that we each carry around with us. This perspective of our "self" would include the declarations of who we are when we say, "I am…" It represents our "storied-up" version of who we have been, who we are, and who we will continue to be. This version of our self-description is built on years of our own internal "self" or character as we have come to see it, interacting with the world, the people in it, the circumstances we encounter, and further perceptions of who we are as a result. It has been formed layer by layer in this way since early childhood. For many who seek therapy, their conceptualized self represents the story they are fused with and the viewpoint, or lens, through which they experience the world around them. If your client has a story of herself as a failure, she may repeatedly retreat in the face of new challenges before she has even tried confronting them, and she won't ask for help because her mind tells her it's pointless.

When we speak of self-as-*context* we are referring to your client's stance or perspective while noticing her "self," at any given moment, from the point of view of the one who is doing the noticing. It refers to the part of each of us that notices or is aware of how we feel, what we are thinking, what urges we have, what we see, hear, taste, touch, and feel. From this viewpoint, we are better able to respond flexibly, with a greater repertoire of possible behaviors, to ongoing circumstances.

Focus of This Session

We want to remind our clients of past experiences that connect to their sense of their self as an observer, and thus to develop their sense of awareness in any given moment. Although self-as-context is presented here as a separate topic and focus of this session, you have actually been weaving the concept throughout the previous sessions. Asking your client to notice and label internal events, engaging her in mindfulness and defusion experiences, and allowing space for internal events—each of these contributes to her developing a flexible sense of her "self," or a sense of awareness, within the context of the present moment, not solely from the perspective of her mind and her "story."

In this session we provide experiential exercises to help clarify the concept, and more importantly, to experience being the one who "notices" and is aware. Because our clients' sense of who they are often centers around being "not good enough" in one form or another, we also focus on self-compassion in this session and include a mindfulness meditation to help clients loosen their grip on their conceptualized self and the shame that often accompanies their "self." This meditation has proven particularly evocative over the years. We suggest that you read the entire description of this session and give some thought to how you might want to structure it with a particular client, making sure you leave enough time to process the experience. We will continue with self-compassion in session 9, so you can move anything you don't cover this time to your next session, or omit things entirely if they don't suit your client.

Fictional Client: Cameron

For this session we introduce Cameron, a seventeen-year-old male who struggles with repetitive and intrusive thoughts of being "dirty." In order to reduce his sense of himself as "dirty," he engages in cleaning routines that take hours every day. Over time he discovered that he felt most "dirty" at school, where he has experienced academic and attentional difficulties from a young age and struggled to keep up with his peers. As a child, Cameron's only way to make sense of his struggles was to attribute them to the "fact" that he must be "stupid," since no other reasons were ever offered. In an earlier session, Cameron discovered he has "dirty" and "stupid" in a frame of equivalence, and over time he has reacted to both with increasing anxiety. His cleaning rituals soothe his anxiety in the short term, but do little to "get rid of it" in the long term. Now in his last year of high school, Cameron is becoming very anxious about college and his cleaning rituals have expanded to six hours per day, leaving little time for homework, studying for tests, his part-time job, or socializing with peers. Cameron's life has narrowed to the left side of the hexaflex and the matrix, with experiential avoidance driving his behavior. He feels very guilty for the impact of his rituals on his family and struggles to avoid a growing sense of shame within himself, because of "how stupid I am."

Self-as-Context with Individual Clients

We never actually use the words "self-as-context" when referring to self-as-context in our conversations with clients. Instead, we use words like "observing self," "aware self," or "the part of your self that notices." If you are comfortable with the ACT processes and the use of present-moment interpersonal experiences as they unfold in a session, you could find lots of meaningful moments to help your client build his awareness, like the one you will see in the following interaction between Cameron and his therapist as they begin to explore possible academic accommodations for college:

T (Therapist): I noticed as we were talking about academic accommodations for next year that you changed the topic; and just now you grabbed your hand sanitizer. (*Therapist is curious—is Cameron's behavior a DOT?*)

C (Cameron): Yeah, I guess I did, I didn't even notice myself doing that.

T: Can you notice how you are feeling right now, how your body feels? (*Therapist helps client to be more aware in the present moment.*)

C: I feel dirty.

T: What is this "dirty" feeling like right now? (*Labeling.*)

C: My stomach is in knots and my shoulders are really sore.

T: And what do you notice yourself wanting to do when you notice you are having sensations like your stomach being in knots and your shoulders hurting? (*Using defusing language.*)

C: I want to wash my hands, but the sanitizer will have to do.

T: Who is noticing the urge to wash your hands?

C: I am. I guess you can't see that, it's all inside me.

T: I am glad that you noticed the urge and I wonder if you would consider using LLAMA here with me: labeling the urge to wash your hands, letting go of the battle and being willing to have the urge and the feelings that come up with it, allowing the feelings and any thoughts you might notice, and mindfully coming back to focusing on the session and approaching or moving in a direction that matters to you.

C: I can try it. I need to be able to talk about the stuff I am going to need for college that will help me do the work. I really want to do well in my program, but I'm so scared that I'm just not smart enough, I feel like such an idiot and I really hate this part of myself.

T: That judgment of yourself as "stupid" seems to define you at times.

C: Yeah, I would rather do anything than think about that, but I can't get rid of the idea, so let's try LLAMA.

After allowing Cameron to choose between LLAMA and continued avoidance, you can reinforce "noticing" once again by asking him to notice the impact of his choice as the session progresses. As he makes his way through the acronym, he will land at "approach what matters," which is where values and committed action take hold and help to expand his definition of himself. As Cameron speaks about his distress in noticing and being with the judgment of himself as "stupid," this would be an appropriate moment to weave in the "Not Good Enough" mindfulness meditation outlined later in this session.

We describe within this session several experiences designed to enhance the "observing self," as well as several mindfulness meditations. They likely won't all fit within a single session, and if that is the case, consider saving one of them, the "Snow Globe," until a later session, since it gives your client something to take home. If you are ending or reducing the frequency of sessions, the globe may function as a helpful transitional object.

What Stuck?

The focus of the previous session was "story"—how everything connects to everything, making the battle to delete thoughts and memories one we are certain to lose. Your client may now have a better idea of the broader content of his story, as opposed to individual thoughts, and how easily it can surface in his daily life.

Review of Home Practice

At the end of session 7, your client was asked to continue moving in the direction of his values and to continue with the practice of mindfulness, either formally or informally. As you review home practice with your client, keep an ACT "ear" out for moves toward what matters: many clients make some progress by this point in therapy. Never assume, however, that this is easy for your client to notice, acknowledge, or "feel." Clients often tell us that when we express pride, they "feel it for a second" and then it's gone. Many clients have explained that pride comes in, "meets my 'not good enough' inside and gets kicked out." Many are not accustomed to feeling a sense of accomplishment and have a tendency to dismiss their own achievements, in order to avoid internal events associated with our pride in them, or their own pride. As the clinician, you will want to avoid engaging in a battle of perspective at this point and instead you might ask your client whether his behavior was in the service of values or experiential avoidance. Here perhaps you could also engage in mindfulness around acceptance of feelings, if appropriate. As clients make progress, they often get muddled up in LLAMA and may need a reminder of what they are moving toward, under what circumstances LLAMA can be helpful, and what they are accepting and allowing.

Mindfulness

We engage clients in a brief informal mindfulness at the beginning of the session and then in a more intimate, eyes-closed visualization of "not good enough" later on.

Informal Mindfulness

A fun way to incorporate mindfulness, without judgment, can be done working with the sense of touch, using brown paper bags and household items. We fill each bag with a handful of a particular item such as paper clips, feathers, candies, pieces of tin foil—the possibilities are endless. Take turns with your client, reaching into a bag and describing what you feel, so the other person can guess at what is in the bag. No peeking! Only factual descriptions are allowed, which gives you and your client a chance to notice judgments and to use LLAMA as needed.

Defining Self-as-Context

As mentioned above, we are trying to build our client's sense of self-awareness in the present moment. One way of describing self-as-context that seems to fit for adolescents is to ask your client if he has ever had the experience of studying for a test or reading a text and then noticing that he was not understanding the material. He may have needed to reread a section, or perhaps he became aware that he was not paying attention and needed to refocus. There is the part of him that was studying or reading, and the "observing self" that noticed how it was going, that was aware of whether his efforts were working. With some clients you can suggest that this is not dissimilar to an "out-of-body experience," in which there is a part of him that stands back and watches what is happening, his own "personal fly on the wall."

Experiential Exercises

The following are exercises that may serve to strengthen your client's ability to step into the "observing self."

Matrix

This is a good time to bring your client's matrix back into the room. You can use a recent experience of something he was working on as an example and ask the question, "Who is noticing?" when he brings up values (lower right) that were spurring him toward his goal, or thoughts and feelings that he was avoiding and that define his "self-as-content" (lower left). This encourages him to shift perspective to the observing stance of self-as-context and to notice moments of doing so.

Stickies

This exercise is meant to help clients take a step back from all that is inside and look *at* it, and then make a choice as to what they want front and center, what they want to base decisions on, what matters to them. For this experience, give your client a stack of Post-it Notes, sometimes referred to as "sticky notes," which we just call "stickies," and have him write a single judgment, an emotion, or an urge that he tries to avoid, on a single stickie. On some of the others, have him write a single value or a few words about what is important to him. Once he has about twenty of them, have him stick them on his person, wherever he likes. We typically ask clients to place the stickies only where they can see them, so not on their backs, for example. Your client can then take a look at what he has written and read the stickies aloud. There is a defusing sensibility to this exercise, as he sits and looks "at" what he has written. You may need to engage in some willingness and allowing exercises at this point, such as the "Observe, Breathe, Expand" mindfulness practice, if reading the stickies seems to flood your client with intense affects or thoughts.

Depending on your client's own context, it may be helpful to ask, "Are these stickies your own or were any of them given to you or imposed on you?" For some clients, there is a *felt* sense that the judgments have been with them for a long time, perhaps since they were very young, and that these are not characteristics that they would freely choose for themselves like they would a value. Working through this question can strengthen willingness to have the thoughts and feelings, a sense of allowing or unsticking, and can loosen your client's grip on his "storied version" of his "self."

You can then ask him which judgments, urges, values, or other internal events would be helpful to have "front and center" at a particular moment, maybe when he is trying to engage in values-based behavior, and move those stickies wherever he likes, so they are more in his line of vision, more noticeable. He can then move stickies that are less helpful or less "workable" to a more peripheral position. Cameron chose to move stickies with "stupid," "dirty," and "anxious," to the periphery and placed them on his shirt, just around his shoulders. He moved "determined," "college," and "self-respect" to his legs, just above the knee, so he could "see them easily." In this way, the thoughts and feelings he does not like and that he tries to get rid of through DOTS are still present, but not at the center of his view. Once you've completed this sorting exercise with your client, you can process it in terms of who it is that is noticing the stickies, noticing whether the thoughts, feelings, judgments, and values are helpful or not, who it is that decides which ones to tune in to, and who it is that makes the choice about which ones will drive behavior. There are many other ways to use stickies. Don't be surprised if your client thinks of something new.

Using stickies allows for common language with your client later on, when you might ask him, "Which stickies are you looking at?" as he makes moves consistent with values, or in avoidance of thoughts and feelings.

Snow Globe

Another way of experiencing the observing self is the "Snow Globe." We initially showed a client a snow globe to engage in the concepts, but found it much more meaningful to have clients make their own globe in session.

For this exercise, you will need a canning jar (the leak-proof rubber ring is essential), water, glycerin, glitter, and a large bowl to sit the jar in (because water will get spilled!).

Fill the jar half way up with water, then add a few drops of glycerin. (This is meant to stop the glitter from "chunking" together but we have found it less than consistently successful!) Once the glycerin is in, let your client add glitter. You can suggest to him that the glitter represents the thoughts, feelings, urges, physical sensations, and values that he experiences inside. He may want to have different sizes or colors of glitter, so that one color represents thoughts, and another feelings, for example. You can ask him to say aloud the thoughts, feelings, and values that the glitter is representing as he slowly pours it in. Then, fill the rest of the jar with water so it is just starting to overflow—this is the point when you want to have the jar sitting on the bottom of a large bowl to catch the overflow.

When the water starts to overflow, ask your client to put the lid on it. Then, once it is sealed tightly, have him shake it up and watch as the glitter settles. You can build on this in several ways. For example, as the glitter settles it can serve as a visual anchor and metaphor for mindful watching, guiding your client to use LLAMA to remain in the moment with the settling glitter. One time, in a flash of extreme creativity, we even glued a tiny plastic toy llama to the inside of the lid of a jar, so it was at the bottom of the snow globe when we finished!

You can also ask your client how this snow globe might relate to his sense of himself and his observing self, as well as to the thoughts and feelings he has inside. Is he the plastic llama at the bottom, the water in which the glitter is floating around, or the jar holding it all together, or is he the "self" looking at the globe? As long as he "feels" the idea that he can have a sense of moving back and forth between the "self" who is thinking, feeling, and doing, and the "self" who notices what he is thinking, feeling, and doing, don't get too caught up in terms of how he conceptualizes the elements of the globe.

Not Good Enough

Now that the concept of an observing self is developing, we move next to a mindfulness meditation of "Not Good Enough" that embodies the observer in each of us. It is preferably done with eyes closed. The intent of this mindfulness practice is that either while it is being done or some time later it will generate a sense of self-compassion within your client. This can make acceptance of thoughts and feelings relatively easier. Many adolescents have emphasized the difficulty they have in being kind toward themselves; they often don't feel deserving because their "not good enough" tells them they aren't worthy of compassion and understanding.

This mindfulness experience is based on an exercise we first did with Kelly Wilson, which sparked for us a deeply felt sense of self-compassion and acceptance. We have woven it together with elements from Russ Harris's physicalizing experience (2009). It includes elements of distancing oneself from thoughts, feelings, and memories, of willingness and allowing what surfaces, and of moving toward a sense of self-compassion. As such, it seems to embody every process of the hexaflex. We find it best to move through this meditation at a slow pace, allowing ample time to notice internal sensations and really take in the experience. Because it can be lengthy, ask your client periodically if he is still "with you," in case he has drifted off in his mind or become sleepy. You can break the exercise into steps and allow processing after each step, or work through it from start to finish. This script contains details that pertain to Cameron: you can change what you need to in order to make it relevant to your client.

> *Let's each bring our mind back to last week's session, when we worked on "story" and the sense we have of ourselves as not good enough in some way. Can you notice where in your body that sense of yourself as "stupid" or "not good enough" is sitting? Try to stand back and just notice that sense of yourself as not good enough, noticing what "not good enough" looks like, what size "not good enough" is, what color, what the surface texture looks like, whether "not good enough" is moving or still.* (Ask your client to describe what his feelings connected to "not good enough" look like.) *Let's breathe in and out from the place where we feel our "not good enough" and try to allow some space for the feelings. Notice thoughts and judgments that may arise, labeling them, letting them stay, making room for them, allowing them, as often as you need to, and shifting back to*

looking at feelings. Now imagine taking "not good enough" out of your body and placing it in your lap, doing so gently, as if you are holding a newborn baby, or a puppy, with kindness, being gentle. Just letting "not good enough" settle onto your lap. (You can refer to the description of "not good enough" that your client gave you at any time in the meditation, such as, "allow that blue ball that is vibrating to be in your lap.") *Notice any thoughts or feelings coming up, as you allow "not good enough" to just sit gently in your lap. Imagine that my "not good enough" is sitting on my lap, too.* (Describe your own if it seems appropriate.) *At this moment, see if you can look at your "not good enough" with a sense of willingness and allowing. "Not good enough" has been there for a long time* (add in the age at which your client first noticed it, if he identified this earlier) *and it isn't going anywhere. Your "not good enough" is part of you. It has grown with you over time and through experience, and it seems to be staying. Fighting "not good enough" doesn't work, so try to look at your "not good enough" with a sense of allowing and understanding and some compassion, if you can. Your "not good enough" is part of you. Try to hold it gently and with compassion. Notice what that feels like for you in this moment—to stop fighting with "not good enough." If thoughts take you away, notice them, allow them to settle, and gently detach, coming back to "not good enough."* (Pause and ask your client what this is like, while he remains eyes closed if possible. You may need to engage in "breathe and expand" again if the affect is intense, and resume when your client is ready.) *Now, let's gently hold our "not good enoughs" and pass them to each other—imagine giving me your "not good enough" and you take my "not good enough" and we will each hold the other's "not good enough" gently and kindly. As you look at my "not good enough," try to let it know that you get it, that it's okay to struggle, that you understand, and see if some part of your face can express that to my "not good enough." Notice how that feels for you.* (Pause.) *Gently shift your focus to knowing that I am looking at your "not good enough" with the same sense of kindness and compassion, and see if you can notice what that feels like. Just allow yourself to feel whatever comes up in this moment.* (Pause.) *Notice what it feels like inside to take in my feelings of compassion for you, knowing what you have struggled with in the past and in the present, knowing what matters to you and who it is you want to be. See if you can let in some of the kindness that I am feeling toward you.* (Many clients tell us that it is easier for them to regard their therapist with compassion, whereas taking in and feeling their therapist's compassion is much more difficult. For this reason, we always have clients imagine their feelings of compassion for the therapist first and then the therapist's for the client, as a way of "gradual exposure" to the affect.) *Now let's say good-bye to the "not good enough" in our lap and imagine passing it back to each other, so that I have mine back and you*

215

have yours. Each of us holding our own "not good enough" with a sense of willingness and allowing. Now, remaining with our eyes closed, just imagine that we are looking at each other, and at each other's "not good enough," and as you do this, try to imagine looking at me and my "not good enough" and conveying some sense of compassion, understanding, and kindness for me and my sense of being "not good enough." Notice what that feels like for you. (Pause.) Now, see if you can bring your awareness to the idea that I am looking at you and your "not good enough" with compassion, understanding, and kindness, and notice what it feels like for you to receive this from me. As you notice feelings and physical sensations, try to give them some breathing room and unclench around them if you need to, trying to find a sense of willingness and allowing for your feelings. When you are ready, gently pick up your "not good enough" and place it back inside, allowing it to have space to be there, not trying to get rid of it. As you take your "not good enough" back, try to hold it with the same sense of compassion you had for mine, and try to feel the compassion I had for you and your "not good enough." Try to regard your "not good enough" with some compassion and understanding for what it has been through. Breathe and expand into the place where you feel it. You can't get rid of it, it is part of you and your "story," and trying to get rid of it seems to make things worse, so just allow it some space to be there. If you can feel some compassion for "not good enough," try to let it know by soothing it in some way, by showing it that you are willing to have it stay with you. It might be something you say or do. Just notice what comes to mind as you show some compassion to "not good enough." (Some clients need time for their feelings to come to rest, so you may want to periodically repeat the instructions of "allowing thoughts and feelings, making room for them, and allowing them to come to rest" until your client indicates that he is ready to end the meditation. Once he is ready, you can continue as follows.) *Say good-bye to "not good enough" in whatever way you like, and then, still with eyes closed, bring your awareness back to the room, noticing sensations where you are sitting, noticing sounds in the room, gently letting your image of "not good enough" dissolve and shifting your focus back to the present moment. As we open our eyes in a moment, try to hang on to the sense of compassion for your self and see if that sense of kindness, acceptance, and compassion can help you choose what to do and who to be.*

Allow an opportunity to process this experience.

Home Practice

As you finish the session, you may want to remind your client of how many sessions remain, if this is an issue, and allow her to choose her own home practice, being

as nondirective as possible. This would be a good time to ask if she would be willing to notice moments of compassion toward herself. You can also ask if she would be willing to allow compassion and understanding from others to find a way into her felt experience, or to notice it from within, toward her "self." And of course, ask her to continue with values-based behavior, either by setting goals, if that is what works for her, or less formally asking her to notice when she moves toward what matters versus when she moves away from thoughts and feelings she does not want.

Modifications for Group

This session works very similarly for working with groups to the way it was described for working with individuals.

Informal Mindfulness

In a group setting, have enough bags for everyone, each containing something very different, and allow each group member to either describe the contents of her bag to a partner, who can try to guess what it is, or to the larger group, depending on numbers and dynamics. As group sessions near an end, we often partner up group members who may not know each other very well, to continue building a sense of safety and connection among members.

Experiential Exercises

Here are some group adaptations for some of the "self-as-context" exercises described above.

Stickies

This can be a difficult experience for some group members, who may feel vulnerable about others seeing their "stickies." If this is a problem, you may want to pair group members with partners and have them share only with that one other person instead of with the entire group. If you do this, consider having anyone who wants to share her perceptions around the experience do so at the end with the larger group. Depending on group dynamics, you may need to remind members to regard what the other is saying with curiosity, openness, and compassion.

Snow Globe

This is a fun exercise in groups, and often brings up subtle and not so subtle moments of comparisons between group members as they evaluate their own snow globes in relation to the snow globes their peers have made. This often triggers a sense of "not good enough" in many group members and gives clinicians an "in the moment" opportunity to engage clients in noticing and using LLAMA so they can return to the moment at hand.

Not Good Enough

This can be done as outlined for individual therapy. Depending on the group, you may opt to arrange the room with chairs in a circle and tables to the sides. Group members have told us that, while not having the barrier of the table between them increases their sense of vulnerability, it also impacts their sense of connection within the room. It provides an opportunity to notice and appreciate the way in which vulnerability and connection come together. In the group setting it is too distracting to have group members reporting out loud what they are experiencing at various points in the exercises. For this reason, we as facilitators keep our eyes open and, requesting that group members all keep their eyes closed, we ask them to raise and lower their hands if they are able to reach a certain point, such as visualizing their "not good enough," so we will know when to pause and allow slower processing members to catch up, and when to move on. We also ask group members to pass their "not good enough" to the person seated to either the left or right. It is a good idea to give each group member tissues at the start, in case these are needed, as opposed to handing them out and distracting the group from the meditation once it is in progress.

Conclusion

By the end of this session we hope that your client walks out the door with a change in his "felt sense" of who he is and how he defines himself, and a sense of compassion and understanding for who he has been and the ways in which he has tried to cope (DOTS). He should have a fairly good working knowledge of LLAMA and how to use the steps to approach what matters in the company of unwanted thoughts and feelings. With an expanded awareness of an observing self, and a beginning ability to stand back from the usual "story" of who he has been, your client may be more able to consent to the thoughts and feelings that have grown up with him and to loosen his grip, allowing a more flexible approach to what matters.

Session 9

Self-Compassion

We have spent one or more sessions on each of the ACT processes: nurturing a sense of awareness, an observing self, the ability to defuse from thoughts, acceptance of feelings, and values-based behavior. We want to pull these processes all together now with our client and galvanize them by engaging in experiences to heighten self-compassion and enhance willingness. If you and your client are moving through all of this in ten sessions, then you have one left after this one, which includes an experiential exercise, review, tying up loose ends, saying good-bye, and questionnaires, if needed. That leaves this session to pull it all together in a way that your client can really embody and remember for the long term.

We strongly encourage you, if you haven't already, to bring a keen sense of awareness to your client's progress with the ACT processes during this session. You might want to incorporate content from past sessions that bears repeating, or elements you did not include because of time constraints, or because they were not appropriate at the time, and so on. If there were self-as-context experiential exercises that you did not cover from session 8 (we included more than what will fit into a single session), the beginning of this session would be a good time to do so.

Focus of This Session

Your presence as a caring and interested therapist will likely have been impacting your client's sense of self-compassion all along. However, we chose to add self-compassion as a specific focus when we discovered that for many clients, fostering self-compassion allowed them to have their first contact with a genuine sense of self-recognition and self-acceptance, displacing, even if only for a moment, a long-held sense of themselves as "not good enough." This can be transformative. But what we found, unfortunately, was that without conscious effort from the clinician, "not good enough" too easily took back the spotlight and self-acceptance shrank out of awareness. Until we chose to highlight self-compassion, this repeatedly happened for our clients, making willingness, defusion, acceptance, and valued living very difficult.

You can follow the session as we outline it below, or weave these experiences throughout your sessions, as you prefer. We have included a few of our favorite meditations to help clients with their sense of self-compassion and acceptance of who they have been, who they are now, and who they want to be.

Fictional Client: Molly

Our patient for this session is Molly, a nineteen-year-old who has struggled with symptoms of depression for several years. She reported frequent experiences of fatigue, lack of energy, and lack of motivation, accompanied by a strong urge to sleep or eat excessively. Molly's excessive sleeping and eating have impacted her ability to function in all areas of her life. She is most upset about the significant weight she has gained in the past year, leaving her with the sense of being unattractive, unlikeable, hopeless, and a failure. Molly's family relationships are characterized by a long-standing history of Molly feeling responsible for her parents. Her parents both struggle with severe mental health concerns and have left Molly with the perception that they are both very vulnerable. She describes an urge to "fix" them, and finds it difficult when she can't control them and "make them better." Molly identified her friendships and academic goals as important to her. She is guided by her personal values of being kind, genuine, compassionate, and curious.

Self-Compassion with Individual Clients

On reflection we realized that very few of our clients regard themselves with kindness, understanding, or compassion in the face of failure, perceptions of inadequacy, or general suffering. Instead, like most humans, they turn to judging, ridiculing, blaming, and condemning, which feed their "story" and keep them stuck. As mentioned earlier, self-compassion was not something we incorporated into our early work, at least not explicitly anyway, until we became comfortable with ACT and in dealing in an ACT way with our own "self" in sessions. We learned along the way, however, that it was important to deal with our own "self" kindly, so that we could support our clients in doing the same. This can be a tricky experience with clients if the therapist has not yet engendered his or her own sense of self-compassion, so we encourage you to proceed only when ready.

For some work on your own in this area, you might consider looking at Tara Brach's lovely book *Radical Acceptance* (2004). With clients, pay attention to moments when your own "not good enough" is taking the spotlight in the middle of a session. You might take a moment to smile at it in your mind and notice how it's kind of trying, the only way it knows how, to help you right now, making a heroic but ridiculous and counterproductive attempt to goad you into somehow being better at being you. Keeping in mind that having this "not good enough" feeling is a universally held human vulnerability can help to reduce its sting. It can also help you to help your client be more accepting.

What Stuck?

The focus of the previous session was self-as-context, and this idea often requires some clarification and review. Engaging clients in experiential exercises from last week, either ones you already did or did not do yet, as well as any you or your client develop in the moment, can help her to sense her "observing self" and get some distance from thoughts and feelings.

Review of Home Practice

At the end of the last session, your client was asked to notice moments when she could feel a sense of compassion toward herself, or let in some of these feelings from others. It is worth spending some time processing this, which can be done within the context of reviewing her moves toward values and her moves away from inner events she does not want. Try to attend to her nonverbal behavior as she tells you about moves toward what matters: does she look animated, are emotions showing up in some way, or is the emotional experience of sharing this with you more flat? Regardless, this is a good time to pause her narrative and ask her to notice how she is feeling as she shares these moments of her life with you. If she appears energized, reflect on what you are noticing and gently inquire as to how she feels, and if she can feel the emotion physically. Often clients are overwhelmed by what they call "good" feelings, such as happiness and pride, and will tell us about their successes, but in a way that dampens down the intensity of their emotions. This may be a form of experiential avoidance that you can work with in the moment.

Conversely, your client may hit a point at any time in the process when she can't achieve a particular goal, and this loops her into her "story," full of judgment and without self-compassion. Some clients may set relatively large or important goals as therapy nears an end, which increases the likelihood of thoughts and feelings intensifying and getting in their way. In Molly's case, she was hoping to study for a test with a friend as a way of moving toward her friendships and academic endeavors at the same time. When her friend was unable to join her at the last minute, she got caught up in her story about herself as unlikeable and a failure and spent the evening in bed instead of studying. Her review of home practice with her therapist went like this:

M (Molly): I went to bed all evening. I couldn't study. It was like I had a pit of black hopelessness in my gut and my head was full of thoughts about what a failure I am. I couldn't write the test today, and I doubt if anyone missed me in class. I even had these daydreams about my horrible future where I fail at everything, it was like a movie just running over and over in my head.

T (Therapist): Lying in bed felt horrible, and you were aware of your "story" coming back along with the feelings in your gut. And now you are disappointed in yourself for not taking the test and you're feeling alone, like no one in class missed you at all.

M: Yeah, it was totally my whole story coming up, it's like a movie I keep watching over and over and I don't know why I listen to it, it just makes things worse, like it did with my test.

T: And although you notice yourself getting pulled into it, it sounds like it's hard to stop following your story or stop yourself from going to bed.

M: Totally, I guess for awhile, even though I felt awful in bed, maybe I thought it would feel more awful to try and study, or to text my friend back, or another friend, I just got so down on myself that I couldn't imagine anyone wanting to be with me. It's that vulnerable feeling we talked about before, going to bed felt awful, but being vulnerable is something I can't stand, I never let those feelings stay because it feels like they will smother me.

T: So using DOTS felt bad, but moving toward your values by studying or connecting with someone leaves you vulnerable and this seems unfamiliar. You aren't willing to have those feelings of vulnerability, they are just too scary.

M: If I'm vulnerable, people will get to know me, and they'll find the "not good enough" inside.

T: It sounds like you are pretty stuck. If you avoid being vulnerable, it's great, no one will see your "not good enough," but to avoid this you end up using DOTS, which feels horrible and you don't do the things that matter to you, or be the person who matters to you.

M: It's that matrix, isn't it, I'm stuck on the left side again.

T: It sounds like it. Any thoughts about moving to the right side, toward what matters?

M: I could try LLAMA, and I guess I am stuck at the second "L," because I am not willing to have feelings of vulnerability, but if I don't have them, I can't do anything.

T: Did you feel vulnerable with me last session when we did the "Not Good Enough" meditation?

M: Yeah, that was tough, it's hard to be with someone who knows me and understands, and then still likes me.

T: So sometimes when you are vulnerable, you are understood and liked—not rejected?

M: I guess so, but I have no way of knowing, so I predict I'll be rejected.

T: I guess you won't know until you try. Others' reactions are not in our control, so it could go either way. The question might be, are you willing to risk it, to be rejected or treated with understanding, and adapt to whichever reaction you get, for the sake of being the person who matters to you?

M: I would be, if being understood didn't feel so awful too. I guess it's more of an unknown than rejection is. Rejection feels bad but at least I know it.

T: Would you be willing to try another mindfulness exercise with me—it may help to allow some vulnerability and see what happens.

M: (Sighs.) Okay.

Mindfulness

As we have mentioned, living according to values and the sense of connection to oneself that accompanies this success can often be difficult for clients to "take in" and to really feel. You may want to engage your client in an eyes-closed meditation called "Younger You" and "Older You," then move to an open-eyed exercise called "Eyes On," as a way of furthering her sense of self-compassion and her willingness to let feelings such as this be part of her present experience.

Younger You

This is a meditation we first did with Kelly Wilson. It seems to have an impact on our adolescent clients, who, despite their relatively young age, do carry a lot of their past with them and can be most unforgiving of what they judge as their own shortcomings. It goes something like this:

Try to get an image in mind of yourself at some earlier time when you came to know your "story," seeing yourself as being "not as smart" as the other kids, or "not as attractive," noticing what you looked like, where you were, who was with you, what was happening. Just bring as much detail to the experience as you can right now. (Ask your client what image comes to mind and how old she is, so that you can use this information later on in the experience.) *As you imagine the scene, imagine yourself now, at your present age, looking at your younger self, and slowly move toward her. When you are beside her, imagine being at eye level with her, in whatever way that works, looking into each other's eyes. Look into the eyes of your younger self, see in her eyes her sense of being not good enough, of feeling responsible for those around her, her sense that she has of herself as a failure at not being able to fix everyone. Look at the younger you, knowing that she thinks she is not good enough, or that she is flawed somehow, and allow her to see in your eyes, reflected back at her, your compassion and understanding, your knowing that she was doing the best she could at the time. Gaze into the eyes of your younger self and with your eyes let her know: "I get it." Notice whatever feelings come up, and allow them to be present as part of this experience.* (Pause.) *If you get distracted by other thoughts and feelings that are rising up, notice them, label them, and try to step back, give them some room, some space, and let them come to rest. Then, gently shift back to being with your younger self and all that arises in this moment. If there is something she needs from you right now, a gesture, words, whatever it is, try and give her that. And then, continue to look into her eyes and let her see your understanding for what she has been through.* (Pause.)

You can choose to stop at this point, guide your client in dissolving the image of her younger self, and return back to the room and share your experiences, or you can continue seamlessly with the following and then share experiences at the end.

Still with your younger self, hold her by the hand and gently walk with her, leaving the scene you had imagined. Now gently take younger you and cradle her in your arms, like you would hold a baby or a puppy, delicately, carefully, gently. Notice what that feels like. (Pause.) *Now, imagine handing your younger self to me, and as you do, see if you can bring to awareness the sense of compassion and understanding that I have for you and for your younger self. As you hand her to me, imagine looking into my eyes as I receive your younger self from you and hold her gently in my lap. Imagine looking into my eyes and seeing, reflected back, a sense that I get it, that I get you, that I know what it's been like for you, the struggles you have had, the suffering you have been through, and yet here I am, with you in this moment, willing to cradle your younger self gently and kindly. (Pause.) Bring awareness to the idea that we are sitting here together, with your younger self. Notice how you feel in this experience and try to just stay with whatever you notice yourself feeling and thinking, just being in the experience. If thoughts or feelings try to take you away from this moment, label them, don't try to fight them off, just allow space for whatever comes up that might be taking you away from both giving and receiving compassion, make room for thoughts and feelings. There may be anxiety or vulnerability, or other feelings and thoughts, see if you can give them some room to be here with us now so that you can gently shift your attention back to the present moment. Noticing what it's like to have the two of us sharing your younger self. (Pause.) Bring awareness to any felt sense of compassion you may have for your younger self in this moment (pause), just noticing what that feels like. Bring awareness to your sense of my compassion for you and acceptance for who you are, who you have been, and notice what it feels like to allow those feelings inside yourself. If you notice an urge to move away from feelings of compassion, try to stay with it. Breathe into those feelings, into the sense of compassion, and make room for them, try to allow even a little more than you may have in the past. (Pause.) Imagine now that I am giving your younger self back to you, and as I do, take her gently and allow her to settle into your lap.*

You may want to end at this point, allowing your client to dissolve the images and return her focus to the room, open her eyes, and process the experience; or you could continue with the final segment below.

In whatever way you can, imagine placing your younger self gently inside you, letting her get comfortable. (Ask your client if she can feel her younger self inside, and allow more time if needed.) Notice where she has settled. Take a look at her now that she is inside, she may still look like younger you or may change form, either is okay; just notice what younger you looks like and how you feel where she has settled. Breathe and expand around younger you and let her have some air to breathe and some space to be here with you now. If you like, gently place your hand on your body where you feel your younger self. Let younger you come to rest as best you can. (Pause.) Breathing into younger you,

allowing the breath to touch your hand from the inside, and unclenching around
that space, giving your younger self more room. Before you leave your younger
self and this meditation, allow yourself to notice once again if there is something
you would like to do or say to her that you think would matter to her. (Pause.)
Allowing your image of your younger self to gently dissolve, keeping eyes closed,
bring your focus back to the sounds in the room, to sensations of touch and
pressure where your body meets the chair. With the sound of the chimes, we will
end the meditation and open our eyes.

Allow time for processing this experience with your client. It is always interesting
to ask what she said or did to show her younger self some sense of compassion and
understanding. You can ask your client what it was like to have her hand on her body
where she noticed her younger self. Often a client will say she found herself "patting
my stomach" or "rubbing my heart" in a manner that suggests she is soothing herself.
If this experience was particularly challenging for your client, it can be helpful to
notice moments of acceptance and compassion that naturally arise between the two
of you. Ask your client to pause and try to notice what you have said or your nonverbal behaviors, remaining in the present moment together. Engage in "Observe,
Breathe, Expand" to help her take in whatever she feels in these moments, in little
increments, over time. At the end of "Younger You," Molly was able to describe feelings of sadness for her younger self, for what she had been through, and shared that
she told her younger self, "It will be okay." Clients often finish "Younger You" with a
felt sense that their younger self is still inside them, doing the best she can, coping in
whatever way she can. But this way of coping just might not be working anymore,
now that she is older, and the sense of compassion that she has for her younger self
may increase her self-compassion in the present moment. By discovering a sense of
kindness for her younger self, perhaps your client can extend some kindness toward
her present self.

Older You

We sometimes engage clients in the second half of this exercise, called "Older
You," which can add further flexibility and broaden perspective. It goes like this:

Imagine yourself a few years older than you are now, perhaps in your mid-
twenties. Notice yourself in as much detail as you can, including what you are
doing, who is there with you, things that are around you, just noticing as much
as you can as you envision your older self, doing what she dreamed of doing,
being who she wanted to be. Imagine yourself as you are now, next to your older
self. Allow yourself to be close to her, maybe sitting together. Look into the eyes of

your older self. Notice what that's like, and allow her to look into your eyes and notice what that's like for you. Now I will ask you to shift a bit and to imagine being your older self, try to step into her shoes, into her body. Imagine being your older self, looking into the eyes of the "you" that is here now. See if you can feel your older self, looking at you with understanding for what you are going through now. Try to get a sense that your older self understands what life is like for you now. Of course she understands, you are both part of you. Just continue to be in your older self, looking at the "you" who is here now, and let you, as your older self, show a sense of understanding, acceptance, and kindness with her eyes. Now shifting once more, let yourself be the "you" that is here now, the "you" who is nineteen years old (fill in with client age). As the present you, imagine looking into the eyes of the older you, and try to notice and feel her compassion for you. Notice what that feels like. Try to let the feelings stay if you can, breathing around them, giving them some room to settle. As you look into the eyes of your older self, see if you can take in her feelings of understanding for what you have been through in the past, and for what you are going through now. She was there, she knows. (Pause.) Notice how you feel inside as you experience her understanding and compassion, breathing into feelings and unclenching around them. If you notice you are clenching or tightening up around feelings, just try to loosen up, allow room for whatever you notice. Just continue looking into her eyes, allowing feelings, opening up around them, and letting them settle. If thoughts distract you from this, notice them, label what you are noticing, and try to allow them to just be there, making room for thoughts, making room for feelings, and staying present with your older self. (Pause.) As you sit with your older self, imagine that she leans closer to you, strokes your hair perhaps, or rubs your shoulder, whatever feels good for you in this moment, and imagine as she leans over that she says something to you. Try to notice what that is, whatever comes to mind in this moment. If feelings rise up, or thoughts that try to take you away from the moment, just be aware of this, breathe into them, give them space to settle, and gently bring your focus back to the moment with your older self. Try to hear what she has to say. Taking in her kind-heartedness toward you, and whatever feelings and sensations that come with this experience. Try as best you can to stay with your older self, with effort and intention. (Long pause.) Before we end, take a moment to say good-bye to your older self, perhaps there is something you would like to say to her, maybe even something about this experience with her. (Pause.) Now, gently and kindly, allow your image of your older self to dissolve, bringing your awareness back to the room.

Allow time to process the experience after you bring the mindfulness to an end. Sometimes clients will share what their older (or younger) self said to them, and others will not. We tend not to press for disclosure unless our client seems particularly troubled in some way. Often we hear from clients that their older self said something like "You will be okay," "I love you," or "It will work out." Often we find ourselves just sitting quietly with clients after this exercise, supporting them as they continue to try and take in the feelings associated with the experience.

Eyes On

Once your client has settled her feelings from the "Younger You" and "Older You" experiences, we offer "Eyes On" as something you can share between you, making self-compassion and kindness a bit more "present moment."

"Eyes On" has been offered at many workshops in different iterations. If you notice that you have a lot of feelings that come up during "Eyes On" that you aren't prepared to feel, perhaps feelings you avoid, or if you just don't feel ready, don't rush into this. This experience can place both client and therapist in an intimate and vulnerable state, so we highly recommend that you experience "Eyes On" at workshops or with colleagues before introducing it in a session with a client. That way you will have some idea of what the experience may bring up for you, the therapist.

Position yourself directly across from your client, so you are not touching but your knees are close to each other's. You can ask your client if, for the next few minutes, she is willing to be with you, in the present moment, face to face, maintaining eye contact throughout, without the need for facial expressions or gestures, and mostly in silence. Once you are seated and she has consented, "Eyes On" goes something like this, with pauses used as you sense they are needed:

Let's just spend time now, being with each other in this moment. (Pause.) Sitting with each other, close together, in this way, may bring up all sorts of thoughts and feelings. Try as best you can to just notice what comes up for you, labeling thoughts, feelings, and urges, allowing room for whatever you notice, giving it space, and then returning to the present moment with me here in the room. You may notice an urge to look away, to laugh, to smile, to daydream, or any number of things. That's all perfectly normal. When you notice, just label what you are noticing, and try to pause. Don't get caught in efforts to control stuff inside, don't avoid it, just allow space for whatever you notice, breathing into feelings, unclenching around sensations and urges, and gently bring yourself back to this moment together, allowing yourself to share in this moment with me, someone who knows you, who feels compassionate and understanding toward you, sharing this connection together with me, someone who knows of your struggles and your "not good enough," and yet here I am with you. Together, in this moment, sharing the you that has struggled and the you that has dreams. Just staying with me, in this moment, with each other, allowing for whatever shows up as we do so. If you feel a sense of self-compassion or kindness as we sit together, see if you can allow those feelings to stay inside, unclenching around them and allowing them to come to rest. Make space for whatever you notice in this moment, feelings of kindness, anxiety, discomfort, connection, just noticing and allowing whatever comes up for you.

You can repeat or omit any portion of the dialogue, leaving room for silence and the inner experience that comes with being present with another person. Allow ample time to process this with your client, asking her about her thoughts and feelings that got in her way, even for a moment. A bit of self-disclosure may be appropriate in terms of what you, the therapist, noticed during "Eyes On," and how you worked with what surfaced.

This exercise varies incredibly from client to client. Some enjoy the sense of connectedness that comes with "Eyes On," while others feel extremely vulnerable and struggle through every moment. Most, however, report at least a fleeting moment when they were able to take in whatever the experience was, despite the thoughts and feelings that surfaced. This exercise can offer a brief moment to have the experience of willingness and the allowing of inner events that are so important when trying to reduce the impact of experiential avoidance. When your client feels her uncomfortable feelings and thoughts in this way, while staying in the moment, no matter for how long, it offers her this moment to discover and experience willingness and allowing. This is the same process you are trying to help her develop, so that she can allow for thoughts and feelings in her world as she heads toward what matters, toward her values.

For a client who really struggles with this exercise, it is worth spending some time understanding her inner experience. What was she avoiding? Is more practice with allowing feelings or seeing thoughts from a distance needed? If your client struggled to remain present, this does not indicate the exercise was a failure. A surprising number of clients have told us that they remember the experience and they could later "feel" the compassion that was present, even months later.

Home Practice

The focus for practicing between sessions remains. Ask your client to notice how she feels when she carries out everyday activities in the upcoming week and ask her to identify moments when she moves toward values and what matters. Make sure she has an understanding of how to work with thoughts and feelings that get in her way and that can lead her toward DOTS in an effort to make them go away. This is a good time to remind both your client and yourself that sometimes DOTS may be helpful, necessary, or inevitable, and that the move away from DOTS and toward values is something that can also be held lightly, and with flexibility. If she notices herself being judgmental or cruel to her "self" over the days ahead, ask if she is willing to "feel" the exercises she did today—keeping them in mind and finding a way to be kind to her younger self, and to her present self.

Modifications for Group

This session works very similarly with groups to how it was outlined for work with individuals. We offer a few suggestions to tweak the mindfulness exercises within a group context.

Mindfulness

We conduct the meditations much the same as for individual clients, but with some additional consideration to arranging the seating and pairing of group members, when needed.

Younger You and Older You

We tend to conduct "Younger You" and "Older You" in a circle in the center of the room (with no table forming a barrier) with group members facing inwards. Occasionally a group member or two may struggle to engage in eyes-closed experiences; sitting with eyes closed and knowing that other group members may be watching them may not feel safe. In these circumstances, we arrange the chairs similarly, but have group members facing outwards, toward the walls, so that a group member with eyes open does not impact others who have their eyes closed. As with previous sessions, facilitators can ask group members to raise and lower their hands at certain points so facilitators can gauge whether to pause or move on. We may do this when asking members to picture a younger version of themselves, and again later when we ask them to sit with their younger self on their lap, for example.

Eyes On

We have found this to be a bit challenging within groups, due to what we call "contagious giggling." Once a group member starts to giggle, others will follow and the impact can be lost. For this reason, choose your timing of "Eyes On" thoughtfully. We have found it helpful to have a sense of safety established between group members and to choose a moment when they appear somewhat less energized so it is not too difficult to settle into the stillness of the exercise.

We partner up group members based on our assessment of which group member we think could engage with which other group member, which is in turn based on the variety of interactions we have observed over the weeks and the evolving group dynamics. We tend not to let group members find their own partners, because this can set off feelings of rejection and comparison among members that won't bode well for the feeling of safety that is needed. If you have an odd number of group members, you can pair one person up with a facilitator.

On occasion we have found that one or more group members could not tolerate the intimacy of "Eyes On" for any of a variety of reasons. When even one group member is unable to take part in the exercise, we adapt it, positioning members in pairs sitting side-by-side, and facing a wall in the room instead of facing one another.

Conclusion

At this point, we hope your client now has a fluid understanding of the ACT processes, both in terms of when to use them and how to do so. The self-compassion experiences may help to reduce her judgment of herself and others and loosen her grip on her conceptualized self, making more room for self-as-context and increasing behavioral flexibility.

Session 10

Pulling It All Together

In the last session we reviewed the ACT processes, using LLAMA, and helped clients open more space to engage in these by accessing self-compassion. This final session pulls everything together and makes the ACT strategies memorable. We set up an experiential exercise in this session that evokes the thoughts, feelings, and urges getting in a client's way, and we provide an opportunity for clients to practice using LLAMA in order to move toward who or what matters to them. Although you have been doing this in past sessions, we make this multistaged process more obvious and more physical this time by incorporating movement throughout the work.

Focus of This Session

Because interpersonal difficulties are ubiquitous in those seeking mental health support, this final session is likely to be very difficult for both client and therapist. During this last session what we really want to do is pull everything together in an experiential way. There are two main objectives. The first is to engage our client in a movement-oriented experience of LLAMA, which we call "The Walk," in the hope that he can generalize this experience to his daily life.

The second objective is to intentionally say good-bye in a way that provides an opportunity to experience the thoughts and feelings that come with ending an important relationship. The "saying good-bye" part of the session can be rich and meaningful for both client and therapist. Feelings connected to the end of the relationship are likely to be both felt and spoken at this time.

Fictional Client: David

David is a seventeen-year-old boy who has experienced symptoms of depression since his parents separated and his father left the family a year ago. Prior to their separation, David recalls his parents "arguing and fighting all the time." David managed his feelings of anger, sadness, anxiety, and frustration by smoking marijuana and retreating to his bedroom, where he found comfort in his TV, computer, and cozy bed. He had used marijuana recreationally prior to his parents' separation, but his use increased over the past year. David has distanced himself from others and won't allow himself to risk feeling connected, lest he be rejected and disappointed. During this same time, he stopped playing on his hockey team, opted for a new peer group interested only in getting high, and lost his motivation to engage in academic work. David has not completed much of his schoolwork this semester and as a result his marks have dropped. He is feeling hopeless about his future. Over the last few weeks he has stopped attending school altogether and his teachers are calling home to report his absences. This is adding further stress to the family and is especially testing his relationship with his mother. David's academic success was always a source of pride for his parents, and was at one time for him as well.

Pulling It All Together with Individual Clients

In this session, your client will accomplish "The Walk," which is an experiential exercise in which he gets a chance to work with difficult emotions in real time. If you are ending work with your client in this session, however, it's important not to get too drawn into the nuts and bolts of the experiential exercise and lose sight of the reality that ending is the other important focus of the session. Some clients may react to termination with detachment, others may be happy or relieved, and still others may react with some degree of sadness or anxiety. You may have a sense of what to expect based on what you have heard from your client over the course of his therapy about his connections to others and separations from them. He may engage in DOTS to avoid what he is feeling. His past experiences will likely give you a hint of what to expect and even what to be on the lookout for. Your client is not the only one who may struggle with this session. It is important for you as the therapist to be mindful of the possibility that, based on your own context, you may be uncomfortable at this moment with ending relationships. This may result in you yourself using DOTS and in avoidance of both your own and your client's feelings.

What Stuck?

The focus of the previous session was self-compassion. It may be helpful to know if your client remembers "Younger You," "Older You," and "Eyes On," and the impact of those experiences a week later. Since there was not a lot of new content last session, you may want to spend some time at the beginning of this session reviewing any material and concepts that you think necessary, or engaging in exercises and meditations that you omitted in earlier sessions.

Review of Home Practice

At the end of the last session, your client was asked to notice how he feels when he makes a move toward his values and what matters to him. Along the way, was he able to take in and experience feelings of self-acceptance? You may also have asked him to be aware of judgments he made about himself over the past week, especially those that lead toward avoidance and DOTS, and to try and let go of judgments in favor of kindness and self-acceptance. If he engaged in behavior that was values based, you may have an opportunity to pause the session and inquire about how he feels in that moment with you as he shares his success. If he struggles with his sense of willingness to experience the accompanying emotions, this would be a good time to move to the acceptance-of-feelings meditations from session 5 or any of the self-compassion experiences from session 9. Keep in mind that many clients struggle not only with anxiety and depression, for example, but also with "good" feelings such as self-acceptance and a sense of accomplishment.

Mindfulness of Five Senses

Because this is a relatively packed session and the last one, a simple "Mindfulness of Five Senses" may be helpful here, just to get oriented to the work ahead. If there are other mindfulness experiences that you have not done yet, or some that merit repeating, go right ahead!

A simple exercise, bringing mindfulness to the moment and serving to "ground" your client, can be done by bringing to mind five things for each of the five senses. Ask your client to sit and notice five things he can see in the room, five things he can hear, five things he can feel, and so on. It is usually harder to identify smells and tastes; you may need to have some edible things handy in your office. Just going through the process of focusing on each of the five senses brings mindfulness to the body and the immediate surroundings. This will help with the awareness that will be needed in the next exercise.

The Walk

Over the years we have developed different iterations of what we call "The Walk," adapted from Hayes's "Passengers on the Bus" (2005). "The Walk" is a physical exercise designed to incorporate LLAMA as clients head toward what matters. Here we provide one version, which you can adjust depending on the size of your office.

Before starting this experience, ask your client to draw or make some kind of visual image representing his long-term goal on paper (or any other medium that seems appropriate). For our adolescent clients, "long-term" is often a matter of weeks or months, not necessarily years. You can ask your client to make sure his goal is "SMART," as explained in session 4, and ask him to incorporate his values somewhere in the picture. Next, have him write down on a piece of paper the thoughts and feelings that tend to get in his way, and hand that paper to you. Alternatively, you can look at his matrix for this information, if he has one. Hang your client's picture on the wall in your office, preferably somewhere that he can walk toward and stand close to. Then, with both of you standing as far from the picture as possible, begin "The Walk" toward the picture of his goal, toward what matters. We have small offices, and so have had to use a somewhat circular path in order for "The Walk" to be long enough to incorporate all the work before we get to the goal picture. (This means we "walk" in a circular pattern, which seems to mimic what most of us go through anyway, as opposed to a linear movement from start to finish!) If you have a larger space, you may want to use a linear path, which is easier and clearer.

Ask your client to move slowly toward the picture while you walk beside him and engage him in talking about his goal and his values. Keep the conversation focused on actually taking steps toward valued action. Through transformation of stimulus function, just looking at a picture of his goal or talking about it, even without it being physically present in the moment, will elicit feelings and thoughts that are connected to the event. Walking slowly and talking about his goal will also elicit thoughts and feelings that threaten to take him away from what matters and toward avoidance. You can check in periodically and ask, "What are you noticing now?" If your client gets looped into thoughts and feelings, ask him to let you know about it verbally and by stopping (in a small office, your client will be smashing into his goal if he doesn't stop every time thoughts and feelings arise). If talking about the goal does not get him stuck in thoughts and feelings, you can use the information on his matrix (lower left) or the list of things that would get in the way that he wrote out at the beginning of the exercise, and repeat these thoughts and feelings aloud as he walks.

As your client gets hooked into these inner events, help him use LLAMA to restart his walk once he has labeled, let go of the struggle, found a sense of willingness and allowing of thoughts and feelings, and returned mindfully to the present moment, approaching what matters. This is an opportunity to incorporate any and all ACT metaphors and experiential exercises that you have shared over the past nine weeks, as David's therapist did with him:

T (Therapist): Can you tell me about your picture?

D (David): Yeah, it's me getting my English project done. Even though I haven't been to school, my teachers are going to let me hand stuff in late. I really want to get this done so my mom will get off my back.

T: That's a pretty good reason. But is it the only reason you want to get your project done?

D: (*Thinks.*) No. I'd like to pass. I know I have to pass—not just pass, I have to get decent grades if I ever decide I want to go to college.

T: Oh yeah. I think you said when we did the matrix that you might want to go to film school. You said you'd like to write film scripts, right? And I think you said there was a pretty important reason you wanted to do that? Can you remember what that was?

D: Yeah. I said something like…expressing what I see wrong in the world through stories, and making statements that way about what needs to change to make the world better…is kind of what I'd like to be able to give…to contribute, sort of. To try and make the world a better place.

T: And that's pretty important to you, right? Important enough to make you take some steps toward your goal? Even if uncomfortable thoughts and feelings come up?

D: Yeah. I guess so.

T: So, can you go ahead and start? Try taking some steps. Walk toward your goal on the wall there. If thoughts or feelings come up that get in the way, just stop.

D: (*Takes a few steps then stops.*)

T: What's happening?

D: Writing film scripts…it's not just something I thought I'd like to do. It's more like the only thing I ever wanted to do. (*Stops—tears starting to come.*) But I'm so far away from that right now. I'm failing.

T: So, when you think about what matters to you, about going to film school in the future, and needing to get your English project done, your mind gets tangled up in thoughts about failing school.

D: I just think about how high a bar my English teacher has, and how easy it would be to write some crap she doesn't like. And then I don't know where to start. It seems like anything I write would be garbage.

T: Hmm. Does this sound like a familiar story?

D: Yeah. The story of me as a failure.

T: Any other thoughts come up with that?

D: Yeah. That I'm basically stupid and boring and I have no original ideas.

T: Okay. You have thoughts coming up that you will write garbage, you're stupid and boring, and you have no original ideas. Then what feelings come up with those?

D: Down. I feel down. And really hopeless. Like it's never going to get better.

T: So down, and hopeless. And then another thought, *It's never going to get better*.

D: Yeah. That's pretty much it.

T: So let's use LLAMA with all that. Can you remember how we do that?

D: No! ...Oh yeah...start with Label...and we just did that! I'm having feelings of being down and hopeless. And thoughts about writing garbage and being stupid and boring, not original.

T: Good work! Sounds like you have noticed your "story."

D: Yeah, I did. The second "L." Let go. I'm imagining I'm pulling the switch on the wall to stop fighting with down and hopeless and garbage and all the rest. To stop trying to push them away.

T: Awesome! Then what?

D: "A" for Accept. Make space for them...and I can't do it. I want them gone. (*Head down.*)

238

T: Wow. There goes your mind again. The problem-solving machine. Trying to fix it when you feel uncomfortable. That's another thought. "I can't do it." Can you thank your mind for that thought? (*Therapist is coaching defusion strategies.*)

D: (*Smiles and nods.*)

T: And is that thought taking you in the direction of your values—of making a contribution—or is it taking you away from your "story" and the feelings that come with it?

D: Away from my story. Big time. Because I feel awful as these thoughts come up, like I just want to get out of here, I can feel it in my chest, like I can't breathe.

T: Is there anything you can think of that helped to let thoughts and feelings settle so you could just let them be there?

D: Something about breathing, and making room, I think we did it with our eyes closed.

T: That sounds like the "Observe, Breathe, Expand." Do you remember how we did that? (*Therapist is coaching acceptance strategies.*)

D: (*Sighs.*) Yeah. Sort of. I just look at the thoughts and feelings. Notice my mind coming up with all the thoughts. Notice the feelings in my body. Let them be there, give them more room. Was that the "Hedgie" thing?

T: It was, exactly, can you do that?

D: Yeah. When I remember my mind is just being the problem-solving machine and it's trying to fix it so I won't feel down, it's a little easier to take.

T: And the feelings?

D: Seeing them. Breathing into them. Trying to let them be there instead of shoving them down. Oh, yeah, and trying to make space for them—to give them more room.

T: Okay! Could you try and do that now? (*Pause.*) How's it going?

D: Sort of better. It's better not fighting with everything. The feelings aren't as bad when I just look at them straight like that. And it's better with making space for them. I am imagining Hedgie in my hands and giving him more room. I feel like I can breathe.

T: Okay! Then what's next in LLAMA?

D: Mindful. Staying mindful of what's going on in with my senses, right now.

T: What do you notice?

D: I see the bookshelf over there, and the door. I can hear birds outside. I can feel my chest still a bit tight, but not like it was. I notice my thoughts and feelings are still inside, but quieter, and I notice my goal on the wall, with my values. My "story" got triggered, I guess because there really is something making me anxious, my grades, but this matters to me so I need to keep going.

T: Like that cue card we did awhile ago, when you move toward what matters you also get anxious—because it matters, you don't want to screw it up?

D: Exactly. So I'm going to try and move toward my values and my goal—finishing my English project. Writing my project is a goal that matters to me.

T: How does that feel now, to be thinking about that?

D: Still awful. But I feel like I can start writing. Writing something at least. It might not be good but it's going in the right direction.

T: Okay. You want to go for it? Ready to start walking again?

D: (Pause.) Okay. (Starts to walk, then stops.)

T: What's happening? More thoughts coming up when you move toward your goal?

D: Yeah. More thoughts about how it will be garbage. And stupid and unoriginal. But I can see how it's just my mind coming up with DOTS—if I think I'm stupid, I can avoid the work. My mind is just working now to fix the problem and take the pressure off me. So I can make space for all that and just write something.

T: Great! So, are you ready to take some more steps toward your goal there?

D: Almost, the thoughts are pretty big—my story is growing again.

T: Anything you can try to get that sense of looking "at" your story so you aren't so caught up in it?

D: I can try "Bubbles," I liked that one, just imagining thoughts in bubbles, and letting them float around, and I can stand back and watch them, that usually helps.

T: Great, try that and let me know when you are ready to try again.

D: Yup. I guess. (*Walks forward a few steps, then stops.*)

T: What's happening?

D: More thoughts about how stupid I am. And now how pretentious I am. As if I had anything to contribute! Like, who do I think I am?

T: So, okay. You're noticing a new thought, *Who do I think I am?* Any feelings with that? (*Notice the defusing language.*)

D: More down feelings. Kind of crushed.

T: Wow, crushed, uh? So what are you going to do?

D: (*Sighs.*) Just realized…my mind really *is* working overtime. It *really* needs to fix this! It's like…playing a game with me. It's coming up with a reason to stop every time I start. And I've just got this huge weight crashing down on me here (*points to his chest*).

T: So, how do you want to deal with that? Do you want to head toward what matters, or go in the direction of avoiding your thoughts and feelings—you can't go in both directions.

D: I don't want to avoid, it's just so hard. I can try breathing into my feelings, it helped earlier. And make space for all the thoughts, too. The "pretentious" part. The crushed feeling. It's all just more of the same. And I can just keep restarting…every time the thoughts make me stop.

T: So, let's see what that looks like! If you can make space for all those thoughts and feelings, and take them with you while you start writing, go ahead. Walk toward your goal and if you're ready, you can even reach out and touch it.

D: (*Thinks for a moment, then smiles and starts to walk again.*) I just go to my computer and start to write. Even if my mind is saying it's garbage. Even if it's telling me I'm pretentious. (*Walks toward goal.*) Yeah. I can do it. (*Takes the last steps forward, reaches out, and touches drawing.*)

T: (*Giving David a high five.*) Way to go! You did it! Great work!

This exercise can be used, as you can see above, as a kind of combination: a final recap of all the work and a graduation ritual for ending therapy. Since you get to literally "walk" with your client through all the dark places he will traverse when he tries to move in a valued direction, it gives you an opportunity to help him remember the strategies he has learned and to coach him in using them in real time. When you are done, you can take a moment to celebrate success here with a "high five." If it seems appropriate, and doesn't take too much away from the celebration, you can also debrief and go over in more detail what was getting in his way, how he used the strategies, what worked, what didn't, and what else he might be able to do when facing the obstacles presented by thoughts and feelings in real life.

If this is your last session, this exercise can reinforce the connection between client and therapist, because you are going through a shared experience together. So the exercise gives your client an opportunity to finish therapy with the experience of both success (in using LLAMA to reach a goal) and connection. It creates a natural moment of culmination for the work. Your next tough task is to finish and separate.

How to Say Good-bye

Ending therapy can be incredibly meaningful and difficult for both client and therapist. For our fictional client David, this session will be particularly difficult because of his recent loss and his tendency to disengage. We begin this process with an eyes-closed mindfulness exercise and follow with a few additional ideas for saying good-bye that you may want to incorporate into your existing practice of saying good-bye.

Mindfulness of Ending

Endings can be difficult for both client and therapist, and either may engage in avoidance strategies that take away from the richness of the experience, away from the sweet and the sad. To help you and your client connect with whatever comes up in this moment, the following eyes-closed mindfulness meditation may be helpful.

As we sit together with our eyes closed, let's take some time just to be in the present moment, during our last session together, letting our minds remind us of experiences we have shared—moments that have been a struggle and those that have touched us. Let's bring to mind what we appreciate about our relationship, our work together, and each other. As we do this, noticing how we feel about ending our sessions and not working together each week anymore. Noticing what emotions come up, what feelings arise. As we sit here together, let's be aware that we are ending, that we need to say good-bye, noticing any thoughts and feelings that might take us away from this moment, make us veer away from good-bye. Maybe there are even other moments of ending that are getting mixed up in this one and taking us away from this moment now. As we become aware of distractions, let's just label them, accepting that they are there, finding our sense of willingness to have thoughts and feelings, not judging, just allowing them to have space and come to rest inside, not fighting with them, not getting hooked into them, but just letting them come to rest. And then turning our attention gently, and on purpose, back to the moment, this moment of ending between us. Returning as best we can to the moment, aware of how we feel to be ending and aware of our thoughts about ending. When we end the meditation, let's try to be the person who matters to each of us as we say good-bye.

Once the meditation draws to an end, spend some time processing the fact that therapy is coming to an end and addressing what emerged during the meditation. Was it difficult for you or your client to stay with this fact? What took you away and how did you each move through the meditation? Sometimes saying good-bye can be enriched by sharing appreciations or bubbles, as described below.

Appreciation

It can be helpful to reflect on your client's progress over the course of sessions and what qualities you noticed in him as the work unfolded. What did you appreciate about him? He may want to share what he appreciates about you or he may choose to stick to what he appreciated about the work more broadly. We often give clients a chance to share personal reflections or thoughts, reminding them of LLAMA if they are struggling with feelings in particular as they contemplate sharing what we, as therapists, mean to them.

Bubbles

Some of our clients have a real affinity to the "Bubbles" exercise. If so, we have on occasion given them a bottle of bubbles to take home after the last session. Use your judgment as to whether and how this sort of "transition object" may be useful for your client.

Home Practice

If this is not your last session, we suggest letting your client guide his own practice between sessions. This may take the form of formal goal setting or less formal "noticing" of how he feels when he moves toward values and away from inner experience. If this is your last session together, you may want to spend some time talking about next steps and the obstacles that are likely to arise when your client attempts to take them.

Modifications for Group

"The Walk" can be done in many ways with groups of adolescents, and the process of ending in a group context can be complex given the number of relationships that are ending.

The Walk

We describe below several iterations of "The Walk" that we have used in our groups, starting with our first, an adaption of "Passengers on the Bus" (Hayes, 2005). These versions make use of each and every group member, giving them different roles depending on what they are willing to try. Regardless of how you do "The Walk," we have found it helpful, before starting, to have each group member create a visual image of a goal he is moving toward, with his values incorporated into the image somehow. While some group members enjoy this opportunity to engage in something creative, others find the experience more aversive, their minds looping into comparisons about how their creative expressive ability or their drawing skills compare to those of their peers. Keeping an eye on your clients as they make their images may give you a good "in the moment" opportunity to guide them in using LLAMA.

Passengers on the Bus

This version of "The Walk" came about as our first attempt to physicalize "Passengers on the Bus" in a way where group members could all take on active roles and have fun at the same time. We had accumulated a collection of very soft, small, colorful, fluffy pillows that we were convinced would be useful at some time, and this was it! "Nerf balls" or fist-sized soft foam balls or blocks would do just as well.

We would explain the exercise like this:

As you can see, we have arranged the chairs a bit differently, like they are seats on a bus. We are hoping that someone will be willing to be the "driver" while everyone else is a passenger. The idea is that the driver is heading toward what matters to him, and he can put a picture of that on the wall in front of his chair. The passengers will be the driver's thoughts and feelings, the ones that get in his way. As the driver heads toward what matters, the passengers will repeat thoughts and feelings that usually lead the driver to DOTS. Just to make sure you get your driver's attention, you can gently bop him with the fuzzy pillows, or lob them up to the front of the bus, as you are repeating his thoughts and feelings. (Facilitator will scoop up pillows and return them to passengers quickly so that this can be repeated.) *And so that you know what to say, we will ask the driver to put a different thought or feeling that gets in his way on each of these pieces of paper, and then we'll give one piece to each of you, the passengers. One of us facilitators will help the driver use LLAMA to get to his destination.*

After explaining what was going to happen, we asked one group member to be the "driver" and assigned the remaining members as "passengers," each armed with a fluffy pillow. We gave the driver a piece of paper for each passenger and asked him to write one thought or feeling that tended to get in his way on each piece. We found that when we engaged group members in this experience in the last of the group sessions, they were already aware of each other's internal events, and this supported a sense of willingness to share in this way. Having arranged the room like a bus, we had the driver hang his picture on the wall in front of his chair, and positioned a facilitator next to him to guide him through LLAMA. The second facilitator sat with the passengers to help them with their role in the exercise, fetching and returning pillows as needed.

As the passengers repeated the thought or feeling that was written on the piece of paper they were each holding, the driver allowed himself to get hooked into what they were saying, hooked into what his mind told him. You can ask him what he would like to do with these pesky passengers. Many drivers will want to engage in a debate, or kick the passengers off their bus. Allow them to do so, and then ask, what happened to the bus they were driving, and the goal they were heading toward? If you feel so inclined, you can make "bus swerving off the road" noises to playfully suggest the outcome! If this is not the case, you can instruct the driver to indicate when he is hooked into his thoughts and feelings by taking his hands off the wheel. This is the cue for the facilitator to help the driver use LLAMA to reach his goal. When the driver is ready, he can take hold of the wheel and start to move his bus toward his goal once again. This process often needs repeating a few times before the driver reaches his goal.

If you try this exercise, you will find that once a driver reaches his goal, you will want to take a few minutes to process the experience. You can ask passengers to hand the driver back his papers, and as each group member does so, ask if he or she and the driver are willing to look each other in the eye, linger for a moment, and try to take in a sense of whatever emotions arise. As the driver takes his papers back, we ask him to do so gently, treating each paper as a part of himself that deserves kindness and understanding, as opposed to crumpling or ripping them and throwing them in the garbage. The time taken for one round of this "walk" varies considerably from one group member to another. If you have time, ask for another volunteer to be the driver.

While the struggle for the driver—with his feelings of vulnerability, anxiety, and possible embarrassment—seemed obvious to us when we started, we quickly realized that the passengers also struggled, and in unexpected ways. The most difficult part for the passengers was their desire to "take away" the feelings that came up for the driver. Our drivers often told of feeling anxious and at the same time overwhelmed with feelings of joy and a sense of efficacy as they were able to work through LLAMA and reach their goal. Passengers often wanted to hug the driver, and we learned to ask, "What are you noticing inside when you want to hug him?" We found that they often wanted to "make him feel better," not recognizing that he was feeling emotions that had been long hidden and were actually welcome. Some passengers were able to share in the feelings of accomplishment with their driver. For other passengers, allowing these feelings within themselves was too difficult and they moved instead toward experiential avoidance. Common avoidance behaviors here included disengaging eye contact, exaggeratedly hugging the driver, finding some other way to distract themselves at the moment of celebration, or dissociating. Sometimes a group-based acceptance of feelings was needed at the end of the experience.

In addition to wanting to avoid feelings that surfaced during the experience, passengers often said they felt "guilty" for "saying what we did" (feeding back the driver's thoughts and feelings) to the driver. Time to process the experience may open up a dialogue among group members that allows passengers to detach from their judgments and use their five senses to really take in what the driver experienced. So far, each of our drivers has described the experience as helpful: the passengers really did mimic their mind and body in a way that helped the drivers work toward their goal, for which they were grateful. When our passengers got out of their heads and out of their story, they realized that the driver was in fact far from upset with them.

Struggles notwithstanding, there are certainly benefits to being part of the "chorus" of passengers. Many group members share common thoughts and feelings that derail their lives. Saying aloud the thoughts or feelings that passengers have been given by the driver allows for some degree of defusion, compassion, and acceptance, while passengers are moving toward their values as a group member and supporting each other.

We stuck with "The Walk" in this original "Passengers on the Bus" iteration for a while, and then adapted it as time went on. Nevertheless, the results and struggles have been much the same as those described above. Group members often return for a follow-up session and tell us that "The Walk" had a lasting impact, regardless of their role in the exercise. They report that having peers "mimic" what goes on inside their mind is intense enough that they "feel" the emotions they want to avoid; making it as close to an "in vivo" experience as we could provide when their end goals were not something they could move toward in real time in the group, such as writing their exam.

The Walk Without a Bus

For the next iteration, we took away the chairs and the bus and opted for something that allowed more movement for everyone. In this version, we ask for one person to be the "walker" (instead of "driver") who moves toward his values-based goal, while the others form a "chorus" (instead of "passengers") of his thoughts and feelings. We position the "walker" and the "chorus" at one end of the group room, with the walker's picture of his values and goal hung on the wall at the far end. We ask the walker to slowly move forward toward his goal, with a facilitator beside him, ready to assist when needed. This is much the same as described for work with individual clients, with the chorus of group members added in. As the walker moves toward his goal, members of the chorus form a semicircle behind him and repeat what is written on their little pieces of paper. The second facilitator stays back in the chorus, to prompt them. When the walker gets hooked into what the chorus is saying, the walker signals this to the facilitator by stopping, and the facilitator helps the walker engage in LLAMA. When the walker stops, the chorus is prompted by the second facilitator to continue repeating what is on their papers, but at a whisper so the walker can hear the facilitator who is coaching him through LLAMA. When the walker is ready, he starts to walk once again toward his goal. The second facilitator signals the chorus to raise their volume again. The walker may need to stop several times and receive coaching again before he reaches the far wall and can touch his goal. Many clients do this literally, by placing a hand on the visual image.

Hockey Tape (We're Canadian)

Yet another version involves hockey tape, which is a wide, cloth-backed tape with a colored surface, available in several colors. If you can't get this, you could use duct tape (also known as "gaffer's tape") which is a wide, cloth-backed tape with a shiny silver surface. Failing this, or for something less expensive, you could just use masking tape. Really what you need is any strong, wide tape. We aim for ones in bright colors or fun patterns, which are more engaging.

For this version, you again need a "walker" and a "chorus," but this time you will work with the tape arranged on the floor in a "Y" shape. Place the open ends at the top of the "Y" toward the far end of the room. Hang the walker's goal on the wall above the top right arm of the "Y" and hang a list of commonly used DOTS on the wall above the top left arm of the "Y." The walker and the chorus begin as they did in the previous version, at the near end of the room, away from the goal, standing at the bottom of the "Y." As the walker becomes looped into thoughts and feelings that take him toward avoidance, you as the facilitator can ask, "Do you want to go to the left or the right?" We used this version before we knew about the matrix, but once we added the matrix to the group, the "left" and "right" distinction pulled in a lot more content and was even more powerful.

The Matrix

Our last iteration to date involves the matrix, again using hockey tape, this time to map out the four quadrants on the group room floor. This also requires a second color of tape to make a squarish sort of circle in the middle for the person who is "noticing." Position the "walker" in the middle "circle" (very hard to make with tape) and have the other group members position themselves in the lower left quadrant, ready to repeat the walker's thoughts and feelings. We don't put anyone on the right side of the matrix in this experience, so that clients get a felt sense of just how loud, overpowering, and compelling the left side can be, and of how hard it is to keep the right side (values and goals) in mind while the left side is clamoring. As the walker gets hooked into thoughts and feelings and wants to avoid them, he can move to the upper left quadrant and choose one of his DOTS to avoid the lower left. Facilitators can help the chorus to continue its role and the walker to "notice" and make choices, using LLAMA as a guide to the processes. After coaching with LLAMA, the walker will eventually be able to move to the lower right quadrant, where he can notice his values and then proceed to the upper right quadrant, his place of committed action.

After processing whichever version of "The Walk" you have used, the group is coming to an end. This is something that deserves special attention.

Good-bye

There are many ways to say good-bye in therapy groups. In addition to the mindfulness meditation outlined under the individual section, we have added a few things that our clients really enjoyed and that you may want to add to your own list of favorites.

Cards

Prior to the last group session, we gather pieces of colored paper, if possible thicker than regular printer paper, and write each client's name in the middle of one of the pieces, or fold it in half, like a card, and write names on the outside. After "The Walk," we give group members time to write something on each other's cards and then give each card to its "owner" to take home. We suggest that they write about qualities in one another that they appreciated, risks they have seen their peer take, what the peer's presence meant, or what they will remember about that person. As the facilitator, you may want to write in each card during the group or put your thoughts to paper prior to the group meeting. Depending on group dynamics, you may want to consider also having cards for the facilitators that clients can write in.

Appreciation

You can ask group members to share what they appreciated about the group overall, aloud, near the end of the session. As facilitators, you may want to start this off so the clients get the hang of it. You may also want to ask that each group member share what they have appreciated about the member sitting to their left (or right), allowing a few moments for them to reflect before sharing.

Conclusion

As sessions draw to a close, we remind our clients that they have guided audio of mindfulness meditations to practice with and make sure that they have our contact number in case questions come up in the future. (All audio files are available for download at http://www.newharbinger.com/33575.) We often schedule a three-month follow-up session for both individual clients and group members. In the follow-up session we review movement toward values-based goals and engage clients in any experiential exercises that seem relevant to struggles they are experiencing at the time. We also repeat questionnaires at the three-month follow-up.

Good-bye and Good Luck!

We hope that this book will be helpful to you as you move forward using ACT with your clients. Please feel free to use it as a starting point for improvising in your work and developing more metaphors and exercises that speak directly to them. We have enjoyed sharing our experiences with you, and wish you a meaningful, enriching journey with your clients!

Acknowledgements

We would first like to thank Kelly G. Wilson for his faith and friendship over the years. Without these, this book would not exist. We were surprised when Kelly suggested we write a book, and both pleased and stressed that the folks at New Harbinger agreed. As of now, we're feeling relieved that the project is all done!

Thank you to everyone at New Harbinger for making this as painless as possible—your patience, commitment, and support are appreciated: Catherine Meyers, Tesilya Hanauer, freelance copy editor Ken Knabb, Vicraj Gill, Fiona Hannigan, Michele Waters, and freelance proofreader Susan Vdovichenko. Special thanks to Chris McCurry and Niklas Törneke for reading over "ACT Basics" and the RFT section in particular so we could sleep at night. Appreciation to our ACBS community for being so darn welcoming, for inspiring us, and for sharing what they have learned over the years. A special thank you to our managers, fellow clinicians, and graduate students at Trillium Health Partners (THP) who supported our efforts and gave us the opportunity to take a chance. To the parents at THP who entrusted us with their precious adolescents, and to the teens themselves, it has been an unforgettable journey.

—Sheri and Mary

They say it takes a community to raise a child. I would like to thank my entire community for helping me raise this book. To my home team: Jerome, Peanut, and Charles, thank you for taking care of my spirit throughout the process. And thank you for never asking, "How's the book?" through clenched teeth, despite the long hours I spent glued to my computer. Maya, thank you for puppy love! Heartfelt thanks to my extended family and friends for refueling my confidence and for simply being there. My road to ACT was paved by a timely suggestion from my analyst, RK, to explore mindfulness—which I did—that led to my discovery of ACT. For this, as well as his unfaltering support and confidence, I am eternally grateful. To Mary, my colleague and coauthor—nothing deepens a friendship like writing a book together—thank you for your patience, humor, and acceptance of all my neuroses! Most of all, this book is for Joyce—I hope it makes you proud....

—Sheri

I want to thank my colleagues at The Hospital for Sick Children for their bemused tolerance of my initial ACT rant, followed by generous, welcome support in working with ACT. Huge thanks go to Sheri for the constant patience and understanding she offered when illness and loss interrupted my work on the book. The kindness she showed in lifting the load when I was not able is so appreciated. I could never have kept going without the exceptional support of all my friends. It has been like oxygen. I really value the presence of my family and David's through all this, and thank them for being there with me. But most of all I am deeply grateful to David, whose love made everything possible.

—Mary

References

Brach, T. (2004). *Radical acceptance: Embracing your life with the heart of a Buddha.* New York: Random House.

Dahl, J. C., Plumb, J. C., Stewart, I., & Lundgren, T. (2009). *The art and science of valuing in psychotherapy: Helping clients discover, explore, and commit to valued action using acceptance and commitment therapy.* Oakland, CA: New Harbinger Publications.

Dalrymple, K. L., & Herbert, J. D. (2007). Acceptance and commitment therapy for generalized anxiety disorder. *Behavior Modification, 31,* 543–568.

Erikson, E. H. (1959) *Identity and the life cycle.* New York: International Universities Press.

Greco, L. A., Baer, R. A., & Smith, G. T. (2011). Assessing mindfulness in children and adolescents: Development and validation of the Child and Adolescent Mindfulness Measure (CAMM). *Psychological Assessment, 23,* 606–614.

Greco, L. A., Lambert, W., & Baer, R. A. (2008). Psychological inflexibility in childhood and adolescence: Development and evaluation of the avoidance and fusion questionnaire for youth. *Psychological Assessment, 20,* 93–102.

Halsted, E. (2015). Stretched to the limit: The elastic body image in the reflexive mind. In J. Petrucelli (Ed.), *Body-States: Interpersonal and relational perspectives on the treatment of eating disorders* (pp. 79–91). New York: Routledge.

Harris, R. (2008). *The happiness trap: How to stop struggling and start living.* Boston: Trumpeter.

Harris, R. (2009). *ACT made simple: A quick-start guide to ACT basics and beyond.* Oakland, CA: New Harbinger Publications.

Hayes, L., & Ciarrochi, J. (2015). *The thriving adolescent: Using acceptance and commitment therapy and positive psychology to help teens manage emotions, achieve goals, and build connection.* Oakland, CA: New Harbinger Publications.

Hayes, S. C. (2005). *Get out of your mind and into your life: The new acceptance and commitment therapy.* Oakland, CA: New Harbinger Publications.

Hayes, S. C., Levin, M. E., Plumb-Vilardaga, J., Villatte, J. L., & Pistorello, J. (2013). Acceptance and commitment therapy and contextual behavior science: Examining the progress of a distinctive model of behavioral and cognitive therapy. *Behavior Therapy, 44,* 180–198.

Hayes, S. C., Strosahl, K. D., & Wilson, K. G. (2012). *Acceptance and commitment therapy: The process and practice of mindful change* (2nd ed.). New York: The Guilford Press.

Jensen, F. E., & Nutt, A. E. (2015) *The teenage brain.* New York: HarperCollins.

Kabat-Zinn, J. (1990). *Full catastrophe living: Using the wisdom of your body and mind to face stress, pain, and illness.* New York: Bantam Dell.

Kabat-Zinn, J. (1994). *Wherever you go, there you are: Mindfulness meditation in everyday life.* New York: Hyperion.

Kovacs, M. (2011). *Children's depression inventory: Technical manual* (2nd ed.). New York: Multi-Health Systems.

LeJeune, C. (2007). *The worry trap.* Oakland, CA: New Harbinger Publications.

March, J. S., Parker, J. D. A., Sullivan, K., Stallings, P., & Conners, C. K. (1997). The multidimensional anxiety scale for children (MASC): Factor structure, reliability, and validity. *Journal of the American Academy of Child and Adolescent Psychiatry, 36,* 554–565.

McCracken, L. M., MacKichan, F., and Eccleston, C. (2007). Contextual cognitive-behavioral therapy for severely disabled chronic pain sufferers: Effectiveness and clinically significant change. *European Journal of Pain, 11,* 314–322.

McHugh, L., & Stewart, I. (2012). *The self and perspective taking: Contributions and applications from modern behavioral science.* Oakland, CA: New Harbinger Publications.

McKay, M., Lev, A., & Skeen, M. (2012). *Acceptance and commitment therapy for interpersonal problems: Using mindfulness, acceptance, and schema awareness to change interpersonal behaviors.* Oakland, CA: New Harbinger Publications.

Polk, K. L., & Schoendorff, B. (2014). *The ACT matrix: A new approach to building psychological flexibility across settings and populations.* Oakland, CA: New Harbinger Publications.

Raes, F., Pommier, E., Neff, K. D., & Van Gucht, D. (2011). Construction and factorial validation of a short form of the Self-Compassion Scale. *Clinical Psychology and Psychotherapy, 18,* 250–255.

Roemer, L., & Orsillo, S. M. (2007). An open trial of an acceptance-based behavior therapy for generalized anxiety disorder. *Behavior Therapy, 38,* 72–85.

Roemer, L., Orsillo, S. M., & Salters-Pedneault, K. (2008). Efficacy of an acceptance-based behavior therapy for generalized anxiety disorder: Evaluation in a randomized controlled trial. *Journal of Consulting and Clinical Psychology, 76,* 1083–1089.

Titchener, E. B. (1916). *A beginner's psychology.* New York: Macmillan.

Törneke, N. (2010). *Learning RFT: An introduction to relational frame theory and its clinical application.* Oakland, CA: New Harbinger Publications.

Törneke, N., Luciano, C., & Valdivia Salas, S. V. (2008). Rule-governed behavior and psychological problems. *International Journal of Psychology and Psychological Therapy, 8,* 141–156.

Twohig, M. P., Hayes, S. C., & Masuda, A. (2006). A preliminary investigation of acceptance and commitment therapy as a treatment for chronic skin picking. *Behavior Research and Therapy, 44,* 1513–1522.

Twohig, M. P., Hayes, S. C., Plumb, J. C., Pruitt, L. D., Collins, A. B., Hazlett-Stevens, H., et al. (2010). A randomized clinical trial of acceptance and commitment therapy versus progressive relaxation training for obsessive-compulsive disorder. *Journal of Consulting and Clinical Psychology, 78,* 705–716.

Wells, A. (2009). *Metacognitive therapy for anxiety and depression.* New York: The Guilford Press.

Wetherell, J. L., Afari, N., Ayers, C. R., Stoddard, J. A., Ruberg, J., Sorrell, J. T., et al. (2011). Acceptance and commitment therapy for generalized anxiety disorder in older adults: A preliminary report. *Behavior Therapy, 42,* 127–134.

Wilson, K. G., & DuFrene, T. (2008). *Mindfulness for two: An acceptance and commitment therapy approach to mindfulness in psychotherapy.* Oakland, CA: New Harbinger Publications.

Wilson, K. G., Sandoz, E. K., Kitchens, J., & Roberts, M. E. (2010). The valued living questionnaire: Defining and measuring valued action within a behavioral framework. *The Psychological Record, 60,* 249–272.

Wolfe, D. A., Jaffe, P. G., & Crooks, C. V. (2006) *Adolescent risk behaviors: Why teens experiment and strategies to keep them safe.* London: Yale University Press.

Zettle, R. D. (2007). *ACT for depression: A clinician's guide to using acceptance and commitment therapy in treating depression.* Oakland, CA: New Harbinger Publications.

Zettle, R. D., & Hayes, S. C. (1982). Rule-governed behavior: A potential theoretical framework for cognitive-behavior therapy. In P. C. Kendall (Ed.), *Advances in cognitive-behavioral research and therapy.* New York: Academic Press.

255

Sheri L. Turrell, PhD, is a clinical psychologist living with her family in Toronto, ON, Canada. She is passionate about her clinical work with adolescents, helping them move toward a life that matters. Turrell is primary investigator, working in collaboration with Mary Bell, for studies of group-based acceptance and commitment therapy (ACT), and is developing a mobile ACT app for adolescents. She runs a full-time private practice, and enjoys being a consultant and trainer for graduate students and mental health professionals who are interested in learning ACT. Turrell teaches ACT at the university level, where she also facilitates therapy groups.

Mary Bell, MSW, RSW, is a social worker in Toronto, ON, Canada. Currently affiliated with The Hospital for Sick Children in Toronto, Bell has had a private practice in Toronto and Singapore. Collaborating with Sheri Turrell, she continues to evolve an acceptance and commitment therapy (ACT) approach to working with adolescents and their families, and is developing an ACT app for adolescents. She loves to share ACT with clients and other practitioners.

Foreword writer **Kelly G. Wilson, PhD**, is professor of psychology at the University of Mississippi. He is a central figure in acceptance and commitment therapy (ACT), and coauthor of the landmark *Acceptance and Commitment Therapy*. Wilson is among the most sought-after ACT trainers. His popular experiential workshops touch thousands of clinicians and students each year. Find out more at www.onelifellc.com.

Index

W

Wade Through the Swamp metaphor, 141–142

walking, mindful, 189–190, 198, 200

The Walk exercise, 234, 236–242, 244, 247–248

The Walk Without a Bus exercise, 247

Walser, Robyn, 20

"what stuck?" question, 56

willingness, 31, 120, 133–146, 152–154; experiential exercises and metaphors on, 137–146; exploring with clients, 136–137; focus of session on, 133; group work on allowing and, 153–154; home practice assignment on, 152–153; individual client work on, 134–146, 152–153; mindfulness meditation on, 148, 149–151; self-compassion and, 151, 152; values related to, 137. *See also* allowing

Wilson, Kelly, 2, 9, 44, 77, 107, 149, 200, 214, 224

Word Link exercise, 192

Word Webs, 31, 193–198

workability, 14, 56, 168, 179

Wrinkled Sock metaphor, 138–140

writing, mindful, 79–80

Y

Yarn exercise, 203–204

Younger You meditation, 224–226, 230

Z

Zettle, R. D., 138

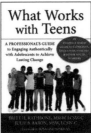
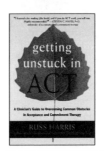
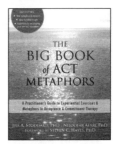

Register your **new harbinger** titles for additional benefits!

When you register your **new harbinger** title—purchased in any format, from any source—you get access to benefits like the following:

- Downloadable accessories like printable worksheets and extra content

- Instructional videos and audio files

- Information about updates, corrections, and new editions

Not every title has accessories, but we're adding new material all the time.

Access free accessories in 3 easy steps:

1. Sign in at NewHarbinger.com (or **register** to create an account).

2. Click on **register a book**. Search for your title and click the **register** button when it appears.

3. Click on the **book cover or title** to go to its details page. Click on **accessories** to view and access files.

That's all there is to it!

If you need help, visit:

NewHarbinger.com/accessories

new harbinger
CELEBRATING
40 YEARS